# OUR SUSSEX PARISH

BY

## THOMAS GEERING

WITH A NEW INTRODUCTION BY

### RICHARD KNOWLES

COUNTRY BOOKS

Published by Country Books
Courtyard Cottage, Little Longstone, Bakewell, Derbyshire DE45 1NN
Tel/Fax: 01629 640670
e-mail: dickrichardson@country-books.co.uk

ISBN 1 898941 83 1

*A catalogue of titles published by Country Books and Ashridge Press
is available upon request.*

Printed and bound by: Antony Rowe Ltd.

# CONTENTS

SOME PERSONALITIES IN OUR PARISH

SKETCHES AND TALES OF OUR PARISH

# LIST OF ILLUSTRATIONS

# THOMAS GEERING

Arthur Beckett, who was something of an authority on Sussex literature, declared that *Our Parish* by Thomas Geering was his favourite Sussex book. He was browsing through second-hand books in a shop when he first came across it and he only had to peruse a few pages to realise that he had found a rare treasure. He was also puzzled, for it was a book that was completely unknown to him. The copy he had discovered was titled *Our Parish: A Medley* by T.G.H. and had been published in 1884. From the signature following the preface he saw that T.G. was Thomas Geering and he deduced that the 'H' referred to Hailsham. He made a point of finding out about Geering, who had died many years earlier, and had the good fortune to meet the author's daughter, Emma, who was still living in Hailsham.

Beckett devoted the best part of a chapter of his book, *The Wonderful Weald*, to Geering's work and his readers began to look for copies of *Our Parish*. Unfortunately, these were both rare and costly. Beckett then persuaded Methuen to republish the book and it appeared as *Our Sussex Parish* in 1925. It is, essentially, a collection of essays and the 1925 edition differs from that of 1884 in that Beckett grouped them under three headings, 'Our Sussex parish and its institutions', 'Some personalities in our parish' and 'Sketches and tales of our parish'. Beckett also excluded a few of the essays as he thought that the earlier book had been too long. More recently, in 2001, Piccadilly Rare Books of Ticehurst issued

*Thomas Geering*

a limited edition of just 100 copies.

Thomas Geering was born in Hailsham in 1813 and lived his whole life in the town. His father, also Thomas Geering, came from Alfriston where he had begun his working life as a shepherd's boy and a ploughboy before becoming a shoemaker. In November 1812 he married Elizabeth Holman, the eldest daughter of a yeoman of Hellingly, in the Ebenezer Chapel at Alfriston and in the following year they moved to Hailsham.

Young Thomas received his education in Hailsham at the 'Academy' of Thomas Weston and he tells us that it "was THE school of the place", despite Weston's self avowed fondness for sherry. When drinking he had been known to say, with a touch of humour, that he wished his neck could be as long as his arm!

When he left school Geering was apprenticed to a Hailsham currier and in due course took over his father's business. It had been prospering and when his parent's died he inherited a house and a shop in the High Street. The business continued to prosper under his management and he was able to build a workshop where he employed a number of men. He was, as he explains, one of the *elite* of the town, for they had no squire and tradesmen were the only aristocracy in Hailsham!

Thomas Geering was widely read and Arthur Beckett was convinced that the *Essays* of Lamb had influenced his style. His favourite leisure activity seems to have been going out with his dog and gun but he also a good flute player.

It was only in 1879, when Geering was well into his sixties, that the idea of being an author dawned on him. He had just become acquainted with a writer who had moved into the area and was allowed to read some of his manuscripts. Geering began to ask himself why he should not also write, but he was hesitant. He wondered what he could write about because he had had no adventures; he had never even lived outside the parish. Happily, he overcame these inhibitions and proved that he had a natural ability. Most of the pieces that make up *Our Parish* first appeared in the columns of a country newspaper. They were then collected under the title *Our Parish: A Medley* and five hundred copies were published in 1884. These were sold under paper covers at eighteen pence or with a cloth binding for half-a-crown. Sales were slow and it was not a financial success. It was only a quarter of a century later, when Arthur Beckett drew it to the attention of a wider public, that its merits were eventually recognised.

Richard Knowles 2003

## PUBLISHER'S NOTE:
This edition follows the story sequence arranged by Arthur Beckett. The first story, 'An Old Sussex Bookseller', was not included in the original Methuen edition. It appeared in the Sussex County Magazine of January 1927.

## ACKNOWLEDGEMENTS
I must record my thanks to the following people:
Richard Knowles, for permission to use his introduction on Thomas Geering from They Wrote About Sussex (Country Books 2003), and for drawing my attention to 'An Old Sussex Bookseller'.
Tony Wales of Horsham and Albert Gearing of Keymer, who kindly made their editions of Our Sussex Parish available to me.

# PREFACE TO THE ORIGINAL EDITION

Since I resolved to go into print, I have discovered that the most serious part of an author's task is his preface. At least it has been so in my case. I have made half a dozen attempts, and as many failures. I could not get on, though the necessity of the thing appeared to be paramount. I found myself in a dilemma, inasmuch as for various reasons the book must have an introduction. First, to issue it without a sponsor would be pedantic and defiant. If I solicited indulgence this might be considered meek-hearted and maudlin. If I apologised for shortcomings, I should be "lackadaisical," and asking for compliment. And if I said I had been prevailed upon by friends, I should be betraying those kindly disposed people. So, as the thing in some form or other had to be done, I have resolved to state a few facts, and leave the outcome of my mental meanderings to the care of that blind goddess who presides generally over fate and fortune.

And now to the point. It was in the summer of 1879 that the possibility of my one day becoming author first loomed upon me; that I set out on my perilous journey into the land of letters. About that date I made the acquaintance of a gentleman who had settled in our neighbourhood, and we became friends. His fate was to write for the Press, and by his aid and kindness I obtained a peep behind the scenes. He allowed me occasionally to read his MSS. This was the first opportunity of the kind that had ever happened to me, and I was delighted. Books had always had a special charm, but here was the maker of them, and I adored the man. To me he was a god. I had never before been in at the birth, almost at the conception of an idea. Here I saw the first blushing offspring of the mind brought to the light of day, and lying all naked and exposed before me on a clean sheet of paper. Here was virgin life – pure, unspotted. The censor had not used his shears, neither the critic his bitter ink and poisoned pen. The well was untouched, undefiled, and I drank freely. It was then I first felt the divinity stirring within me. Here it was I saw the "stuff" articles were made of, and I said, "Cannot I write also?" But I had no subject, and less knowledge. I had never lived out of the parish. I had had no adventure, had never built castles to tumble about my ears; and, better than all, I was no philosopher. In short, looking back, I found the greatest romance of my life had been when I went out to *shoot* a CROCODILE, and upon this daring deed I resolved to try my " 'prentice hand." This was my first subject and my first article, and the medley that has followed goes to account for, and to make up the contents of, this book. Here is the true history of its origin.

And now to my readers I subscribe myself respectfully,

THOS. GEERING

Hailsham, 1884

## AUTHOR'S INTRODUCTION

The history of our parish in the present century [1] may be summarized in two words, viz., the barrack-yard and the brick-yard. Then we were military and stagnant; now we are social and progressive. Then we were roused by the drum and the trumpet; now by the ring of the trowel and the rattle of the saw. Then, by the early marching of the tired soldier; now by the tramp of the workman to his daily toil. Then it was the halting place of the brave; now it is the home of the free.

Onward! Onward! was the cry as the troops hurried to meet their comrades, drawing from all diverging lines to the centre at Dover, ready to give their lives in a foreign land, at the stern call of duty; and there, too, they died grandly for a huge chimera, never attained nor attainable—"Balance of Power."

When the monarchs had driven Bonaparte to Elba they clapped their hands, laughed, and said, "The work is done; we must meet and rejoice. Visit England, and do homage to Brother George." One incident in connection with this visit of the "crowned heads" may be noticed here. On the return homewards of these wonderful people, the Emperor of Russia, the King of Prussia, and their suites, passed through Horsebridge on Sunday, June 26, 1814, for Dover. The cavalcade halted at Amberstone House, then the residence of —— Rickman, Quaker, farmer, and owner. Emperors and Empresses alighted, and the Hailsham farm-house became the resting-place and shelter of royalty. The beautiful Quakeress soon after became the mother of a third son, and according to imperial request, the child was named Alexander.

[1] i.e. nineteenth.

13

The reminiscences relating to "Our Sussex Parish" will be nearly limited to this date. The writer, having no other record than memory to draw his facts from, will not venture deeper into the misty regions of the past.

The history of a parish must, like that of a nation, be the history of the people; so it will be my object to introduce circumstances and characters all having some bearing upon our collective and individual life, and if we can produce no distinguished specimens of humanity, we can at least show our representative men, such as the poet, the painter, the athlete, the cricketer, and our famous pugilist. As we proceed some minor lights will spring up demanding our attention. There will be one or more adventures that may become stirring, according to the narrator's power of delineation; and there must of necessity be a ghost story or two, to show that we have not lived outside the domain of the marvellous. Further, the reader may be assured there will be but little of invention, and that the whole has some foundation in fact.

1884.

# THE OLD SUSSEX BOOKSELLER

*Shortly before she died, Miss Emma Geering, Thomas Geering's only daughter, presented Arthur Beckett with some unpublished stories by her father. Among them was the following tribute to an old Lewes bookseller, James Butland, who died in 1882.*

What a medley of minds and capacities do we not find in a second-hand book shop! What contrarieties and contradictions, what controversies and rabid vapouring, what soul-stirring and enduring verities! What mysteries and conundrums are there unsolved and unanswered! A very witch's cave and a wizard's castle filled with all manner of spells and mental allurements, where fact and fancy become bedfellows; the necropolis too, where the dead speak.

Again, what a paradise is the place where the old and the withered are looked doatingly upon and worshipped, while the young lie languishing, to die early. Here, too, is found the gamut of the human mind, from the lesser to the greater, from the greater to the greatest.

What a dusty, musty place is the old bookseller's shop, where no housemaid with her brush or broom, nor old-fashioned house-wife with her goosewing, dare enter. Here confusion reigns and disorder appears to justify herself. The shelves are overburdened and more than filled with all sorts and sizes. The binding is as varied as the authorship. Colour and material go for nothing — all here are welcome and fraternize, from cloth to russia and the ever-enduring vellum. The counter is ricketty and creaking with the heap that can find no other resting-place, the pile being so high that the seller and buyer get glimpses of each other only through niches and chinks, or over the uneven top ranges of volumes. The window is sparingly set off with stale theology, chiefly controversial, old histories and biographies of forgotten heroes, and any other book having a quaint or illuminated frontispiece here exhibits itself, inviting the lounging, longing book-worm to open the door (which, as a rule, is shut), and to search out some coveted author to fill up a vacant place on the shelves at home.

To the dreamy lover of books, what an attraction has the place — this stronghold of knowledge, this accumulation and concentration of all the eddying thoughts and soul-pulsations belonging to the past and present. And what a delight, too, must be the life of the bookseller, to be ever among his best beloved, his heart's treasures, where he revels his time away — he who accumulates with a lighter heart than when he sells and parts with some of his special favourites. It is then his heart-strings are touched, then he feels a pang and a sorrow unknown to any other trader, for, though he loves money much, he loves his books more.

A curious, quaint character was my old friend the bookseller; and where, for miles round is the man or woman who is bookish, who did not know him and his shop? But alas! he is gone, and where now shall we find him? We may follow him in our fancy, but we all know he is not to be found, we can gather no more from his lips, neither shall we hear his voice ever again. Would that we knew more of the tale of his life, of his struggles, success and enjoyments, far away from the country of his birth, the beautiful Devon; of his country rambles in Sussex, visiting his numerous patrons, of his intercourse with the intellectuals of the country — in short, his tale of "the battle of the books."

Reader, you will have learned ere this, that it is James Batland, the old bookseller of Lewes, to whom I am paying my devotions and attempting to do some honour to his memory. Years have now passed since I first saw his quaint figure, diminutive and deformed. He was then out on a business excursion, a dozen miles or more away from his home, before the rail had knit us together, and when a poor man had to use his feet, and make the best he could of a trading journey. He was perambulating our street and once seen he was a man not to be forgotten. The occasion of his being a dozen miles from home was a sale by auction. There being a long list of books he was on the look out for bargains. After this I lost him for years, and when we met again it was in his old shop in St. Michael's.

I have, through life, been somewhat bookish, it has been one of my weaknesses. I never could resist the temptation or attractions of an old book shop, and so, here and there, I have picked up a few odd volumes. Cheap, they must be, for I bought to read. The contents concerned me more than the covers, uniformity stood not in the way of adding to my collection, and therefore I patronised James Butland. My first visits were purely business ones. I had a want, the craving would not be denied, and thanks to the old book-seller and his shop, he has satisfied many of my needs.

Up to the present year, in my occasional visits to our country town, I have looked in, and my last volume was purchased there. The last time I saw my old friend he was seated at the head of his counter buried in books and covered with snuff. Stricken and sorely afflicted, palsied and almost helpless, there he sat, an object to sympathise with. To whom can we compare him? My knowledge of character and appearance does not furnish me with his duplicate. With lean cheeks and lacklustre eye, there he sat, his tall hat dropping backward on to his shoulders, while his head fell towards his chest, his knees and his chin both in advance to meet each other.

His long arms and hands were hanging listlessly on either side, and the god he adored, was, as ever, before him. There, at the end of the counter, lay his snuff. Not in gold or silver, or in box of any other material, but in the paper in which his daily allowance had been purchased. There it lay, open. When his moment came he had no time to unclasp and raise the lid of any box; and more, he required breadth and space wherein to deploy and to obtain enough. But enough he never had. His lean and lank fingers, as they drew the dust together, revelled in the task of conveying it to the nose; his coat and vest, which had once been black, had become brown, whilst his nether garments and shoes followed suit. The floor too, around him was covered with the bewitching particles. The whole man, both inside and out, was absorbed and had given up — it was a surrender to the demon and a complete victory. The powder, had it been detonating, would, years ago, have blown up and destroyed the devotee; his Moloch would have devoured him.

As Boniface, in the old play, told the Irish captain that he had eaten his ale, drunk his ale and slept on his ale — declaring it to be Burgundy and worth ten shillings a quart — so our old friend could say this, and more, for his idol. But dying, as he did, at eighty-one, who can say that the indulgence shortened his life? We will rather conclude that, though it did not give him vigour nor add marrow to his hones, it tended to prolong his days by yielding him some comfort by way of diversion and who, after this, would deny him his snuff? Towards myself, he, in our little dealings together, excelled in two virtues, patience and civility. The time taken up appeared to belong to the visitor; if the minutes ran on to the hour he be grudged neither.

In striking contrast was this behaviour to that of the London bookseller towards a country customer, who, once upon a time, in my own person, was attempting to cheapen an odd volume or two of Charles Lamb. "Lamb," he pettishly exclaimed, "goose, I see, sir, is more fitted to your capacity." The countryman laughing at the jest, quickly paid the price asked, pocketed the volumes and bolted out of the shop, but he never again ventured to face that snappish man.

What do we not owe to the bookseller and his books? To be easily and cheaply supplied with this mental aliment, this necessity for the healthy mind — for among all his fellows the reading man has the advantage every way. Life with him who loves books and makes them his companions is, at all times, active. In his solitary chamber — it may be the prison cell — he is never alone. He has made friends who will not forsake him. He may call them to his presence again and again, and they dare not refuse. He can converse with whom he may select, and be instructed or annexed in proportion to his capacity of appreciation. To the blind even, the one solace above all has been the knowledge of books. Has not Milton told us, in never-dying verse, of "Wisdom at one entrance quite shut out?" "Yet not the more," he says exultingly, "cease I to wander where the muses haunt clear spring, or shady grove, or sunny hill."

Upon one of my visits our old friend gave me striking proof of what habit and use may do for us. I remarked upon the number of books he had about him. He replied, "I have ten thousand beneath this roof," "But," I said, "do you know what you have?" "No," he answered, "yet if you name any book and the author, I can tell you if I have it, and can hand it to you." It was upon this visit that he told me that among all poets and poems Dante and the Divine Comedy were his special favourites.

In a slight obituary notice in the "East Sussex News" it has been remarked that had Dickens known him he would have made a volume out of his person and character, and surely, among the twelve thousand who nestle around their proud castle he will not soon be forgotten. Now, after shaking off the "mortal coil" if it should be our old friend's fate to be situated in those middle regions between the Elysian Fields and Tartarus, and the longings for earth and old associations, which are allowable there, come upon him, can we not fancy him, ghost-like, visiting in the glimpses of the moon his old dwelling, sitting at the end of his counter, counting the old bookshelves, and drawing with his bony fingers the snuff together, waiting for the new clock of St. Michael's to chime out and strike the "witching hour" when night and morning meet? But we will not anticipate a disturbed future, and bidding him adieu, say "May his bones and his spirit both rest in peace."

# OUR SUSSEX PARISH AND ITS INSTITUTIONS

## THE CHURCH

On the apex of a spit of land, rising with a gradual ascent from the confines of Pevensey Level and running due east and west, stands our church. The tower is exactly six miles from the sea, and the base one hundred feet above high-water mark. If you will walk out to the north-east about a mile you will see with what nice care the spot was chosen. The high road from Marshfoot House traverses the ridge of the "Hog's Back" and shoulders, and by a gentle curve and descent lands the traveller into the town, leaving the church on the right hand. From this point the surface slopes away in all directions, giving a full and clear view of the country from ten to twenty miles all round. From the top of the tower the look-out, if not romantic, is wide and varied, and by a little amount of searching we find we are the nucleus of many an historic spot.

Will you accompany me in an imaginary walk round? We will start from a point westward, where we see Mount Caburn, "Sovereign of Sussex hills," the bluff and hoary sentinel — ever watching, never tiring guardian of the ancient town of Lewes. We narrow the circle, and come on to the beacon tower of Firle — guardian over the domain of the Gages. Draw nearer home, and we have the old dwelling of the fat Abbots of Michelham. Michelham

*Michelham Priory gateway tower*

Priory, with its watch-tower and the surrounding moat and glistening waters, glide southward, and we find the mossy, unbroken covers of Abbot's Wood, perhaps primeval, or a residue and a remnant of the old wealden forest, whence the bygone owners of the Priory drew in summer their firewood, and in the winter their game, now the stronghold of the foxes and the foxhunter's trial of patience; for the cover is so strong, Reynard does not care to break, but will prefer to die, if die he must, at home. Here, too, the naturalist may wander, capturing by night or by day his beautiful but fragile prey. Forming a good background to these woods rise the South Downs, glowing with a purple hue in the summer light, and veiling the setting sun as he blushingly takes his evening dip in the laughing ocean.

Perhaps a reminiscence or two, and a little dallying by the way, may be here indulged in. On the north front of the hill is to be seen the Wilmington Giant, stretching at full length, with staff in hand, on the the soft turf, showing the outline of his vast proportions, and the "green path," a ledge stealing by gentle and skirting rise from

*Michelham Priory moat and tower*

the north to the hill-top, over looking the spot where once stood Wind-door Mill. Twice have I seen her in flames, and that for the last time. "She" will now never be rebuilt. The latter mishap was brought about by a strong sou'-wester in the night. The brake failing in its grip, away went mill and all to destruction. I opened my eyes about 6 a.m. to see one of my oldest acquaintances expire in flames, leaving only a lifeless lump to mark the spot where all my days I had seen the sweeps swing round in merry mood.

I witnessed, too, the first conflagration. At that time I was on a visit, and sleeping under the roof of my poor old grandmother in her thatched cottage close to the shadow of the hill. Sweet are the memories of childhood! There was at that time, as now, a sheep-yard close in front of the old house, and the poor widow was, as she said, "frightened out of her wits" by the glare of the fire. She thought the yard and all was ablaze — and what would become of the ewes and lambs! She would in a moment be off for the shepherd, when lo! the sheep and the yard were both untouched, and all there was safe. The light from the burning mill made everything as bright as day. The cause of this fire has remained a mystery. The night was calm; neither lightning nor thunder, nor any other reason, could be assigned. Fifty years after the event rumour said, on that night the mill had been robbed by two men from a distance, and a load of corn carted away, and to prevent suspicion and discovery the building had been fired by the robbers' hands. A troubled mind made the confession as life was departing. So said my informant.

To the south of the mill is Deep Dean, a desolate yet beautiful hollow. The steep sides, to the eye of a stranger, look dangerous, but the shepherd boy, squatting and tucking his arms across his knees, will slide on his heels to the bottom and call it fun. From the northern end, which is an abrupt and forbidding termination of the gorse, we have a good view of the soft and mellow south-western opening into a wide spreading valley, soon to be lost in the surrounding expanse of Down.

You must pardon me if I linger here. My father was a shepherd boy on these hills, and he early awoke my fancy by the tales he told of his boy-life; of the "Little Dean" and the Deep Dean; of the sheep he tended; of the old shepherd and his well-trained dog; of the timorous wheatear; of the trapping of these delicate birds; of his playing and lolling until he fell asleep in the hollow of the turf that goes to make up the Giant's head; of the clouds flying up hill for fine weather and rolling down hill for wind and rain; of the wreck of the wheelbarrow — how he was tempted to drive it down the hill front, a short cut for home, and how, to save himself, he had to let go the handles, and how the thing bounded and rebounded, and was smashed up till not two sticks hung together.

That old cottage of my grandmother was to me a paradise, with the gardens, the hedges, the birds' nests, and the outhouse, partly occupied by Master Levett, the basket-maker. He was known as "Old Twigs," his tame rabbits munching and poking their noses between the slits of the hutches; his eel-pots and the slimy prey captured in the neighbouring Cuckmere. I have stood by as he turned his catch into a tub of ashes, to quiet them ere he skinned

23

and weighed and bunched them off in pounds ready for market. The basket-maker was famous for his wicker eel-pots. I am told his art of making them is lost to the locality.

A low wall of rough flint, with a slit, in lieu of a gate way, for entrance to reach the house, bounded the garden close by the high road. A honeysuckle and a rose hung trailing over a rude wooden porch that stood guardian at the front door, the overhanging eaves of thatch giving shelter to numerous sparrows, and these had in winter nights to look out for ugly visitors — the bird-catchers with their nets; the roughly brick-paved living-room, with the meagre furniture — a few ash-built rush-bottomed chairs. The old arm-chair had its standing in the left-hand corner of the fire-place, though the last owner died years ago. There was the well-scoured round oak table constantly in its place close to the widow's chair on the right-hand side. As much for ornament as for use, the brass warming pan hung from the wall. The bright face served me for a mirror. These were a few heirlooms. The family Bible had a shelf to itself. Delf ware decked the shelves of the old dresser. A very long and twisted blue or green glass stick, with a shepherd's crook at one end, was suspended by two ribbon loops, each with a bow, in a line with the ceiling. There were several relics from vessels wrecked at various times on the neighbouring coasts — one especially, *The Nympha*, lost in November, I747. By a nail in the wall opposite the open fire-place, where, on the chimney top in summer you heard the flutter of the swallow and the twitter of her song, hung an American tomahawk, said to have been brought over by a returned soldier. His comrade had been scalped, and the Red Indian thrust through with the bayonet, and the hatchet taken from his bloody and grasping hand had found its way, with other tro-phies, to old England with the honest warrior who had avenged his comrade's death. There were two small coloured sketches in glazed black frames, portraits of a daughter and her soldier husband. She had marched with the regiment or troop westward, never to return home again. Her costume was very scanty, and the waistband was carried up as near to the shoulders as possible. Short waists were then doubtless the fashion. The soldier in blue was as stiff as ever was man on parade. The old lady declared both to be good likenesses. Dame Hill (she was a widow the second time) was, among her poor neighbours, a useful creature, and many were the births and deaths she was witness to. To fill up her time she spun wool mops. The whirring of the wheel has followed me through life. I was well up in all the process, the carding, rolling, spinning, spooling, tying, cutting, shaking, and picking out, until the article became as round and level as a trencher, and fit for sale or use. When, at a good old age, she gave up the ghost, the share of the chattels that fell to my father was the family Bible and the tomahawk, and these have, in another distribution, fallen to my lot. The first is religiously kept; the war hatchet is, with other odds and ends, consigned to the garret.

Next we approach Wilmington. As we enter the hamlet from the north we hear the thud of the wheelwright's hammer as he drives the spoke home, and higher up the street the sparks from the forge of the blacksmith hiss at you as you pass by. There is the "Black Horse," the one inn to accommodate travellers, and for the rustics' evening parliament, where, in the back kitchen in winter evenings,

*Wilmington*

25

around a glowing fire, parish and imperial politics are energetically discussed over the "pint and the pot." There was a rookery overhanging the road; but the elms and the rooks, together with the harness-maker and the shoe maker, are gone. The barn, opening its wide doors to the street, is silent now; the sound of the flail is no more heard in the land. Flowers are cultivated wherever a house has a patch of border in front, and as we rise with the narrowing roadway toward the church and the vicarage, the banks on either side are beset with the wild clematis, with its feathery bloom, and the periwinkle, with its glossy leaf and blue blossom, mixed with a variety of wild flowers and creepers. In the trees overhead birds twitter and sing, and give welcome without ostentation. As you emerge from the little labyrinth you are in full face to the Downs, the mountains of Sussex stretching away on either hand. Here is, or used to be, by the roadside stuck full in season, a bank of white violets, short "strigged," stunted from dryness of soil, and the sweetest ever smelt. The church and the churchyard lie high above the roadway, and, to gain admission, a flight of steps, cut in the bank, must be mounted. Guarding the porch stands the grand old yew, beneath whose waving branches lie the bones, if aught there be remaining, of my paternal grand-father and grandmother; and now, perhaps, I may be excused for lingering about this quaint old village and the locality.

Due south we have Beachy Head, and well sheltered by its grand bulk from the south-western winds is the charming town of Eastbourne, which, from our position on the tower, we can plainly see. The growth has been as rapid as the social change is great. Fifty years ago, and less,[1] Eastbourne had but one church and one clergyman, the present venerable Vicar, inducted in the year 1828, with a population of 1,742 souls (according to the clergy list of 1828). Candidates for confirmation then came to Hailsham. There were two doctors, one lawyer, and no printing press. The latter was Hailsham's privilege. We supplied the type for the little "matter" Eastbourne had to set up. It was, however, at that time a watering-place of some note. Lovers of retirement sought out this seaside

[1] Circa 1840

26

*Entrance gateway to Hurstmonceux Castle*

retreat: the heated politician, the wearied philanthropist, the clerk, jaded with uncongenial work at the India Office, the ever-charming, gentle Charles Lamb, sought here to recolour his blanched cheeks and brace his laxed nerves with the invigorating and balmy breezes of the South Downs and the tonic of the sea air.

Turning eastward, we meet Westham and Pevensey, with the grand old castle separating the two parish churches, each with their few attendant houses that go to make up the town. The grey towers and battlements of this splendid ruin, clothed with ivy, nod their heads and wave their hands and arms to us across the Marsh. It was at Pevensey, as all the world knows, the Merry Andrew, Doctor Borde, lived when he wrote "The Wise Men of Gotham," satirizing the Corporation officials, and especially the Mayor. A messenger had handed his Worship a letter. The servant, perceiving his master was perusing the document upside down, drew his attention to the fact, when he, full of magisterial dignity, rebuked the man for his impertinence, declaring he would, while Mayor of Pevensey, read his letters upside down or any other way he chose. The Doctor has bequeathed the name "Merry Andrew" to all succeeding professional jesters. Then we have Pevensey Level — so much changed since Horse Eye was an island, and salt pans, peat bogs, and fish ponds were things of necessity and profit to the neighbourhood — now a grand sweep of many thousand acres of rich pasture, famous in these days for its juicy beef and delicate mutton. To the south of this place are the shining waters of Pevensey Bay, on which rode over, on his grand enterprise, William the Bastard — the Conqueror. On this coast, too, it was that he stumbled and fell, and to reassure his omen-stricken followers, clasping the ground on which he lay, he claimed the kingdom as his own.

Classic ground, too, is Herstmonceux. The church, built on a mound fringing the Marsh, is a clear object to our view, and, with the Castle, is surrounded by historic incident. The mansion in the Park, built from the spoils of the dismantled Castle in 1777, has been the home of more than one notability. The philanthropist and the philosopher — Wilberforce and Bunsen — have there each in his turn found a retreat from the busy hum of town life. The first-named, writing to a friend in Scotland, says:— "How much you will be surprised to find that I am within a few miles of the tremendous John Fuller. It must be surely a wild region that contains such inhabitants — some outlandish place beyond the bounds of civilized society. To explain, I am in a corner of Sussex, and in a place almost as pretty as the neighbourhood of the sea ever is. There is an old castle here," &c. Bunsen too—

> The man of lordly brain and lordlier soul,
> Friend of all hearts and counsellor of kings,
> Found here a quiet and congenial home.

It takes more than a generation to wipe out these and like memories from the neighbourhood. There is a dazzling though misty spell hanging about the remains of such men's lives, and as we cast our eyes eastward, watching the rising sun, their halo rises

*John Stirling*

too, to grace the horizon, and we credit our experience with one joy more by seeing the very trees that have once waved over the heads of these intellectual heroes. The Naylors and the Hares, though all dead or gone from the parish, yet fill the neighbourhood with their inspirations. The triumph of the spiritual over the sensual, of truth over bigotry, of gentleness over brutality and ignorance, the bread thrown upon the waters of doubt by the authors of "Guesses at Truth," has not passed away. It shall be seen after many days. The Rectory and The Limes are both within four miles walk of our church. Men of my day well remember the Rector (Archdeacon Hare) driving his four-wheeler, with his devoted wife, his constant companion, by his side — they were often seen in our street — both pale-faced, looking wan through much watching, both plain in attire, and the well-worn hat of the Archdeacon showed how little he cared for gloss and glare and the outward adornment. I once heard him preach in our own parish church what I considered to be a very dull sermon — prosy, long winded. Little did I ween I was listening to a man who would one day become famous in the world of letters, numbering, as he did at that time among his friends and visitors Arnold, Herschell Landor, Wordsworth, Manning, Bunsen, and Maurice; "that young Luther of a later day," and that Hercules of thought, Thomas Carlyle, wandering and musing, as he himself has said, among the leafy lanes of Herstmonceux; and Stirling, too, son of the Thunderer, of Printing House Square. It was here he robed himself, and joined, as he facetiously called the clergy, the "Black Dragoons."

I knew, too, the "poor cobbler" mentioned by Carlyle, whose after success in life was due to this kind instructor, the good John Stirling. I am a worshipper of mind from the Godhead downwards, and for my heart and head's content I will believe I have seen the poet and deep-thinker ride into Hailsham with his reverend friend, Julius Hare. The "poor cobbler" was very fond of talking of his benefactor, and he has related to me, with wondering and excited eye, with what facility the young curate would compose a hymn or pharaphrase the Psalms of the inspired royal songster, David. Poor Stirling! Here are the last lines he ever wrote:—

> Could we but hear all Nature's voice,
> From glow-worm up to sun,
> 'Twould speak with one concordant sound,
> Thy will, O God, be done!
>
> But hark! A sudden, mightier prayer,
> From all men's hearts that live:
> Thy will be done in earth and Heaven,
> And Thou my sins forgive.

He gave the paper, the verses written with pencil, to his sister; he murmured, too, the two last lines to himself. He appeared to be seeking for something, and said, "Only the old Bible, which I so often used at Herstmonceux in the cottages." He was buried, says the narrative, at Bonchurch. I remember, too, the happy features of Mrs. Maria Hare (Maria Leycester), the aunt of the author of "Memorials of a Quiet Life," and her rubicund coachman — upright, full chested, stiff, and dignified — who for years was her outdoor attendant. The phaeton was often in our little town, and on the box by the side of the driver (a privilege, no doubt) was occasionally seated a boy, whom I now picture as the author of more than one book of travel and incident, besides the Memorials.

I feel an inclination to linger over the memories of Herstmonceux, so full, so rich, so varied of love, war, literature and history from ages past: when King Henry III encamped with his army in the Park, and marching forward, fought the battle of Lewes, was defeated by the Barons, and found himself a prisoner in the Castle that yet overlooks the county town. But my purpose is a call only, a passing call; so we will move on to the cold and sterile north — fit home for the "tremendous" John Fuller. Why the liberty loving Wilberforce styled him "tremendous" I do not know. Probably he was a tremendous Tory, and, for his position in life, he was coarse and obstreperous in his habit and manner. On the left hand, going north through the village of Brightling, is the obelisk — or "needle" as the natives call it — an object which can be distinctly seen on a fine day from our churchyard. As a public man, John Fuller is still remembered by one of his Parliamentary utterances, known as "John Fuller's pull," a strong pull, a long pull, and "a pull altogether," will be useful as a triple emphasis for many a year to come. With one anecdote we will leave him in his cold home, for Brightling, save for its heather-bells, wild thyme, and roses, has little charm for me. The story goes that once upon a time the leading man of the church choir asked Squire Fuller to give a musical instrument or two to assist in the singing. He promised when next in London to see to it, and he took the way to be right by applying to a musical instrument maker for advice in a matter of which he was entirely ignorant. The man of melody

31

recommended a bassoon. "Send a dozen," shouted the patron, and out of the shop he bolted; and down to the village of Brightling, in Sussex, addressed to the churchwardens, came a case containing twelve bassoons for the free use of the choir, more to the chagrin than delight of the rustic singers. Fancy, the first time the Squire appeared again in church, twelve bassoons in a circle in the gallery, each man doing his best with the coy but stubborn instrument! I would rather be away in the fields. However, the gift showed good-nature, which is akin to charity, and that virtue, we read, covereth a multitude of sins. So we will suppose the old Squire to be as good a man as many among his fellows, his neighbours, and contemporaries, and as circumstances would allow him to be. It is evident he thought himself so. His motto was "Honest Jack Fuller."

Farther on to the north-east are to be seen the white houses on Guestling and Fairlight heights, and next inland is the high ground around Battle Abbey, where the proud Saxon fell eight hundred years ago, and Netherfield Toll, high above all surroundings, marking the spot of the Wealden boring, set about to ascertain the strata, and to decide the question of coal or no coal for Sussex, which it did both negatively and positively. To the enterprise and honour of Mr. Henry Willett, of Brighton, is due the final solution of this geological problem. Further to the north-west is Heathfield, the church of which parish, and of the monument standing in the Park, we have a good view. Heathfield has a distinct history as the centre of the defunct Sussex iron mines and foundries, and it may here be noted that in cutting the railway, in 1879 and '80, through from Hailsham to Tunbridge Wells, many of the old pits were run into, and the outline of their circumference exposed and clearly displayed. Then we have Warbleton parish, its church and church tower, the prison-house of Richard Woodman and, others who were burned on School Hill, Lewes, in the year 1557. We are completing the circuit, for the western section offers no spot of note, save the Laughton Woods, the roosting-place of thousands of rooks,. which at the gloaming congregate from all points to these covers for the night. But we have passed over Chiddingly and its noble church tower and spire, beacon for many a mile by sea and by land; also the parish and

*Warbleton church tower*

home of Richard Lower, a man of more than local fame, author of the popular tale in verse of "Tom Cladpole's Journey to Lunnon," and many other rhyming, humorous, and witty things in print, which give the writer character and claim not to be forgotten by the public. Mark Antony Lower, his second son, the somewhat famous archaeologist and county historian, claims Chiddingly as his birthplace and early home.

We have now from the summit of our church tower, looking over the battlements, taken a survey varying from ten to twenty miles in radiation. We have passed from west round to west again. Let us descend and sum up the result. If in the bird's-eye view we have obtained of our little town and surroundings we have no architectural ruin, no monumental tower, no tumbling ivy-clad walls, nothing to point to belongings of the past, save the very modest Priory Chapel of Otham, near Polegate, now, and for many years, used as a farm stable; if we have no rocks nor rivulets; if we are lacking in groves and cascades, and grand old trees and shady paths; if we have not the picturesque that the residents of some localities have to boast and to be proud of, we are at least the centre of a circle of rich and varied scenery, and surrounded by spots made famous by historic incident and lore. We have seen in the distance the deep blue sea, soft hills, smiling pastures, undulating landscapes, farm home steads, rustic cottages, curling smoke mounting from many a chimney peeping out from among surrounding orchards; and the lark sings as blithe and as wanton above our heads as he does over the grandest mansion and the best-kept parterres.

## GOD'S ACRE

It was a pleasing sight in years gone by to see the rustics of the parish assemble on a Sunday afternoon and hang about the church door ere they entered and took up their seats, all dressed in the smock-frock and hobnailed boots, and with hair cut straight across the forehead and all round as though a basin had been clapped on the head as a guide to the scissors of the homespun barber; and I well remember these same youths passing the reading-desk, with chin almost resting on the breast, "demure and grave," many of them dropping the Curate a reverential bow as they followed each one on to his appointed place. Behaviour since that time has somewhat changed, but reverence, if not so demonstrable, may be deeper. One thing is certain: the smock-frock and the hobnails are never now seen or heard within the portals of the church door. Fashion, following close upon the heels of progress and means, has banished the rustic garb. For dress 'tis hard now to know the maid from the mistress and the manservant from the master.

I pity the man, if any such there be, who can escape without emotion a visit to the shrines of our "pious ancestors" as they lay embalmed in the dim religious light of our grand old cathedrals. The most rigid or rabid denominationalist, as he gazes upward to the centre of the high vaulted roof, is touched, and becomes mute in wonder and admiration, almost with love, as he treads the pillared aisle and hears the

Pealing organ blow
To the full voiced choir below.

And so in some degree it is with our rustic life in our own parish church. If veneration for the ritual is changing or passing away, there is no change in veneration for the building or for God's Acre. All this-is sacred and hallowed. We may forget some living acquaintance, but here are friends we shall never forget. As I pass daily among the graves some occupant of the cold and lone home rises and stands before me — not shrouded nor ghostly, nor wan, nor weary. I see them, and hold converse with them as of old. We walk the paths together, but talk on no new subject. Their present is my future. We touch not that mystery. It is some episode of the past that engages our thoughts and tongues for a few seconds: it may be the glimpse of a beloved child who has risen and is standing before me, or sister, brother, or parent who is awakening and tightening the cords of broken and almost forgotten love; it may be a mother's or a wife's caress, or it may be a father's rebuke. And so we people our brains with associations of the past. The reverie is salutary, and our loved ones retire to their cerements.

Such are some of the influences by which our churchyards will ever be dear to us. I am touched as I pass the last resting-place of the widow Slye. Under a mausoleum of plain stone lie the mother, her five maiden daughters, the maiden sister, and Aunt Marthana, and the blind bachelor son, William, all mingling together in their common dust, waiting the last trumpet-call. On the opposite side of the pathway is the tomb of two other bachelor brothers, Mathias and Pearson, the first named decidedly the eccentric man of the parish. Excepting the mother, I knew them all, though the birth of the eldest daughter, Mary, carries us back more than a century. Inside the church, on the south wall, is a tablet to the memory of the mother, the daughter, Ann — a strong-minded woman — the ruling spirit of the family of old maids and bachelors, and the blind son and brother, Mr. William, as he was always called — a man of varied information, well read, easy in conversation, more than clever in figures, and always cheerful. "So little is it in the power of physical evil to deprive us of our enjoyment." Mr. Slye was in the habit of walking miles in every direction, "led by a thoughtless boy," and was well-known and thoroughly respected. Within the hearing of a whisper or a sigh are other graves that awaken memories. To the right is the renovated rail stretching over the bones of our first parish schoolmaster, Francis Howlett. On this rail, from the poet who it is said never wrote one bad line, and never said but one good thing (Oliver Goldsmith) our Vicar has in happy paraphrase paid a tribute to the memory of the old master and to his profession:—

> There in the former vestry skill'd to rule,
> The village master taught his little school.
> But past is all his fame — the very spot,
> Where many a time he triumphed, is forgot.

A good test as to the quality and position of the inhabitants of a country parish is the state of the churchyard. Ours is of the medium order — more inclined to poverty than to fame. We have no "storied urns" to look up to, nor animated bust gazing down on the passer-by; no tomb but of the plainest order and pattern; neither marble nor granite pressing recumbent on a rich man's bones; no truncated column, that most suggestive of all memorials, telling of early life cut off and the blighted hope of loving parents; no order of rank save one solitary squire; no epitaph worth transcribing; and if we ever had a village Hampden or a mute, inglorious Milton, their resting-place is unknown. To me the most regrettable fact about the old burial-ground is the lack of trees. Would that some self-denying man, at the time the foundations of the church were put in, had planted a memorial tree — a yew. At the ordinary growth such a tree would now be in its prime, and we should have something beside the pleasure to the eye to carry us back in thought to the old, old time —

> When the Monks came up from old Marshfoot,
>     Each man to ring his bell,
> And they rang with zeal, and rang with skill,
>     And they rang the changes well.
>
> And the Monks would listen on Michelham Tower,
>     For those bells were of good renown,
> And few there were that could compare
>     With Saint Mary's of Haylsham Town.
> E. H.

The Marshfoot Monks, perhaps, are not verities, yet the poetic instinct may be as trustworthy as more sober prose narratives relating to the past.

Until the Rev. Hobart Cannter, our second resident Vicar during this century, about the year 1850 planted a few on the north boundary, we had not a tree to wave its branches in the summer sun nor to cause the wind to whistle in the wintry blast. See now the crystal dew as the drops, in a spring morning, hang on the tender leaves; listen to the twitter of the bird,

>     With golden wing and satin poll;

hear him invite his mate to their summer home, for high up in the sycamore at midsummer you may see their nest and hear the unfledged cry, "More, more." Stretch yourself on the turf beneath and watch the unfolding buds of the chestnut, and you will hear the unbroken murmur of the honey-bee, the murmuring of gladness and the satisfaction of a hundred workers. Perhaps you will ask yourself whence they come and whither they go; what finger-post directs them to their homes, for though miles away, each will be there before sundown. This is a mystery, and, as we reflect, we thank the Rev. Hobart Cannter again and again. Planting trees is a self-denying act. It is for posterity we then work. The man who does this graceful deed does not expect to see the full glory of his work. But he shall have a share. He shall not be forgotten when he is in his grave, He shall be remembered for more than one generation.

Speaking for myself, I am a worshipper of trees — the sturdy trunk, the brawny limbs, the leafy fingers, the hoary head; and, as I approach a veteran — poor as I am at a bow — I can uncover my head and become reverent. My wish is that we had a few grand old elms in our churchyard, beneath whose shade man might linger and worship. The general appearance of the place, and the habits of the people surrounding, have of late years very much improved. I remember when journeymen shoemakers and blacksmiths from the workshops adjoining played cricket in their dinner hour, improvising sometimes a tombstone for a wicket, and when all manner of things, with a total disregard to decency, were done with impunity. Until the present Vicar's time the herbage was let to the butcher for sheep-feed, and, when a fresh supply of mutton for the shop was needed the slaughter-house door was thrown open, even on a Sunday morning, and the victims were driven in. Then the graves and all about the place were worse than neglected. Thistles, docks, nettles, and any weed rioted and revelled on dead men's bones; the graves were broken, and grass grew rank and was never mown, and no one appeared to care for the place except for a profit and convenience, to obtain fees, and to put away the dead. It is true we had those semi-ghostly men, the churchwardens, to meet all requirements. The Vicars —resident or non-resident — made £5 a year by letting to the butcher. It was the Vicar's freehold, and should not a man do as he pleased with his own?

Since the closing of the ground for burial purposes a gradual improvement has taken place. The parish has responded, and at this time a neatness unknown previously is creeping over the surface, and that which was a few years ago a disgrace and a rebuke is becoming a satisfaction and a pleasure to look upon. Here is a question: At what time was the churchyard encroached upon for building purposes? There can be no doubt but it has been — that the houses of the street on the church side are nearly all, from one gateway to the other, standing on old burial ground. At various times the building of new houses on the sites of old foundations, and cellar diggings have brought to light many human remains. In one instance an entire skeleton was dug out, and so late as the drainage of 1879 the workman, in running a trench up the passage to the blacksmith's shop, brought to the light of day the perfect jaw of a child with full set of sucking teeth, which teeth were being displaced by a second crop from beneath. To speculate upon the number of years passed since these interments would be a rash venture. However, this may be taken as certain, that some of the old houses now gone have, according to writings relating to the different properties, an age running up to three or four hundred years. Now, the church, it is pretty certain, has not been built over six hundred years, and we have no evidence to point to any earlier structure for public religious purposes. Before that time we were dependent upon Hellingly for the benefit of a "cure." Where, then, was the burial-ground for the people? We will leave this puzzling question a legacy to the next generation.

How and when was the church despoiled of its western frontage? It may be added that the present smithy and house were built by John Ellis about the year 1810. Before this date the old shop was close to the street, and the sparks from the anvil from the force of the hammer flew out at the open window across the then unpaved footpath into the roadway. The ground on which the present workshop stands was then a back-yard, with a fine old pear tree growing in the centre. It may here be noted that the iron frame on which hangs the sign of the "Crown Inn," as good a piece of anvil work as you will meet with in a long day's march, was made at this shop by John Ellis.

Standing east and looking west, we see the church, as a whole, is a building of four distinct gables — the chancel, vestry, lady chapel, and the nave. Each has within the last five years undergone repair, restoration, and rebuilding — first the south front, in 1869; high, pointed, arched windows being substituted for plain, square, white-painted, oak-framed ones. These old windows were separated by roughly-hewn yellow sandstone groins, and a red-brick parapet surmounted — save where the porch cut it into two divisions — the whole length of the front. This was the work of a resident tradesman, and had been standing about a hundred years, the whole being as unchurchlike and out of all character as could well be. Next the vestry was rebuilt on the old foundations, and with the old material, broken stone — an honest restoration; next the lady chapel — a restoration in character with the vestry. This chapel is embellished with a figure painted east window dedicated

*Hailsham Church from the entrance to the High Street*

40

to the memory of the late Vicar, Rev. G. G. Harvey. The south chancel painted window is in memory of three deceased sons of the late Vicar, and, like the east window, is the pious gift of the mother and widow, Mrs. Harvey, as is also the rebuilding of the chapel. Next the chancel was partially restored, and decorated with an illuminated east window, the gift of Frederick Sherwood, Esq., of Ersham Lodge. Next the north front, an honest restoration — painted windows in lieu of others, cut off at the turn of the arch, roof restored, the overlapping eaves being replaced by stone parapet to match the south front.

The restoration of the tower is a great success. The most captious and keen-sighted would be baffled to find fault. The turrets and the battlements were all taken down and entirely rebuilt, and so happily is the new blended with the old, that one would, looking up, hardly believe the thing had been done within the last dozen years. We are proud of our church tower, so square, so perfect, of so good proportions, so ample from the base to the height. Surmounted by the centre vane, and guarded at each angle by the four small ones, all on a fine day glittering in their coats of gold, give the place a pleasant and cheery appearance. To the eye of a stranger approaching, especially from the south, the place has a somewhat inviting aspect and beguiling character. The tower is built of hewn sandstone (probably taken from the "Quarry pond," the only bit of sand rock we have in the parish), interposed with squares of broken flint. The workman must have been master of a special art with these boulders. Many of them, if you observe, are duplicates, and, as I imagine, have been broken in the hand and laid or placed in the mortar forthwith. How was the breakage effected? Many are cut as true as though a pair of shears had passed through them. Except the south front, all the works have been brought to maturity and finished, and the expense has been met by the superintending care of the present Vicar, Rev. F. C. Harvey.

There is on the roof of the church a patch of slate which may cause a question to be asked when there will be no one to answer or reply. Here is the history. In the year 1836, November 19, a mighty storm swept over the South of England. Buildings were unroofed, trees torn up by their roots, barns, churches, and many other structures blown down, and casualties happened, many of which are now forgotten. One among our own was the unroofing of the church. The wind came from the south, and the tiles, like sear leaves, flew over into the parsonage field, leaving rafters bare and the roof looking most desolate. This, of course, was not a tithe of the loss of tiles in and about the place. Many roofs required new covering, so a sharp-witted man, Thomas Burfield, then about 27 or 28, and owner of more than one house that had received damage, seeing the dilemma, mounted his horse and rode off ere the wind had settled down, to the brickyards at the Dicker, and bought up all the tiles he could, as he said at the time, for love or money, and so, there being none others to be had, the church roof became patched with slate.

How well the massive walls of the tower bear the wear of six hundred years! There is no breakage nor crack in the whole structure. The angles and the buttresses are as true now and as unshaken as when the tower passed fresh from the hands of the builder. On the south front are several indentations in the stone which for years have been a puzzle to me. I have walked past again and again and asked myself, "Whatever can be the meaning of these cup-like holes?" until one morning, my brain and my fancy taking a leap, I said, "Can these be bullet marks? And, if so, did any of the shots strike the flints?" And behold, so it is. Several of these flints are smashed, starred from the centre where the impact of the force fell. By general consent now these holes are considered to be the result of musket or pistol shot, fired whether in wantonness or in executing a dire sentence we cannot tell.

To me the most interesting person employed on the works was the artist workman, John Pepper, of Brighton. See him on the scaffolding erected over the belfry door, with mallet and chisel in hand, as he digs out from a square projecting stone the living features of a man, and then, after the order of Nature, the woman follows. These heads must have been the creation of the workman's own mind, formed within by his own fancy. He had no copy to guide either his eye or his hand, but by degrees, what with the chip ping of the chisel and the blows of the mallet, both rude implements, two perfect heads and faces — male and female, creations of his own brain-power — come out and give life to the cold stone. I stood by and watched the progress, and gradually both form and characteristic expressions became developed. The male grew stern and noble, the female soft and benign — impersonation, I said, of Justice and Mercy.

## OUR HOUSES

I remember when, on the 14th of May, 1849, the railway was opened from Polegate to our town. Gentlemen, railway officials, and strangers, visiting us for the first time, remarked that our houses had been built for King John's men. The public dinner was held at the "Crown" in the old market-room, the ceiling coming down so much that visitors upon entering felt half impelled to stoop to save the head. A heavy, hot dinner, a room full of company, with the overhanging lath and plaster just above your skull — what more oppressive? Eaters, drinkers, speakers, all feel the despotism.

The rooms of our two principal inns, excepting the new market-room at the "Crown," are of this order, and so also are all our houses that belong to bygone architecture. Enter where you will, the ceiling may almost be reached by the knuckle joints. In winter the glaring gas changes white into black, the unventilated room becomes oppressive, making night hideous. In all our new houses we have improved upon this, and may now extend our vision ten or twelve feet upwards. We are escaping the dilemma of the sailor who, when I was an inquiring boy, told me he had sailed so far that he could not put a sixpence between the crown of his head and the sky.

"Poor fellow!" I said; "how not?" "Because," he added, and relieved me, "I had not a sixpence belonging to me."

The street now styled "High Street" is a make-up of odds and ends. Our ancestors, one would think, had neither method nor eye to order, each man following his own plan. Or, perhaps, they were bound by circumstances, and the result was to them advantageous, though at this date it appears to be a great muddle.

We have more than one house standing end on to the road, as if shy and bashful; another turning its back that way, as if in contempt and derision; and if we do meet a few looking us full in the face, and our hearts begin to soften, we directly come across another giving us the cold shoulder, crooking the elbow and turning the traveller out of the direct line of march. There is the "corner," almost an acute angle, twisting out suddenly from south to west, with the ugly old house taking up the most prominent position in the town — a dingy, worn-out old place, without any charm to awaken that veneration which usually attaches to age, and especially to ancient architecture. It ought, years ago, to have made way for another and a better building. But perhaps I am a little hard on my old neighbour. It may be, that it looks a shadow, or a part only of its former glory; but it has, no doubt, a life of several centuries, and if its history could be told, we might revere what we now deride. The original half-timber basement has been supplemented by brick covered over by yellow wash; the woodwork above, with the sectional plaster and the quarried casements, tell of bygone respectability and character. On the south front are projecting timbers, that carry the second floor slightly over the base, which timbers, years ago, carried the extending covering still farther out, overshadowing the footpath.

This was the meeting-place for gossips — fellows of the grosser sort, lounging here, cracking their coarse jokes on innocent passers-by. It was at this spot they joked Master Budgen on the colour of his breeches. Twice on a Sunday he walked this way from Cacklebury to church. Fortunately for this good man, and especially for his nethermost parts, he had at that time a son who was coachman to a nobleman, and this son sent the father, periodically, his decarded plush. A consignment having arrived, the old man started next Sabbath, dressed in a pair shining black as jet On sighting him, the rowdies shouted out: "Here comes old Budgen as black as a coal." The old fellow thought he would, in the afternoon, try a change of garment, so he put on red, and the lads then shouted louder than ever: "Here he comes again, all a-fire; bring water, he is as red as a live cinder! He looks like lightning! He will be burnt up!" This joke, if tame, may be given as a type of street behaviour at the time.

Whether it is more than surmise I know not, but rumour asserts that at one time the high road ran athwart and behind this, to us famous, "corner," thus leaving the crooked place somewhat alone in its glory. The old shop, with its sweets and sours of every hue and shape, has time out of mind been popular with all girls and boys, and in many other ways the "corner" is an important place to the Hailshamer. It is our radiating point from which we measure distances, and many other things depend on the "corner." It used to be protected by a heavy post and railing to keep off reckless drivers, and when "improvement" swept away the guard, the good woman of the house said she should never be safe again in her bed. However, the old place has outlived, scathless, her fearful and trembling heart.

Over the way, southward, stands the old Workhouse, for age and character a sister building to the corner. The roof covers a mass of mutilation. Excepting one, all its old eyes have been put out, and replaced by modern substitutes of many shapes, sizes, and colours. What was originally a good chimney has become an iron-bound hotch-potch — a mass of plaster and the ever-abominable yellow wash. The only thing remaining entire is the north gable, ornamented by an outside looped oak rafter, with pendant carved post. Who can tell how many centuries have passed by since the old house was the village inn, the "Fleur-de-lis," where the pilgrim, on his way to some holy shrine, was invited to shelter and rest for the night — to take a seat at the open fireplace and partake of "cakes and ale," when the floor was strewn with rushes, and the fire from the yule log roared high up the chimney? All this may have happened, but we have no certain knowledge of the character, and pretensions of this old hostelry. The sign is somewhat suggestive, representing a lily, the hieroglyphic of majesty. Was the original owner or patron the descendant of a follower of the great Norman, and the sign adopted in homage to his nation and parentage? Local tradition affirms that we have at the present time many among us and in our neighbourhood, our tall men and women, who have Norman blood in their veins. Strangers coming among us often remark that there is on the south coast more than an average of tall men and fine women.

On the open space known as the Market Square, and about midway between these two old houses, stood, until about the year 1800, the Market Cross, a structure of bricks. Dangerous to traffic was the verdict upon which the old place was condemned and demolished. Besides being the mart for fish, provisions, earthenware, and other domestic necessaries, the town crier made the ledged base his rostrum. Here he sounded his bell ere he sonorously delivered his message, made his bow, took up his fee, and said, "God Save the King"; and here the parish beadle, cocked hat in hand, gave notice of vestries and other important parochial matters. But wonder of wonders, it was at this place that banns of marriage (many years ago, mind) for this and surrounding parishes were put up and published, telling that Jacob Johnson and Mary Drew wished to become husband and wife, and asking if any among the gaping crowd or passers by had any objection to make; if so, they were then and there to declare it.

The old Workhouse, fifty years ago, was the last refuge and home of the unfortunates of the parish — where the aged toiler and the worn-out wife or widow sought a place of shelter to die in; where the thriftless unmarried man, who all his days had nought to do but to live, and spending his all as he earnt it, retired unabashed, to be kept by his more thrifty neighbours; where the wanton, together with the betrayed and deserted, withdrew to become mothers and to rear the offspring of illicit love; where the fatherless and motherless children of many names and homes found food, shelter, and clothing; where the maimed soldier and worn-out sailor met again to quid and to smoke, and tell oft-told tales of love and war, of lust and rapine; and the dribbling, stooping idiot found his home and his greatest enjoyment, with his back to the wall sunning himself, and the daft, letting off his unpremeditated, almost unconscious humour, set the company of idlers, young and

46

old, in a roar of laughter.

Oliver Mills was the jester and rhymester of the Workhouse. In his young days he had been drafted for the Militia. When at drill, putting the muzzle of the musket to his shoulder, Oliver said in his own rhyme —

> He cut such a figure,
> A-pulling the trigger,

that the drill-sergeant sent him home again. He was too bad even for the awkward squad. At Christmas, for many years, he was our chief caroller. On Boxing Day evening we children, as well as fathers and mothers, expected to hear him tune-up at the street door. Poor old fellow! There was sure to be a good deal of ahem-ing and haw-ing, as he was certain to have a bad cold; but, husky as he might be, his hoarseness soon melted away under the genial influence of a little mulled home-made port — the ever famous elderberry.

The housewives of those days prided themselves on the quality of their home-made wines. The process of making, the age, the quantities, and sorts — from grape cuttings to parsnips — were the points which over a friendly glass these good women delighted to discuss and dwell upon, and if you only praised their beverage it was enough to establish you in good favour ever after. There was, too, in this, as in many other matters, a dash of rivalry and commendable pride. If you could compare favourably with their neighbour's make, you further enhanced your position as a person of discrimination among good liquors; and who could refuse the quiet, kind invitation of the mistress of the house, when she put forth her sparkling gooseberry or blushing two-year-old currant, which had cost her so much time and skill? She had fortified it, too, with a little brandy, and would demonstrate its strength by throwing a few drops on the fire. Who, I ask, after all this, could refuse? I have suffered the just penalty, over and over again, of thus partaking and praising when I knew I should suffer in sickness and headache; and though I detested the liquor, it was years before I could muster courage to say the word "No."

It was not so with our friend Oliver. A little good liquor could do him no harm. It appeared to tighten his relaxed muscles, to brace his nerves, to brighten his dull eye, to loosen his tongue, clear his throat, mellow his voice, and to re-make the man altogether. The wine lit up his flagging confidence, and it was then he sang from a full heart and with the greatest vigour. His songs were those of the festive season, and all of the olden time — "While shepherds watched," "Christians awake," and "God rest you, merry gentlemen," made up his programme; and when he had sung these and pocketed his fee — for which he had always a ready eye and hand — Oliver thought it time to seek other patrons. He had his special houses, where for years he received a hearty welcome. To tell the truth, the poor old man was but a sorry singer; but he had no rival. He was our only solo serenader, and this post of honour drew many a penny into honest Harry's pocket from old acquaintances whom he chanced to meet. I saw him borne to his narrow home in the churchyard on the tottering shoulders of four old men, fellow-inmates of the Workhouse — a pauper's funeral! There were no mourners, and but one attendant — an old woman in her garb of blue, the pauper's livery. The bell tolled its most melancholy note, and the coffin sank into the grave without a tear to follow it. Oliver's relations had all gone before him. It was then the earth became his best friend, and received him. The surface of the grave is now level with the sward. No one knows the spot, and in a few years his name will be forgotten.

## OUR COTTAGE HOMES

These old homes, standing away in the fields, lead us to think about the inmates and their lives — the lives of the farm labourers. How distinguishing a term is labour! — if not the first, the second cause whence all our good things flow. Without it, barrenness and want; with it there should be plenty and contentment. Sad is the lot of the man who has "nothing to do." Such is the fate of many of the younger sons of our aristocracy and our country squires, born never to know the privilege of being independent. Not so with the too-often-despised farm labourer—the man bred to work. The

*Old cottage in Hempstead Lane*

tenth son is on a level with the first, and the lesser is equal to the greater. There are no exemptions nor privileges in this family. To the first and the last the fortune is equal, and all the intermediates have a like share in the heritage, to work to obtain the necessities of life; and happy — ah! happiest — is the man who has a willing heart and able hands to do so.

> He that will not live by toil,
> Has no right on English soil.

What more dignified than honest labour! The toiling, plodding, earnest man of the fields, tied by never flagging affinities to the spot on which he was born, has never roamed, and never perhaps sighed for change, though it has been but scant fare with him all his days. He was one of many sons, and took his lesson early at the plough, where he whistled, it may be, for want of thought, his boyish days away. He is an old man now, and has become the father of many boys and girls, and the table has been too often but scantily supplied. The mother has had her "hands full" keeping the children tidy and clean, and the goddess of health has rewarded her by painting their glowing, laughing cheeks a ruddy hue. See the father in the village on a Saturday evening, clean-shaved and robed in the last new round-frock, with his basket by his side shopping; and see him as he returns up or down the street with the good things for the coming week — bacon, cheese, butter, and it may be a bit of tobacco; and he may also call at the tavern and wet his lips with a pint of beer, but never more, and only on shopping nights. Somehow, I suppose, he learned the notion from his father. He has considerable faith in the virtue of beer, but he wisely says, "You must not take too much"; and a pint is his limit. See such a man, I say (and I am thankful I have known a few such), and you see one of the happiest men in the universe — never in debt and never in fear. To-morrow is Sunday; he reveres the day, and goes to church or to chapel. Probably he is a Dissenter (Baptist, Calvinist, or Methodist). His faith is strong, and his hope equal to the future. The morrow finds him refreshed, and ready again for the coming six days' toil. The master salutes him in the morning at his work, and the man, with no averted eye, freely returns the salutation.

I say I have known a few such men — would that they had been many! Visit these in their homes, and you need have no fear for your senses; neither sight nor smell will be offended, everything in and about the house is "as clean as a new pin." You could eat your food from off the brick floor of the kitchen. And see, too, what a taste for the fine arts. Pictures are on the wall, testifying to the fact that mankind are one. It is the tailor who separates us, and cuts us up into sections. The eye and the heart are the same through all grades, and from the hovel to the throne we are touched by the like influences — beauty is alike for all. There is one striking innovation to be seen among the old furniture, the round deal table and the rush bottomed chairs. The sofa or couch is the result of the latest effort at fashion and indulgence. You rarely now enter a decent cottage without seeing this representative of ease and luxury. The youngest of the family, the last one at home, stretches his limbs upon it on a winter's evening as the mother sits darning, and the young daughter is crocheting or knitting by the light of the oil lamp; and the father, scanning the "People's Edition" for the latest news, lifts his glasses to look at the old clock standing against the wall opposite, and warns the household that it is time for bed.

There are good people to be found who object to these innovations, these lamps, this embroidery, and other fancy work; but while the girls are so employed with the needle they are not romping in the street, neither is the boy, while he is on the lounge, spending his money and spoiling his morals at the beershop. Good, honest couple! They have worked hard, and are wearing away, and, becoming old, their bones are bare of flesh. The man's shoulders project, and the waistband hangs loose about his hips; his legs have become shanks, but the face maintains a healthy glow. He has lived in the open air, in the cottage, in the fields; his regrets have been few. He is innocent of all knowledge of town life, he knows nothing of shares, or discounts, or dividends, of competition, bad debts, balances, or credits. If he has a few pounds in the Savings Bank, it is a small total for his long life. But amidst all his shifts, and wants, and struggles, there is now about him that which no city man can rival. He has but few grey hairs. Time has dealt tenderly with him in this. As a rule, his locks, if thin, are unblanched, while the country tradesman, at the same age, is grey.

Of late years a great change for the better has come over the home condition of the farm labourers. There are some yet among us of the class who, in the early part of their married lives, worked for nine shillings a week, and on this miserable pittance reared the family, rarely few in number, for like the proverbial poor curate, the poor labourers are generally blessed with children; We look now on these men of nine shillings a week as curiosities, as we would on mummies or fossils — relics of an age of trial and endurance, and wonder how ever the thing was done; how father, mother, and eight, or perhaps ten children could be raised, and started in life upon such slender means. But behold, the father and mother are alive, and the boys and girls (now men and women) are around us, and life is more satisfactory with them. The emancipation has come, the shell of the chrysalis that bound them has broken, and the full man has come out. It may be with a rude independence of manner and thought that shakes the old world conventionalities, but this rudeness in due time will work itself off. We have, happily, done with doles and coals and soup kitchens, and consequently in a great degree with servile meeting, and greetings, and bowings, and curtsies, and more honesty of life is the blessed result. I will not prognosticate, nor go into questions either economic or political. Every effect has its cause, and some causes of the change in this case are patent enough. The burden had become too much for the bearer; contrast in condition was getting to be unbearable. Outside sympathy and help was springing up, the crisis had come, and speaking generally, whatever may be the opinion about the lesson and the plan of the teacher, the hour and the man had arrived when Joseph Arch mounted the wagon on Wellesbourne Common, and told his fellow Warwickshire labourers how to win — and won the labourers of England have.

I have always had great sympathy with farm labourers. I am but one remove from them — my father was a plough-boy. I have all my days lived among them, and if I have witnessed many of their failings, I can testify to many of their virtues: to honesty, constancy, humanity, and sobriety. They are, have been, and will be the backbone of the country. Conditions may change, but there will never be wanting men to cultivate the soil. "Depend upon it there are more good men in the country than we suspect, especially among the poor," said the poverty-stricken curate in an old tale. In sketching the lives and habits of our bygone farm labourers the narrative might be prolonged; true characters might be drawn of various hues and shades. As it is among all other classes, so there will be found to be with these, some individuals to blame, some to praise, some to sigh over, and some to laugh at. The drunkard and the sloven there must be, and it is as certain the proud man and the fop will be also among them. Some will be — some must be — fashionable. Fashion then, as now, was all-powerful, and it is hard, up to the present time, to find the man or woman who can withstand the influence. "Custom will be king." "I shall die," said the young lady of our day to her agitated mother, who dreaded the expense, "I shall die if I do not have a seal-skin jacket."

And so, looking back at our fathers' foibles, let us be charitable. Good dressing, let us hope, is oftener a sign of self-respect than of a weak mind. Fifty years ago top-boots were "all the go." The tradesman copied the squire, and why should not the labourer copy the tradesman? Like all other fashionable raiment, top-boots — when once a man got his feet into a pair — became so comfortable and easy that the wearer did not feel dressed out of them, and so, too, thought our farm labourer. From Monday morning till Saturday night he followed the plough, or made hedges and ditches, or thrashed and swung the flail and rattled out the corn. Then he dressed as became his work. He lived frugally, and drank little beer; he was proof against all common temptations, and saved his earnings, or might have done so, against a rainy day, had not the demon of dress beset the way and lured him with his charms. "If the blacksmith and the tailor," said he to himself, as he mused upon the case in the fields, "wear top-boots and broadcloth, why not I?" And so he concluded, as he could pay for a fit-out, to the tailor and the bootmaker he would go.

Well then, in his day, in our parish, for show and figure this man stood at the head of his class. Sunday was his great day — when, in blue cloth, swallow-tail coat and white vest, drab kersey breeches and top boots, with streamers of ribbons floating at his knees, and, to cap all, frill-fronted shirt to adorn his manly breast, he showed himself in the churchyard a few minutes before service began. Then it was that he looked the satisfied man. Strangers seeing him would not expect to find him on the morrow making a ditch or grooming a set of cart-horses; but this was his fate, and his great blessing through all was to be contented with his lot. He knew no ambition beyond it, and he put on no airs of superiority among his fellows. To his duties in the fields he was ever constant, and above all, he was a good Churchman, and as such he gathered his greatest fame and the laurels that wreathed about his brow. He, too, was musical, and if he failed for want of mechanical skill at the bassoon, nature yet sustained him. He was gifted with a powerful voice, and his greatest pride was to be heard at church. For year she was our leading male treble doing the Psalms and the anthem, the women, as was the country custom in those dark days, singing the seconds. "Fortissimo" was our friend's forte, and well he obeyed the rule — all other voices paling beneath his crashing tones. His voice alone more than filled the church, and at times in Jubilate he has been heard, on a summer morning, distinctly in the street. As a matter of course, among us he was a well-known character, and if with the haughty few he failed to win sympathy and respect — his only marked weakness being love of dress — his well-spent life might have atoned for this. The weakness may, perhaps, be accounted for by the law of survival, he being a descendant of a broken-down family who had, a few generations gone by, stood high in the parish. However, he was not without patrons and friends who, in their caprice and jocularity, good humouredly nicknamed him "Prince," and by this high-sounding term he was generally known. Ere he was an old man death came, and he was taken to his narrow cell and laid beside his father and mother —

Where heaves the turf in many a mouldering heap.

So where he was born there he died, and our church yard holds and owns the bones of our model labourer.

## OUR OLD LANES

I have a word or two more to say about these dear old places, and a few other matters connected. Taking the round southward, onward from west to east, we pass or cross at least a dozen. Years ago these all bore one, or rather two, unvarying characters — dismal in winter, charming in -summer, especially those little used for cart traffic where the year round the turf was green and unbroken by hoof or wheel; where " tots" of hazel, oak, and white-thorn had run, off from the line of the hedge, and had taken up positions as chanced in the wild life of a country old lane; where the primrose and the violet nestled, and found shelter and warmth among the decaying leaves of the past autumn; where the modest bluebell hung its head, and nodded to its younger though more proud and showy neighbour, the rams horn where the daisy and the buttercup made up their bed in the moss and slept together, while the grasshopper chirped and the nightingale sang them off to sleep, the owl and the bat keeping watch during the night, and the cuckoo calling the hour of sunrise for the morrow.

When I was an idle schoolboy such, especially, was Hawk's Lane — a by-way leading from one good road to another, little used for horse or cart, backed up on either side, first by Hawthyland Wood and then by Hawk's Wood; the smuggler's safe retreat and the beggar's home for the night; where the tent fire crackled and the smoke curled and wreathed over head among the trees. Hawk's Lane is the only one that has escaped the improver's hand. But that which has been denied the road-surveyor fell into the jaws of the Inclosure Commissioners (Scylla and Charybdis, those cormorants that have swallowed so many of our odds and ends), and has been given up to Nature. The entrance is now barred by a gate, and if by tempting appearances you should be lured to pass over, you soon become involved in a labyrinth. The wood has swallowed up the lane or old roadway. Of the latter there is neither beginning nor ending; the twain have become one, and live together.

I sometimes now in season visit with my dog and gun (my last and dearest hobby) this old haunt, the haunt, too, of my boyhood, and stand in the winter months watching in the mazy ways as the beagles drive the rabbits across the "ride." It was here I shot my first head of game, and here, too, when a boy, I found a partridge's nest full of eggs, and delighted took the lot home, to get into a grand scrape. It was here our auctioneer, Thomas Roger Willard, lost his staunch pointer, "Bess." (He told the tale, so it was said, until he believed it true.) He discovered her skeleton, together with the bones of the covey, the following spring. The birds would not rise, neither would the bitch move, so, game-like, they all died there together. This is not the only marvellous tale that can be credited to Mr. T. R. Willard; but we will let his fame rest on his staunch pointer "Bess," and the flat grave-stone that covers his bones in the northern confines of our churchyard. It was here, at the entrance to Hawk's Lane, that I used, when a lad, to spend my Saturday afternoons with a family of boys whose home was the very old cottage now standing in the garden, with the very same old pear trees on its front, and now occupied by a member of the same family — a nephew of my old companions and playfellows. At that time there was a slip of unenclosed turf — no such slips to be had now—which we made our playground, where, among other ways of killing time, we manufactured rude pottery, and baked it as best as could in a kiln of our making, where also on alternate Saturdays we burnt, or tried to burn, into lime, bits of chalk, picked up from the roadside, that had fallen, in passing, from the farmers' wagons; and here, too, we kept our anniversary with home-made squibs (feeble things) of Guy Fawkes, which *fête* wound up, for the year, our out-door revels. The old cottager and his wife "Joan," deserve a note. In every way a thoroughly worthy couple; they obeyed the earliest injunction — increase and multiply — twenty-two children, all told, being the fruit of their union. The old lady died at the age of eighty-five. A head-stone in the Baptist Chapel-yard marks the final resting-place.

Hawk's House at that time was the home of an authoress, Mrs. Duke. Her volume, "Something New of Men and Manners," is a collection of fugitive pieces, original, critical, humorous, historical and satirical — the book issued from the Hailsham Press; and though the author was ambitious to become a teacher and a satirist, her shafts fell harmless enough. Her memory has almost died out.

One object of the lady's notice was a near neighbour, a Calvinistic preacher, whose chapel at Horsebridge was within earshot almost of her home. Her feathery barbs fell harmless on the minister's mailed shoulders — as harmless as a "snowflake in a river." As well, for success, might she have attacked Behemoth. Thomas Pitcher was too well-grounded in his opinion and faith to be shaken by any arguments Mrs. Duke could use. He had friends here and a meeting-house, Providence Chapel, in "Terry's Yard," where often sounded "pulpit drum ecclesiastic." He was well known for many miles round as a stern Calvinist. To me he was the Sir Hudibras of the time and the locality, a genuine, representative man, one who had "rather fallen than fled." He belonged to a family of blacksmiths, and was brought up to the trade, and was used to hard blows. It was said by some that he carried the habit of the shop into the pulpit, when he made it rattle and crack with the rapid thump of his clenched fist, and made the room resound, too, with his denunciations of the non-elect. He was not a clanking weak-kneed Christian. He kenned the road, and saw the end clearly. When Calvinism was to me a grim reality, I have both at home and at Horsebridge, in his own chapel, heard him preach and pray, and I recall now his earnestness and his consistent life and labours. It was then a solemn moment as he mounted his pulpit stairs, his head hanging over on his left shoulder, his heavy lip dropping, his eyes half shut. Breathless and silent sat the people as he took his seat and drew his heavy hand steadily over his grizzled, cropped head, and as he groaned in silent prayer for help for the duties of the day every man present felt the influence. His opening prayer was a supplication for all men, all had sinned, though none but the chosen vessel could be brought in and be saved. The sermon was a trial alike for the body and the soul. As he warmed, sweat drops hung on his brow, his cheeks became livid, and his eyes flashed. He was then filled with the Spirit, and if he had a message of mercy and of salvation for the few only, and he smiled, he hesitated not, though with tears, to remind the wicked many of the everlasting fate of fire and sorrow that awaited the non-elect. Our lady authoress drew no prize when she attacked this spiritual giant. He passed her by quietly; he may have said, "Lord forgive her, she knows not what she doeth." And surely it were best, be we giants or be we dwarfs, for every man to be allowed to dwell at peace in his own mental castle, whether he has inherited the strong hold from his ancestors, or whether it be retreat from the common fold that circumstances and convictions have driven the possessor into. I plead for liberty of thought, of opinion and conscience, to be done unto as I would do unto others.

The costume of our friend was as consistent as his life. He showed his reverence for his calling by the constant use of the conventual black and the white neckcloth minus the shirt-collar. In person he was of the Hudibrastic type, bulky body, glowing cheeks, and prominent bulbous nose.

But heigho! I have quite run away from my old lane. We will now make short work of it. I have but one other visit to make, namely, Marshfoot Lane. Here forty years ago the hedges met overhead all the year round. I have, standing in the middle of the roadway, gathered hazel nuts from the overhanging boughs. So bad was the road that once upon a change of occupiers at Marshfoot a waggon with a load of implements stuck fast. The tools were removed piecemeal and taken to the farmhouse, but the wagon remained mud-bound the whole winter. Now Marshfoot Lane is our best summer and winter promenade.

## OUR INNS AND PUBLIC-HOUSES

Many are the memories, if not romances and legends, that hang about our inns and hostelries, those most stable of our institutions. Perhaps even before the church they held sway among us. What would a village or a hamlet be without the public-house, that first-fixed product of incipient congregated parish life, the traveller's rest, the social man's recourse and refuge, where he may spend his spare hours soothing his troubled spirit, descanting upon local and imperial wrongs; where he may be independent of grade, the cut of his coat or colour of his necktie, certain, if he is civil in his behaviour, of having the same meted out to him again? But I am not to be the apologist of the system. Let us take things as we find them. Man, being gregarious, must have a common meeting-place, be he poor or be he rich — the public-house for the toiler, the club-house for the independent man, where any matter may be talked over, if not finally settled, where refreshments may be had, and the thirsty soul gratified, if not satisfied.

For the number of our inhabitants we have no lack of inns, of "Good Intents" and "Travellers' Rests." Our most noted roadside inn is the "Red Lion," on Magham Down, the half-way house leading on to Gardner Street. Here you rarely pass, but a cart or waggon, one or more, is standing on the open half circle in front, the horses patient enough, while the attendants are "refreshing" themselves after a fatiguing journey of two miles from the railway station. The team has turned off of its own accord, and settled down in front of the ever-open door, where the landlord is standing ready to serve his well-known customers. Years ago, this old whitewashed house, with its Red Lion sign, a furious-looking beast, swinging in the wind, was kept by the widow Easton and her well-known son, Joe. Who now remembers the peculiar twist of Joe's lip as he turned out his ready joke and set the room in a roar? And who also their best customer, the rhyming blacksmith over the way? —a round-eyed, fierce, wild-looking man, rarely seen out of his ragged leathern apron, but, withal, as gentle as a lamb; he who made his own songs, and sang them to his own tunes, to the stroke of his hammer, as the sparks flew out of his shop window; or of an evening, in the inn kitchen, when he lit up the company with his unpolished lays, when the not prudish maid-of-all-work slyly listened through the keyhole, laughing at the broad jest about some love affair that had come to light, and had provoked the blacksmith's satiric muse.

Those free-and-easy days have, with the old land lady and her son, passed away, together with the open "Down," the home, time out of mind, of the ass and the goose; when the heather bells, wild flowers, and thyme covered the unenclosed surface, and the old fashioned beggars pitched their tent in peace, having then no fear of the policeman before their eyes. Again, where now stands the "British Grenadier," eighty years ago stood a barn, and the man is yet alive, and among us, who was born ten years before the one was taken down and the other built. This inn, as the name implies, was an outcome of the barracks, a necessity, no doubt, of the times, and a legacy left us of the war that closed in 1815. Since barrack-life, the most striking character belonging to the "Grenadier" has also passed away. Then, when all tramps within a radius of ten miles gathered together for the night, the house was a real refuge for the destitute. Tired and weary they might be, but a merrier lot never met. There of an evening, in the common room, was herded together as motley a company of scoundrels and cheats, of knaves and liars, schemers, soft talkers and hard swearers as the eye ever looked upon or fancy bred. The one-legged turnpike sailor, who but an hour before had sang on crutches his war-song with most stentorian voice in the town, now, with both legs perfect, might be seen dancing a hornpipe to the strain of the blind fiddler, who had as suddenly and as mysteriously been restored to his eyesight; and the worn-out soldier, minus an arm in the street, now ready, as he ever had been, to fight for his honour with both hands and arms all right and at liberty. Here, too, was the broken-down scholar, in shabby, threadbare black who, lacking moral courage and principle, had become an outcast and a vagabond, the companion of the vilest, and the ready penman, the professional begging-letter writer, a man well versed in touching phrases, as false as they were fair. Here were organ-grinders and hurdy-gurdy grinders, owners of monkeys, bear dancers, acrobats and tumblers, ribald song-singers, sellers of Catnatch and Co. by the yard, singing by the hour in the street to groups of children and idle fellows, and many other artful dodgers, together with hawkers of catchpenny dying speeches and confessions, professedly made beneath the beam of the gallows, all these traders, one way and another, seeking our coppers, and to tell the truth, we gave them liberally. Here was a company of all the talents, and despicable in many respects as they might be, they were not without an admirer and patron. It was a whim of one of our tradesmen to spend his evenings in the common room, declaring "that there was to be found, among the tramps, the best society in the place," and Tom the tailor was no mean judge. He was of good presence, and intelligent, a keen observer, a good story-teller; and this may be said to his credit — he was no drunkard, and further, he was never vulgar enough to laugh at his own jokes. He, too, was as proud a man as any among us. See him fresh from his shop board, vault ing up our street to meet his ever-varying evening company, and you might say Tom thought himself one of the lords of creation.

Pride in his port, defiance in his eye.

However, since Tom's days all has changed. "Casuals" have been invented and patronized, and the "Grenadier" has assumed a new character. If society has suffered, let us hope the old inn has not. I, whose first wail of infancy was heard within a few yards of the creaking sign, and who, all my days, have looked the old inn in the face, can testify to the good character of the "Crown," our premier hotel. I remember at least a dozen landlords, all good neighbours, but without any touch of romance hanging about their lives or character. Times have run smoothly with the "Crown" — a plain, uneventful history. As market house, it still maintains its supremacy, and, of course, on market day it is the centre of attraction, where assemble specimens of pure Sussex folk — good, honest, stalwart men of the south, whose phrase and words to a stranger may be marked by many a peculiarity, but, of course, such as we deem to be good and proper English. There has been but little innovation. As fifty years ago, so now are to be seen those who represent their great grandfathers, of the same class of hard-working men; farmers, a few in the time-honoured smock-frock — thrifty, honest men — types, many of them, of the Puritans of old, lovers of the truth and of liberty, and as ready now, as their fore-fathers were, to fight for it. They are easy, quiet men enough in all business matters, but rouse them on points of faith, and you will find you have lions to battle with.

One well-known character who used to disport himself in front of the "Crown," the auctioneer, is gone, and has found no successor. The mantle of Ody Wenham has fallen on no man's shoulders, yet the owner had power and a character that carried him over many a year. Who, among the fraternity of those days, could collect a company and command attention equal to our old friend when he appeared on the joss-block in front of the inn on a market day? And who now, among our young and aspiring professors — knights of the ivory hammer — can rival him as he indulged in fancy on the many qualities and uses of the various lots he offered to the public? Who can equal his finesse when drawing another bid from reluctant, stubborn competitors, especially among the ladies? How he would show them twenty uses for an article intended for one only, and by a few skilful touches wind up his harangue by some original rhyme, insuring the good humour of the company, as his hammer fell and he called out the name of the lucky purchaser. Though no poet, he was very fond of his own jingle. Here is the notice attached on special occasions to his office door—

> Ody Wenham begs to say,
> On every Hailsham market day
> He being a licensed auctioneer,
> He writes and takes in orders here.

I write of the past; the present to me is far away. Let another, years hence, when the trifles of to-day silvered over by time, may have been born to the parish, — let him who will, pick up the thread of our history and make his record. The narrative may be a welcome one, so let us, turning again to the bygone, introduce a dilemma of the dinner-table that happened at our old friend's round the corner — the "George." At that time the saint-hero figured in glowing colours in front of the house, with the dragon vanquished beneath his feet. When James Bray Baker, our celebrated cricketer, was the landlord, and the house was owned by the Lewes brewer, the handsome George Wood, then the "George" was known for its good catering, the setting out of the table, the variety of the dishes, and the quality of the wines. Why should these points be forgotten? Dinner, of whatever quality, is a most important event in any man's life, be he at home or be he dining out, be he young, middle-aged, or approaching that cavity into which we all retire. Dinner is the base, the pillar upon which we all build our everyday hope. It is, above all, the thing we work for, the point of time, the meridian of the twenty four hours between rising and setting, getting up and going to bed, towards which man's thoughts are centred, his hope gravitates, on which his peace of mind depends. Then when the table is spread, the chairman seated, the blessing asked, the attendants demurely standing by, waiting orders, what smiles, what satisfaction girdle round the room.

And so it was when our old friends met at the "George " to celebrate the twenty-fifth anniversary of the Hailsham Prosecuting

Society. This was the red-letter day of all the year. Alas! how many of our old institutions have died out. We have had, to my knowledge, during the last fifty years, that anti-Malthusian lying-in club and baby-linen basket, the soup and coal club and committee, our street driver and beadle elections; but all these have gone. I remember the last beadle being buried, and his hat and his staff went with him; his occupation was gone, and very few now among us can tell his name or the colour of his livery. But the Prosecuting Society stood at the head of all. At times it forced itself upon our notice by offering a reward to catch a thief. Men and boys beheld with a thrill the announcement "Twenty pounds reward," in very large type, and we held our breath as we stood by and saw the bills posted on the walls.

But it was the annual dinner that gave the Society character and the members position among us. And had it not been for one of these dinners the Hailsham Prosecuting Society would long ago have been forgotten. The members were few — a score or so — the principal men of the place. The Curate, though a bachelor and a lodger, being a member, he, of course, on these festive occasions, took the head of the table. It had been a time-honoured custom that when the cover was lifted a turkey should present itself, and on the occasion I am writing about, as the chairman remarked, "What a fine bird, gentlemen," all eyes turned towards him. He found many patrons — plate after plate went up for the turkey. "It is done to a turn," he remarked. The seasoning was abundant, the flavour excellent; all hands and mouths were active. "A little more stuffing, waiter," said the fourth on the right-hand of the chair. "It is good," he remarked to his next neighbour, as the plate returned well replenished. This gentleman had not gone in for the turkey, he had chosen beef — a cut from the sirloin; but just then, turning his head, he exclaimed, "Bless me if your stuffing arn't puk-needle!" In an instant all knives and forks fell with a clash into the plates, and a general consternation ensued. "What did you say, Mr. Kenward?" asked the terrified chairman. "Why! say, sir, that your stuffing is nothing in the world but puk-needles! have plenty of 'em at home in my yard. Ha, ha, ha!" laughed the old farmer. The company, as well they might be, were horrified; curses ran deep round the table. "What is to be done?" said they one to another. The Dissenting minister, divining the cause, counselled forbearance, sagely remarking, "It is an accident, gentlemen, I think, not likely to happen again, and things might have been worse if—" Here he made a sudden pause, and advised the landlord to be sent for, the whole company blustering up. The fat, fair, full-bodied, short-legged landlady soon entered the room. The cook was arraigned, and by a few scathing questions from the indignant mistress it came out that though, luckily, the woman had drawn the bird she had neglected to uncrop it. The bird had gone to the spit with the last meal within it, and thus the peculiar flavour of the seasoning was to be accounted for. Here lay the secret. The mystery was solved. "Things might have been worse." Luckily, the company were well-disposed, and not over fastidious. The plates and the residue were quickly removed, the host, rubbing his hands, apologized handsomely, an extra glass of sherry washed down the needles, the next course came on, and a pleasant evening was spent; and every year after, until the Society expired, was the turkey examined by a jury of five before the knife was applied or the party sat down.

## OUR BARRACKS

In a conversation with our oldest inhabitant, I learnt that our barracks were built about 1800, and that the "Barrack ground" before that event was part of the common; that scrub-furze, short, sour grass, wild thyme, and emmet hills[1], were the chief produce and covering; that the horse, the ass, and goose had undisputed possession, and roamed at pleasure; that "anybody" cut the herbage, and carted it away for their sole use and benefit, chiefly for "litter." Also, that the "British Grenadier" was built about that time, taking the place of an old barn that stood where the inn now stands. When I was a boy a man by the name of Wood kept this inn. He was very popular with all young fellows. He had a strong

[1] Ant hills

relish for birds, and would purchase any taken to him. Owls and hawks were his favourites, as he said these were the best flavoured. His fixed price for either was three pence each. At this time, and later, the house was a general rendezvous for tramps; for making money it was considered to be the best in the parish. Of an evening our little town swarmed with these degraded people, and the beds at the "Travellers' Rest" were generally full.

But though I detest tramps, the old-fashioned beggars of my boyhood I look back upon with some degree of veneration, they being professors and bred to the art. They were at that time an institution in the land, and had their rights. They belonged to the picturesque, and were looked for. The old lanes and the byways were their heritage, and rural life was not complete without them. In some old hollow lane, and beside some well-known spring or rivulet's side, you might see the curling smoke rise from their encampment, the blazing fire and steaming kettle hanging on the three sticks, the tent pitched for the night, and the spoils of the day spread out for supper. We will make them a present of our suspicions, and forgive them, too, if they will us, as it may be they have taken a trout from the stream, or snared a rabbit in the wayside hedgerow, to-help make up a variety for the evening meal. They deserve something, as all showmen do, for the view they have given us of one extreme of our civilized life. We thank them, and say goodbye.

## THE TRADESMEN

A word now for my own class. We chiefly live in our own houses, and by far the greater number of the places of business belong to the occupiers. We are free from landlordism and the influences of the upper classes. We have never had a resident magistrate save and except John Mynn, of Searland, and as a consequence, we have none to bow down to. We have very few Mac-Sycophants here. Many years ago our old lawyer, in a first conversation with a new Vicar, told him, with a caution, that Hailsham was a little republic; and our "old doctor," at a more recent period, in introducing a tradesman to a stranger, said: "One of the *élite*." The trade, he added, is our aristocracy, and so I make it out that we live in the home of the free; and, like all free people, our society has a healthy tone about it.

How can a man be morally and mentally free and honest when at every turn he has to duck and to bow, and to speak, if he dares speak at all, with bated breath, to his superiors in position? It is a life we have not been accustomed to. We are not to that manner born. We are not so over-conventional; we are a stiff-necked and an outspoken people, and generally hate shams. In short, we are nothing more nor less than circumstances have made us to be. We are not any better than our neighbours and brothers, and we are not proof against idols, only we have not, nor ever have had, any idol to bow down to. My general observation through life compels me to the conclusion that we are a happier and a more honest people in the absence of the squire, or the overshadowing influence of earl, marquis, or duke.

> The rank is but the guinea stamp,
> The man's the gowd for a' that.

And I am ready to sing or say with the philosophic poet —

> Worth makes the man, the want of it the fellow;
> The rest is all but leather and prunello.

## SCHOOLS AND EDUCATION

The question of education, which had been lingering on for six years, resulted in the completion of a set of schools for boys and girls, with residence for master and mistress. The erection of the buildings has been carried out by the authority of a Board, elected in 1875. This was forced on the parish by an order from Government, demanding extra accommodation and means, from the old sources failing, the rates have been requisitioned to supply the need, and a Government loan has been effected for the sum of

£3,250, at 3½ per cent, repayable in fifty years. Thus we have passed the first stage, and established the necessary room for the teaching of 150 children of each sex. The application of the Education Act of 1871 has been the cause of a considerable amount of feeling. The looming in the not far distance of an increased rate has stirred some of our people to the quick, and at the election of the second Board, in 1878, the cry for economy was raised by both candidates and voters as a test and guarantee for future rule and manage ment. There were eleven candidates for the five seats, and the old Board was completely upset, two only of the old members being returned.

Then came the election of 1881. The economic Board had failed to reduce the school-rate. The voters were disappointed, feeling ran high, and the question who were to be the five honoured men for the next three years ran as an echo through the length and breadth of the parish. Whatever may be said about the expenditure, whether wisdom or folly predominated, there can be no doubt that the schools and the master's house are a credit to the place, the, architect, and the builder. The site is the very best round about the church, and it is to be hoped, that if the present do not appreciate all that has been accomplished, the next generation will look upon what has been done with pride and pleasure, and esteem the building not only for being an ornament, but a blessing to the place.

Until the "Free School" was built on the northern edge of the common, and paid for by voluntary contributions, in 1827, the old vestry at the north side of the church, a poor, miserable, cold, dingy place, was the schoolroom for the parish and for children of both sexes, the churchyard being the general playground; and at the northern base of the tower stood the office for all, the drainage running off into a ditch almost close to the church wall, and passing the door way until the moisture became absorbed by the earth in the journey onward. An iron pipe, from the stove within the room, pushed its dark muzzle through one of the square windows that admitted the scanty light for the master and the children to work by. The door was rickety and in slits, and with a damp brick floor the accommodation was altogether wanting in space and comfort. The master, in addition to that responsible office, was clerk and sexton besides, being at once our guardian and guide from the cradle to the grave. There was this good point in his character: he was no pedagogue; he was natural, and shone by no borrowed light. He was not pretentious. His learning made no one about him envious, neither was he ever known to be sighing for more. He did his duties quietly and patiently, said "Amen" with reverence, and at the grave, when the Curate pronounced the universal fate, no man could let the earth fall on a coffin with a gentler hand. He belonged to a family who had once held a good social position in the parish, and the effect had not died out in his generation. There is a pride that lingers after the estate has vanished, a self-respect that asserts itself in spite of the untoward circumstances which bring a family to poverty — the sins, or misfortunes it may be, of fathers which visit the children even to the third generation. The depths of such men's thoughts are rarely probed, neither are their sorrows recognized. Standing aside to let the hurried pass, and settling down to humble but respectable avocations, avoiding the grossness of mere manual labour, they let life pass with the consolation that the lowest has not been touched. Such was the character of Thomas Tutt, our schoolmaster, parish clerk, and sexton; and if he gave no lustre to his office, the office did to him, and in this way I hold his remembrance in respect. He was the last who held the triple appointment. Peace be to his bones! They lie in the sunny part of the church, and a descendant there is yet who knows the spot.

The first Church schoolmaster whom we have any reliable information about is Francis Howlett. His advent here was somewhat remarkable. Being one of a party of strolling players who arrived in the place on a professional tour, he gave up the buskin and settled down to quiet domestic life, married a wife from the neighbourhood, and ultimately became *factotum* of the parish. At that time it was no uncommon event for a party of players to arrive in the town, and they were always welcomed. The south coast then was a camp — the military outnumbering the fixed population. Diversion was necessary, and willingly paid for. If accommodation could not be had at the inn, a barn was speedily improvised into a theatre. The opening would be announced in the street by beat of drum, and tragedy, comedy, and farce were kept up according to patronage bestowed. If a party could manage to hit the public taste, and become popular, they would maintain their hold for weeks, it might be months, but the end was too often, financially, failure. The break-up of such a party is well described by a local writer of the time. The "Man of the Rocks," [1] the Rev. Richard Mitchel, Vicar of East Dean, in a letter to the "Lewes Journal" — Lee's old paper, now the "Sussex Advertiser," — says: "This morning a wagon passed the door conveying from a barn in the last town to a malthouse in the next the wardrobe of a company of strolling players, their thunder and lightning, pasteboard crowns, wooden sceptres, poisoned bowls, daggers, etc., etc., in short, the whole theatrical apparatus and stock-in-trade, excepting only a few articles which, in consequence of a want of due taste for such exhibitions in the inhabitants of the place, had been left in pawn. In front of the carriage sat a tragedy-queen or two, and at a respectful distance behind a mute candle snuffer and train-bearer. The greater part of the dramatic troupe followed on foot. Hamlet's ghost and one of the witches in Macbeth brought up the rear, with a large bundle under each arm."

This is without doubt, though a little cynical, a true picture of the poor player's exit — camp and baggage; and it was from a similar party that our schoolmaster separated himself, giving up the boards and the footlights, and settling down for life in our town, and it must have been with a pang of sorrow that he parted from his companions. I have great sympathy with players. I hold them to be closely allied to some of the best instincts of our nature, and to be a much maligned people; but they need no apology, theirs being, next to the priesthood, an ever-enduring profession. They are Nature's children, and we cannot do without them. Man begins life with a rattle, and passing through he must be tickled, if it be with a straw only. Humour and comedy are forces that gravity

---

[1] Mr. Mitchel's pseudonym is A. B.

itself bends and bows down to. Who can read Hood without emotion? — with tears for the pathos, laughter for the humour, and admiration for the lesson he always teaches.

Francis Howlett, comedian, schoolmaster, postmaster, tax-collector, vestry clerk, printer, travelling librarian, musician, and general referee, became a trusted and honoured man in our parish, and living to be over eighty, departed leaving no enemy behind him. As may be supposed, he had a large store of anecdotes always ready, and many a tale is yet told of his great tact as a story-teller. He, too, was a man of mark, as wearing a pig-tail, and he did not consider himself dressed without the caudal appendage. As a musician, he was an anomaly — no very uncommon character — showing great devotion and but little ability. Arriving one evening after a seven-mile walk, being late, and entering hurriedly where the bandsmen had assembled, he tripped and fell headlong into the room. His hat, clarionet, wig, and pig-tail all parted company, much to the owner's chagrin and the amusement of his musical companions, who burst suddenly into a roar of laughter; but our friend after an emphatic and expressive address to all in the room, soon recovered his usual placid tone. The wig readjusted, he was himself again, there being nothing vindictive in his nature. His grave is near the eastern gateway in the churchyard, and is yet overshadowed by a rail; but soon unpausing Time will leave no man to say, "I knew Francis Howlett."

When I was a boy Howlett kept the post office, whither I was sometimes sent with a letter. The old gentleman, coming forward, always appeared to be pleased to take the money. Eightpence, prepaid, was the postage to London. Then, among working people, there was very little gossipy letter-writing, and few of this present generation can appreciate the advantage of the postal change and accommodation in contrast with the old system. The following extract taken from a letter of the old time will partly show the shifts people were put to to avoid the expense of postage. The writer says: "Mrs. B — called last week and offered to post any letter in London for the boys. The cost of letters, having so many boys and girls as we have, is very great, and we took advantage of Mrs. B's

— kindness and consideration to send three by her." This was a good all-round practice among friends. At that time London had a twopenny postal delivery. So we see the letters cost the sons twopence each instead of the mother two shillings. There was, too, a privileged class who could *frank* their own letters and also their friends. M.P.'s, naval and military officers, magistrates, etc., had the favour. Many a poor person has walked miles to get a letter franked, and sons in the army and navy writing home would get an officer to frank their letters. This shows what we have passed through, and the great advantage of the penny post. There was an attraction at the post office that pleased my boyish eyes, and lured me to go there whenever a chance offered — this was the post-man's clock. Mounted on the top of the pendulum, and showing itself in a crescent cut in the face, was a ship in full sail that kept sailing ever, ever, evermore. This was a sight that pleased my young eyes and mind very much. I would linger and stare at this wonderful ship, with her bellying sails; but it was the motion, so steady and true, that puzzled my young brains. I knew then nothing about pendulums.

I will refer to two other schoolmasters only — one for his virtues, the other for his failings — Charles Jackson and Thomas Weston. They were both my tutors. The first had his schoolroom at the Baptist Chapel, where he was master of the Sunday School, and a most devout and good man he was. It is not always boys look back with much love toward their old teachers, but the effect of C. Jackson's kindness and attention to his boys' welfare has not died out. I know more than one who remembers with reverence the old tutor. I am glad to be able to say in reference to Thomas Weston that, if his habits did not lean to virtue's side, these had not depth enough to interfere with his ability as a teacher, nor to taint his professional respectability. He was convivial and fond of his glass. It is for a dash of humour there is in it that I record the fact. When he drank sherry he has been known to say, "I wish my neck could be as long as my arm," so pleasing were the nerval vibrations caused by the liquor. His was THE school of the place, and the master stood up for the dignity of the profession, and wrote, in large letters, ACADEMY over his door — the present residence of Mrs. Col. Sinnock.

## OUR PETTY SESSIONS

These Courts were held fortnightly at the "George Inn" for many years, in two upstair rooms — one a sitting-room, the other a bedroom. In the first-named sat their Worships, with their Clerk (Inigo Gell, of Lewes). Whenever a case required an attorney he, too, was admitted to this apartment, but there was no space to spare for personal friends nor "Cousin Slenders." The room was consecrated to law and justice.

The Bench usually consisted of two magistrates only — Inigo Thomas, of Ratton, Willingdon, and John Mynn, of Searland, Hailsham, the only resident magistrate we have ever had. There was occasionally an addition from Eastbourne. Once, especially, when I took a look in, I saw a third, so striking in his appearance that I have never forgotten him. My eyes became riveted, and I now believe I saw nothing beside. It was the grand, antique head and face, and the peculiar muscular working of the latter that then held me spellbound. He was very pale, with full and broad forehead, large overhanging eyebrows, the eyes set deep back, and with the slowest possible motion the lids kept dropping, until the sight became deeply buried beneath fold upon fold of the relaxed muscular covering. This rested a few seconds; then the curtain was as slowly lifted, and the eye emerged from a depth that had set me wondering if ever again it would reveal itself. He, too, was an abstraction. He took no notes, neither did he speak. The stranger was Davies Gilbert, of Eastbourne. He, at one time, was President of the Royal Society. His personal appearance, I have since read, drew from Southey the remark that "His face ought to be perpetuated in marble for the honour of mathematics." I never had the gratification of seeing him again. A biographic sketch of him says: "One of his highest claims to public gratitude is the discrimination which led him to bring young Davey from his obscurity at Penzance and to foster his talents." Mr. Gilbert died at

Eastborne in 1839. He owned Town House Farm, in our parish, but some years ago the family exchanged with the Duke of Devonshire for other property.

Inigo Thomas was a man of good average ability, and a discriminating magistrate. He resided on his own estate, the mansion at Ratton being delightfully situate on the eastern side of the Downs, and overlooking the picturesque village of Willingdon, the whole of Pevensey Bay onward to Hastings, the wealden, and a large sweep of country to the north and west. Travelling from Polegate by rail to Eastbourne the residence is at all times an object to catch the eye. It stands in a crescent of shrubs and forest plantations, and has a very inviting appearance. John Mynn, the only resident magistrate we have ever had, was a man of medium ability.

On Session days — market days — prisoners and witnesses both stood in the same room, and at the same bar. An opening about breast-high, made by a movable shutter in the partition wall, was the dread aperture through which the unfortunates looked dolefully upon the grave personages in front of them. Here were crowded parish constables engaged in the prosecution of their several cases, loungers, gossips, and persons who make a pleasure of seeing other people in trouble; and the public room was usually filled up with this medley. There was no special officer to enforce silence or obedience, each one acting for himself. Rural authority in those days did not vaunt itself, striving fairly to do the duties of its office, perhaps at times showing a touch of sympathy with the offenders.

Crimes were then more numerous than now. Highway robbery, burglary with violence, were not uncommon. The venial crime of poaching, the poor girl whose figure bespoke her frailty, drunkenness, fighting brawls, offences against that very solemn person, the night-watchman, also against the street driver, whose office, with his charges against offending owners of stray pigs and cows, has long since died out. Of course committal for trial, summary conviction, fine, and imprisonment followed then as now, but one peculiar mode of punishment, the parish stocks, has since been abolished. This dread engine of torture stood on the margin of the common, and within a few yards of the front of where now stands the "Terminus Hotel." Here was then standing a double cottage, which is built into and forms part of the inn. In front of the old house stood half a dozen shabby poplar trees, sighing and moaning in the unbroken south-west wind. Was it in pity or in derision? Either way, the one in durance could only say, "I can't get out, I can't get out!"

Reader, you have never seen a man in the stocks, and it is now more than probable you never will. This relic of a barbarous age — when we hung men, and *women* too, for forging one-pound notes — we will suppose to be gone for ever. It is remembered by few now, and as a curiosity only. The rural police, or County Constabulary as the force is now called, has superseded the use of the parish stocks and the public whipping-post. The two have vanished together. I have seen both utilized in our parish — the latter, I am thankful to say, once only. I well remember how the dull, purple spots beaded up on the poor fellow's back; how his courage broke down with the first few lashes, and he cried out for pity, help, and forgiveness. He had been accused of a trifling offence, and it was said ever after that vindictiveness had been at the bottom of the cruel punishment. The "cat" was applied by a professional from Lewes Gaol. I do not wonder philanthropists abhor and denounce the use of the lash. The infliction is disgusting, and horrible to witness, and terrible to endure. The culprit was tied to a cross-beam fixed to the finger-post in the centre of our street, and pointing to Eastbourne. He survived the infliction many a year, reared a large family by honest industry, and was known to the last as a cheery old man.

The parish stocks, to me, have quite a comic character. See a man clutched by the heels, thrown on his back on to the bare ground helpless, rolling his head and arms about, fighting with the wind, and sometimes for a change sitting partly on his haunches, with his feet, it may be, a foot higher than his seat, but in no other way punished, and you see him in one of the most absurd situations possible. I never remember a man in the stocks being pitied. He was often laughed at. The boys and girls of the street and idle fellows who thronged about him were his best friends, inasmuch as they helped to while away the time with their jokes and laughter. The culprit lost no cast among his fellows from his punishment. It was often the end of a drunken spree or a fight — no uncommon affair in those days. It was a good remedy to sober a man, and bring him round again to his senses. But the stocks had other purposes. The parish constable and his headborough had no better friend. They had no other lock-up, and the stocks would hold any man safe, be he ever so refractory, who once got clutched by their gyves, and until a horse and cart could be procured to take the prisoner before a magistrate or off to gaol.

## THE CHURCH RINGERS

Again looking back, we may note a few other features and changes. To begin with our church ringers. Then the master tradesman thought it no degradation, but rather an honourable distinction, to be one to minister to the rights of the belfry. To be a ringer was a privilege. I remember but one new hand, and he carried his election by force of prescriptive right and family interest. His father had been one of the fraternity, and a brother stood then foremost man as leader. Each bell had its regular hand. There was the hatter, glover, tailor, shoemaker, and blacksmith in succession, and a few others — odd men to take a turn as occasion required, and one, the street driver, who was always needed to fetch the beer from the tavern. They were all professionally earnest, devoted men, and to do them justice, as a rule — and what rule is not more or less broken? — they were sober men. But the potent god, bred of malt and hops, at times got possession of the brain, and then was the time to take note of the work of the features and lips as the ropes flew up and down.

No wedding was allowed to go by unrung or uncared for. On practice nights and rare occasions they would treat the outside world with a set of changes. Four bells allowed but little variation, yet with, the steady and even pull of the tenor by the tall black smith, George Huggett, and the clear, unerring lead of the hatter,

Samuel Jenner, the old-fashioned peal was considered to be eclipsed by the change of four and-twenty.

The great treat of the year was, when I was a boy, to be awakened on Christmas morning by the early clatter of the bells, and to lay awake watching until midnight on New Year's eve to hear the old year rung out and the new year rung in; and during the whole of my life I have never once upon these occasions been beyond the reach of the gladdening sound. I have hoped to live to hear a fuller peal. I have importuned those in authority upon the subject, but with no success, to add a sixth. Our old ringers would yearly make a house-to-house call, and accept any gratuity as an acknowledgment for their services. What master tradesman now among us would do the like?

## MUSIC IN OUR PARISH

Time was when, and less than fifty years ago, we had but one piano in the parish. This instrument, melancholy in its loneliness, had its home at Sandbanks, the residence of Miss Bristow; and it was she, too, who owned the only covered carriage that then graced our roads. We were not at that time a musical people — that is, in our houses or homes. At the present date pianos, harmoniums, and chamber organs abound. We were then like unto the dry bones in the Valley of Death; we were sleeping, waiting to be called. We had not hung our harps on the willows, inasmuch as we had never heard the stirring sound of the royal instrument. Echo had given us no answer, as we had not invoked the sylvan goddess. 'Tis true the effect of the military band of barrack life had not passed without leaving behind some good result. The murmurs of the far ocean was yet heard in the shell. The sound had never died out, and fancy had at intervals called for more; but all we had to offer, and to keep our lone piano company, was one sad instrument. With the last tramp out of the Berkshire Militia died the sound of the drum and the clarion, and we were left alone to our solitary piano and bassoon,

Since that time we have, instrumentally and mechanically, made great progress — nearly every household of respectability has the piano, harmonium, or organ. In musical execution the vital matter is this — Will the player be found to be the master of his instrument, or the instrument master of the player? From the fiddle to the bassoon, all will depend upon this. I was once delighted with the hurdy-gurdy. The performer had discovered the hidden power of the instrument, and he drew forth sweet sounds with a rapidity and clearness of execution that puzzled and astonished his hearers. He was master of his instrument, and for the time, too, of his audience. So it was with our bassoon player: from the top note to the bottom all came at call and in full tone. For years he had a local fame. He was the focus around which gathered our band, which on a summer evening treated the lower world from the top of the church tower with its strains, and at Christmas made our street and homes merry with the rolling drum and the twanging trombone.

This, too, was the time when we had our anthem at church — the voices accompanied by the bassoon, French horn, and clarionet; and altogether we considered things satisfactory, if not grand. I confess now to a lurking fondness for the old ways. *Let us sing to the praise and glory of God* has an earnest, awakening tone about it; and the anthem was always welcome. Our bassoon player, with one exception, outlived all his musical companions. He never deserted his early love, being a practical musician over fifty years, and until nearly the end of his days would have what he called "a blow." My old friend, Samuel Jenner, died aged ninety. He was to the end a fine, hale, hearty man, and of irreproachable character. The writer of these notes is the one player who has outlived him, he being twenty years his junior.

## CRICKET ON OUR COMMON FIFTY YEARS AGO

Where, let me ask, is the Englishman who will not do homage to the noble game of cricket? Let us, by way of contrast to the present, look back at the game as played fifty years ago [1] on our unenclosed common. That was the time for a merry day, when we

[1] Circa 1830

challenged Hellingly, Chiddingly, Westham, or any other parish, before clubs were known or thought of; when the honour of the parish was the object fought for; when Churchwardens and Overseers were patrons worth seeking, and the Curate would take the head of the table at the dinner or supper; when underhand bowling was the proper form, and before that innovator, Lillywhite, had introduced the break-shin overthrow; when white cord knee-breeches, white stockings, showing off a good pair of calves, and tied shoes, with the chimney-pot hat, made up the swell cricketer's dress; before knee-pads, finger-pads, or any other pads were known or thought of; when the game between parish and parish was pleasant to see, and one might take a part in the sport without danger to life or limb; when a good hearty all-round shout followed a good hit, and the company cheered the field for a difficult catch, and the man at the wicket shared the applause for taking, over the stumps, a well thrown-in ball. "How's that?" he asked of the umpire as the bails flew off. The wicket-keeper knew it was a nice point, but he thought it was out, or he would not have put the question. The umpire hesitated, and appealed to his second-self, an old fashioned farmer, and one who never did anything in a hurry. "Can't say, really; was setting my watch by the church clock, so can't say zackly how 'twas." Of course, "Not out" was the verdict.

In such pleasant ways, in those old days, did we settle our difficult points, and being in earnest, before the stumps were drawn the game would be played out. Tradesmen, farmers, and respectable young fellows of all classes took part, together with our lawyer who — being a crack hand, generally took the lead — and when a match was on, the game would be played by our best men, victory alone being the aim. The dinner might be the stake, with perhaps, in addition, pots and pints, winners and losers sharing equally in the liquor. There were few, if any, teetotallers in those old-fashioned days, with more familiarity between man and man and less drunkenness than at the present day.

After dinner followed the free-and-easy song and toast, not forgetting "Wives and.Sweethearts," and with many a bantering joke, the evening soon passed away. Before breaking up "The health of the Curate " was drunk, all the company standing. Then arrangements would be made for the return match, and with "Better luck next time for the losers," the company parted, the beaten longing for the opportunity to avenge themselves, the victors being a little swollen and boisterously valiant with success and, perhaps, a little extra beer. Our good-natured Curate, with his large heart, thought it no degradation to preside over these rustic parish festivals.

One among the many of our defunct institutions was the "South Down Cricket Club." Very few now among us remember the South Down Cricket Club. The members of this high-toned society met on our common every Wednesday evening — market-day being the special day for a full company to get together to practice, many members living at a distance having business in the place on that day. There were to be seen the Mynns, the Sampsons, the Pagdens, the Ades, the Coopers of Norton, and many others, aristocrats at that time among the farmers of the Downs and the neighbourhood, showing off their manly forms on the turf of the old common. The evening became an attraction, and many a country lass, with her flowing locks, piercing eyes, and peeping ankles, met, doing homage to the noble game and the gallant players, cheering the whole company with their presence and their approving smiles. Then it was, in one case especially, Love got the better of Reason, and one imperious maiden fled from her father's house in the night, overcome with her emotions, under the protection of her lover, assisted by her willing and sympathizing maid, and before the following sundown the runaway became the wife. The conquest, at the time, was given to the credit of cricket, and a fine pair of calves shown off beneath the knee-breeches and white stockings of the gallant player —

What great events from trivial causes spring!

Our one famous cricketer, fifty years ago[1], was James Bray Baker. He being a gentleman county player, of course we thought much of

[1] Circa 1830

him and of his play; perhaps more than he really deserved. All heroes and their doings are apt to be exaggerated. Whatever carping critics or envious players who outlived him may have said, without doubt Mr. B. was a great man among us. That he was exceptional at cricket, of that one proof is that neighbouring elevens objected to him in a parish match. He was a county player, the weak-hearted ones said, and too good for a country party to play against. So Mr. B. was often compelled to stand aside and look on while the honour of his native place was at stake and hung trembling in the balance. Many tales have-been told of his prowess, his hits, his splendid fielding and throws in, and his defence at the wicket. These qualities combined made many a country youth envious, if not despairing. There was too, a slight romance hanging about his life that drew one's eyes and thoughts towards him. He was the first-born of his parents, who were hard-working people living in the parish, while the boy had been adopted, educated, and reared as a gentleman by Elizabeth Hooper, a maiden lady, residing in the Vicarage, who, as the inscription on a tablet in the church tells us, died in 1819, aged eighty-four, and who had lived the whole of her long life in the vicarial home, she being owner of the great tithes of the parish, and of many rich acres of meadow land round about the church. Mr. B. had grown up from infancy to manhood beneath the roof of his lady patroness. He had indulged in many a fancy, was fond of field-sports, kept his harriers, his horses, and was one of the gay troopers of the now forgotten East Sussex Yeomanry Cavalry. In fact, he was for some years the young gentleman of the place, and no doubt our best cricketer. Upon one occasion, playing for the county against the Marylebone Club in London, he is said to have kept his wicket up through one whole day's play, so saving the match for his county. He is also credited with winning one extraordinary single-wicket match against eleven Eastbournites, with one man, William Martin, a shoemaker, to field for him, beating the lot. And after bearing a good deal of chaff and abuse from the defeated party, he is said to have challenged them then and there to single combat with the fist, which challenge the eleven declined, perhaps wisely, seeing that the conquering cricketer was a Hercules for bone and muscle, and moreover, he, like many gentlemen of that day, had learned the noble art of self-defence, and knew when and where to plant a good knock-down blow.

One more incident — this out of the cricket field — and we have done with our hero. The affair happened at the time when Sir Godfrey Webster lived in his own home, the Abbey at Battle. Being magistrate for the county, he had authority to quell riots and disperse mobs. Gardner Street, on a certain day, was in possession of the starving labourers, and other disaffected people. The Riot Act having been read, the Baronet walked into the "Woolpack," the only inn, and ordered all present to quit and be off to their homes. Mr. Baker chancing to be in the house, remonstrated, saying he was no rioter, and that he should not be turned out so unceremoniously. The magistrate, as all the world then knew, was no craven, threatened, and soon proceeded to force, when, in a moment, he found himself sprawling on the floor of the room. "There, Sir Godfrey," said Mr. B., "if I can be of any service to you now, if you choose we will walk out of the house together." Whether the worthy Baronet accepted the kind offer I cannot tell,

Again, as regards cricket, I am inclined to the belief that the game, as a diversion in purely rustic parishes, is wearing out. Time has been when the "cricket field " was a field well-known, where the lads of the cottages met the farmers sons on easy terms, and played away together the summer evening. Looking round, I know now but very few cricket clubs and cricket fields as they used to be. The game has become high-toned and scientific, and to be a player now one must be of independent means, or of sufficient extra ability to become a hired man to play for his patrons and his party.

In our parish, though we have the six-acre allotment, a clear square reserve, with level turf, set apart for ever for recreation, cricket has "gone to the dogs." We have not for years had a game worth looking at, making one almost sigh for a return of the days when two of our tradesmen, the tailor and the shoemaker, always held in reserve as umpires to act for both parties in a match, set off at a table by themselves, each with his pint of beer before him, and each with a long stick and pocket-knife in hand, keeping score by notching, independent of pen, ink, and paper.

We have yet a reminiscence or two lingering in our memory relating to these old games and times — a long hit, a wonderful catch, a drive on into the gipsies' booth, smashing the blue-eyed dolls and the mimic mirrors and toilet-tables. The long hit is deserving a distinct record. Playing Westham, and the sturdy boys and the young men of the " corporation," Hailsham apparently had the game in hand. The last innings was on. But the "glorious uncertainty" was being proved again. The large balance in hand had gradually disappeared. The last man of Westham was in, and six only was wanted to tie. Excitement, of course, ran high; every ball was eagerly watched, when such a "lifter," as "never before was seen," brought the game to a close, seven runs being fairly scored off the bat. Two men in relays went out to meet the man who had pitched up the ball, but to no avail. The game was lost, and the Westham boys have never forgotten the honour of beating Hailsham on its own ground. The striker of this marvellous "hit" was at the time holding the honourable post of oxman on his father's farm. He lived to become a man of mark in his own profession as agriculturist, and doing honour to his neighbourhood and county as a prize-taker and breeder of cattle — the beautiful reds of Sussex.

There are many among us now who, it may be, are too old to join in the field, but would gladly see the game revived and played again on the common. The one rule to qualify, in days of old for practice, was character, neither a man's calling nor the colour of his clothes being then any bar to membership.

## TITHES

The custom of paying tithes by a tenth of the produce had not died out when I was a boy. Then a tenth swath and a tenth shock was left by the farmer on all his corn-growing fields, the tithe-barn being then one of the institutions of the parish. We had two of these buildings. Fifty years ago [1] strange men, with wagons and strange horses, from a strange county arrived, and entering the fields, carried away to these barns the tenth of the cereal produce of the parish. Thrashing with the flail was a job for the winter. The produce became the property of the tithe-owner, John Luxford, of Salehurst, Robertsbridge, and the proceeds of the sale went into the pocket of a man who rarely came into the place, He was generally known as Little Johnny Luxford, being of diminutive stature. He came into possession of the great tithes and certain meadow lands under the will of Miss Hooper, who lived and died in the Vicarage House. What should we say now to such a mode of paying our obligations? Taking a tenth!

## THE CURFEW

Time out of mind has the curfew sounded from the height of our church tower. Years ago the first stroke of the bell was a welcome sound to many a hard-working man. Many of our tradesmen, as the tailor and the shoemaker, toiled until the curfew sounded the knell of parting day. The draper and the grocer kept open even until ten. Early closing now prevails, to the disgust of a few old-fashioned housewives. In summer, if you are on the look-out, you may see the starlings rushing from the louvres at the first stroke of the bell. Use does not entirely reconcile these birds to the clang, but they soon return and settle down again. On a fine, clear evening the sound is heard three or four miles away. We have no knowledge of the beginning of the custom here. Whether the lights and the fires ever obeyed the summons is not known.

The curfew-ringer has always been a man of mark among us. I remember at least half a dozen. They have been bell-ringers, and had become part of the church, and never one left office in disgrace. All have rung on until in their turn death has taken them, up to our present sexton, C. Vine, whose father before him pulled the ropes and said "Amen" for many a year. When I was a boy I

[1] Circa 1830

pitied the curfew-ringer. His duty was, besides, to wind up the clock. Climbing the worn stone steps on a winter evening, and without a light, was a task I did not begrudge him. Though he proclaimed every twenty-four hours, his presence was seldom seen. He was in a measure a ghostly man, and I fancied the ghosts of the church tower held him as their own. I was afraid of the spirits. I shuddered for his safety on winter nights in his journey, until he began to ring; then at the first stroke I believed the spirits all fled, and that not till then would he be safe.

I had a great dread of ghosts. I fancied ghosts roamed at night and came into the street, so that I was foolish enough to be afraid to pass, after dark, the gateway leading from thence into the churchyard. This saddening fear was in a great measure the effect of well-meant religious teaching. The "fear of God" was early implanted in my mind, and the terror and dread of the devil also taught at the same time, and I was held enslaved, being afraid to move about in the dark, either in or out of doors; and to be sent off to bed alone was almost more than I could endure. At that time I knew by heart all Dr. Watts' divine and moral songs, and the thought of the wicked child who "must with devils dwell in darkness, fire, and chains," ruined the peace of that part of my young life that should have been the freest from care and sorrow. Thirty shillings a year, or a penny a night, is the fee paid to the bell-ringer, and no sinecure is the office. We cling to the old institution. Since the church-rate abolition a house-to-house collection is made to meet this and other incidental expenses, and what the law has given up to the free-will of the people to supply has so far been provided. The repairs and the restoration of the tower and the north part of the roof happening in nesting-time, the birds were much distracted. They had had undisturbed possession so many years that the flutter was great among them. The workmen were all strangers, and that fact might add to the general consternation. I fancy the chirrupers recognize a few of their old neighbours — some are so often passing beneath the eaves. How ever that may be, there was a great flying here and there, and so much talking as never before was heard. They appeared to band together to repel the common enemy; the martens and sparrows, for once, were upon good terms. They had no opportunity to be fighting for possession of the same nest-hole; a common trouble made all friends. To hear and to see them and the starlings in their grief was enough to move the heart of an enemy even. Perhaps in asking for help, like many mortals, they exaggerated their grief; but they were not without friends and sympathisers.

## PENSION DAY

Fifty years ago [1] "Pension Day" was a day of note in our parish. The pay-table was at the "Crown." There the old warriors met quarterly. They were all heroes on that day. They had all been to the wars, and many had returned maimed. One had lost an eye, another had sabre cuts in his face, showing, as we used to say, he had not turned his back to his foe. Some were minus an arm, some a leg. One, who had a superb military bearing — a Waterloo man — had his silver medal dangling at his breast, and though his face was pale and rugged with scars, fire yet flashed from his dark eye. He had been with Wellesley in India, and with the great Duke again at Waterloo at the final overthrow of the great Napoleon. All arms and both services were represented. The sailor who saw the Frenchman go down with his ship on the "glorious first of June," and had heard him cry, or said he had, "Vive la Republique." The men disappeared for ever, but the cry has struggled and survived for a century and finally triumphed.

Let us see a few of our old heroes. First we have the artillery man, who had helped with General Elliott, a Sussex man, to hold the Rock of Gibraltar. He was a taciturn, grand-set, staunch-looking man, rarely speaking to his old comrades, taking his shillings and himself off home again. You might see "No surrender" written full in his carriage and character. Upon some special occasion he might tell how he had fired the red-hot shot that played havoc with the French and Spanish war-ships. He had returned to his original calling, a shoemaker; and his only companion on pension day was his trusty dog, a short-legged,

[1] Circa 1830

wiry-coated Scotch terrier. Then there was the gay trooper with his dislocated kneejoint, generally bound over with a red handkerchief, full of talk, and, it may be, some bluster. He had been with Abercromby in Egypt; he was now in the Workhouse, and he would boast and say how he had seen "the Frenchmen run." He had no objection on pension day to an extra tankard, and the liquor often made his poor crippled limb very crooked indeed. Next we had the fearless infantry man, who had followed his captain from Torres Vedras to the crowning victory of Toulouse, where he lost an arm, and returning to his native fields, became again a farm labourer. To see him working with his fellows he never appeared to any disadvantage. He was leading man at the farm — seedsman, stacker, and at a new hedge it was hard to find his equal. Years ago now he was taken to his rest beneath the shadow of the old church tower, and the Vicar (the Rev. G. G. Harvey) pronounced Verral (why should his name be withheld?) to have been a fine example of what a British infantry man should be.

It was a merry day — this pension day — with these men; and if no one among them shouldered his crutch, each in his own way showed how fields were won. We may say what we will — and it cannot be too much — about and against the horrors of war; we may denounce the havoc, the fire and the desolation, the shrieking virgin, the butchered infant and the weeping mother; we may see the bloody corpses, the half-dead and dying soldiers strewing the field; we may sigh with those left to sigh, and weep with the weepers; but after all this the luridness will pass away, and the successful general becomes a hero, and we shall worship him, and his veterans will, as our old pensioners did, command our homage and excite our enthusiasm. Thus, when Uncle Toby swore his famous oath, he only gave us one of the many touches of our nature that makes the whole world kin.

There is but little record left us of our fifteen years' barrack life. The most enduring are two tablets in the church — one to the memory of the old Royalist, Van Courtland, who retired from the strife and struggle of the war of American Independence to find a quiet home and grave in our churchyard. He was barrack master, and occupied the house of the late Slye family. The second is to the memory of Lieutenant Bannell Webb. The cause of his death being sad and somewhat romantic, is worthy of notice here. One can understand, reading the inscription, that it was written by a loving hand:—

> He was
> A friend without guile,
> A soldier without vice,
> A Christian without bigotry,

— a character none too good for the full and almost broken heart of the young widow to dedicate to the memory of her gallant husband. Only a few days before his death she had presented him with a spirited charger, and in his first ride the animal bolted, got the mastery, and Amberstone turnpike gate being in his way, the rider was thrown, and carried to the barracks a dying man.

Our place, being on the line of march from Dover, was frequently visited by regiments en route for the Continent. Then the inhabitants were awoke early by the sound of the trumpet and the rattle of the drum. They also well understood the effects of the billeting system. Now we live in happier times.

## OUR PLEASURE FAIR

The third of June was a glorious day with the bygone Hailshamer. Then the old common resounded with the drum and clarion, the gong and the tambourine. The day was one of high festivity; it was our saturnalia, when all were bent upon pleasure and merry-making. Prudent boys and girls, weeks before, had put by their pence, to add the amount to the annual gift from their thrifty parents, to meet the expenses of this happy time. It was then we went in for lollipops and running paper mills. These were the earliest indulgences of inexperienced childhood. What happy, what merry days! Then followed the penny trumpet and the two penny drum, and we would cut a dash — marching and remarching, braying and resounding. The next would be to mount the gaudilycaparisoned wooden horse and ride in the circle with fellow boys and girls. There was no care then mingled with our joys; "all went merry as a marriage bell." There were no reckonings to make up — no afterclaps. The coppers had been coined for that day and that occasion, and we parted with them freely. Another stage, and the girls mimicked their mothers, purchased dolls and became nurses. The grown-up boys patronized Aunt Sally, and looked longingly at the lemon-shaped and coloured boxes poised so temptingly on the points of the peeled willow sticks. Poor little novices! We rarely obtained a prize, but we were jovial players and laughed heartily as we parted with our money.

This fair of my early days was a revival. The old fair had quite died out excepting one solitary booth for gingerbread and a few other juvenile knick-knacks. About the year 1820 a stir came among our people. Pleasure on her gaudy wing presented herself and put in her claim. There were soon found hearts to sympathise and heads to reason. "What is life," 'twas said, "without some change? Why should man always be working?" Then Saint Lubbock had not lived, and we were a law unto ourselves. The gay goddess so artfully displayed her charms that numerous votaries came to her service. With some people to will is to do, and it came about that the old fair revived and lived again. So heartily was the case taken in hand, that the good-natured Curate, with his beaming face and guileless mind, saw nought amiss, and he patronized with his presence the new-born institution. The day was our carnival. Fathers and mothers, as well as girls and boys, lived for it, and counted the hours as the days rolled away and the time drew nigh again for the fair. We had our dancing booth with raised orchestra, and planked floor for the dancers. This was the meeting-place for lovers. The fiddle screeched, the basses twanged and grunted, as Hodge in his shirt sleeves, with collar unbuttoned, and his Molly at his side, went up and down the middle, or struck off to the tune of the "Triumph" — a great favourite in those days. The hobnails glistened and rattled on the boards as John's heels flew up, so much had he become possessed, while Molly, in her more gentle mode, clung to her partner as they both whirled away the happy

88

hour — to use the phraseology of the day. They had become hot and blowzed, and would retire and take a seat in the drinking booth, to rest and wet the neck with a cordial draught of ale, and to have a wipe up with the cotton — red, white, or blue — handkerchief. Cambric and silks were not in these days sported by the working classes. And who could be happier than these people? Perhaps in less than a year they had become husband and wife, and the first child born. And so these meetings and greetings had their uses; the start in life had been made and many things appertaining were reckoned from the date of this fair. We, too, had our peep-show, where could be seen smuggling by moonlight, the Battle of the Nile, and the last charge at Waterloo, all for a penny. Punchinello and her matchless husband were there. But who can catch and describe the ever-changing wit of that greatest of all comedians, Mr. Punch? I will not venture further than to note his august presence. Then we had Wombwell, with his family of quadrupeds of all grades, from the roaring lion to the chattering monkey, not forgetting the grand old elephant. The monkey, above all, was the boys' favourite — hanging by the tail, catching nuts or any other edibles offered him, but never saying, "Thank you," nor giving a single look of pleasure or gratitude. Sordid creature! How he would munch away! Doubly interesting now is the monkey; for at that time little did we think that "science" would level man down, down, down until Jacko should become man's progenitor, elbowing out poor old Adam and Eve from the post of honour.

I have never, and never can, forget the sensation when I first looked down from the entrance of the stage, after the fat woman had taken my money, upon these wonders of animated Nature. My young heart bounded up into my mouth; I was spellbound and speechless, and almost afraid to move one step further on; but the strains of the brass band close on my left hand reanimated me, and I was soon one among the crowd listening to the showman, as he related to his gaping audience the name, nature, early homes and habits of his varied collection. "Here," said he, "you see in the same den the lion from Africa and the royal tiger from Bengal, both noble beasts in their native wilds. The first can swallow a man as easily as your mother can take a pill; the tiger so voracious and strong that she would steal one of your father's bulls and leap over a ten-foot wall with it in her mouth. Here we have them living together and loving one another — tamed by the art of man, and as gentle as lambs. Stand off there!" he shouted all of a sudden. "Don't touch their paws, or they may scratch you." And so he went on from the elephant to the chameleon. "Come again to-morrow," said he to the boys, "and you will find her black. This is her blue day. Ladies and gentlemen, the chameleon changes her colour every twenty-four hours." Poor drudge! The same unvarying tale. He had grown weary of it, and there was no smile on his face the whole round.

My history bids me say we had tragedy, comedy, and farce by that most interesting of all bands, or companies, the strolling players — "diverting vagabonds," as an old wag of ours not ill-naturedly called them. As robbers are said to smell out money, so these people soon scented out our fair, and the patronage accorded them was enough to secure their regular visit for several years in succession. If it was not edification they offered, it was that which is often better relished. They taught by diversion and amusement, and so these players were ever welcome.

To detail all the wonders of this grand fair would weary one. As the day wore on, and the evening drew near, and the country folk flocked in, it became a very babel of sights and sounds, and as we had no squire to represent the upper grade of country life, and to act as master of ceremonies, precedence devolved upon the good-natured Curate, and from him the social scale descended to the gipsies, and lower still, to the sordid gamblers and the thimble-rig men. See the horrid grovelling face of that man with the roulette table, and though the chances are all against his patrons, greed and care have so stiffened the facial muscle that he is never seen to laugh; he takes his winnings and pays over the losses with the same unmoved countenance. He never smiles — so unlike the thimble-rig man, who is adroit and gay, and will banter his victim upon his want of discernment and his run of ill-luck. This gambling, and properly, is a thing of the past; it is not allowed now for common people at country fairs, and at races only within the "ring," where noblemen and "gents" do congregate, and where the police do not interfere.

Then we had the marionettes — strange and incongruous novelty. The arrival the day beforehand of Middleton and his "poppets," as the boys and girls called them, was taken as a good omen for success on the morrow. All grades honoured and patronized Middleton. In the line he had taken he was looked upon as the king of showmen. No other man, it was said, could pull the wires and make the dummies dance as he did. And true enough it was a pretty sight to see the dolls thread their way through all the mazes of the dance without one false step or move. More correct than their animated rivals, they never trod on their partner's toes. In the play, too, be it tragedy, comedy, or farce, they suited their action to the word with becoming gravity or humour. In fact, they did all, except talk, with precision and grace. I wished they could do the talking part also. It was this talking that made the exhibition farcical. When the mysterious wire-puller carried on the dialogue for all conditions and ages — young and old, from the callous murderer to the tender lover — in a croaking, half-choked, unvarying tone, then the play became an absurdity. But here again I must not be critical. On that day, as said before, we all went in for fun, and we welcomed the old Sibylline utterances. Marionettes, I have read somewhere, were instituted ages gone by to avoid the rigour of ecclesiastical and political law; when from behind the curtain the satirist would be safer than the public actor; when in the dark the oracle spoke and was tolerated, and the puppet, by the imparted force and motion, was made to represent and give embodiment to the impulses, the love, the resentment, and follies of human life.

Gipsies were in great force on our fair day — those strange, mysterious, unapproachable people. I remember them well, and the oak in Hempstead Lane, a solitary tree, around which they camped and lit up their fires. The roadside waste is gone now; so is the oak, and so, too, are the gipsies. These dark skinned strangers, who do not like improvements, never visit us now. At the time I write about their presence was no novelty — men tinkering, women hawking and fortune-telling, beguiling country maidens and drawing the coin out of their pockets; boys and girls begging, scouring the country round about, and for days and weeks beforehand making the fair the climax of their visit to this locality. What questions, what visions of the past, do the presence of these people call up — these lean and hungry looking men and women and shivering, bareheaded and barefooted boys and girls! Inbred vagabonds! Whence do they come and whither do they go? Without a country, history, religion, or morals; born never to rise to well-doing! We may pity them, but they thank us not; for, like all fatalists, these people welcome and cheerfully submit to the customs they were born to and the habits which bind them for life, and it may then run for ever. We may boast of our aristocratic beauties, but go among these poor people if you would have models for the artist, or living features for your eye to feed upon, or the painter to fix on canvas. To my mind I have seen more classic form, unique and of the highest order, in our country fair among these gipsies, than I have ever seen out of it — the young women, many of them, as beautiful in shape as in feature, and as lithe and graceful in motion as a flag in a breeze. Prudes might have called them voluptuous. But withal they were natural.

There was one stall owned by a gipsy, and kept by mother and daughter, "choke" full of allurements for all young eyes. This place in the fair was a great attraction for boys and girls. The latter especially would egg their mothers off to this booth and point out the lovely flaxen-headed, blue-eyed dolls; or if one preferred the dark beauty, here was the choice. The inventory would be too much to attempt. The attraction to some visitors was the dark-eyed widow and her married daughter — the first a grandwoman of fifty, the other about half that age — both tall, upright and majestic. It was evident from their poise of body and self-possession that liberty and they had, all their days, been play-fellows. We will not talk about black hair, nor eyes, nor olive complexion, nor oval face; these marks of race were all in perfection. Add to these the heavy finger-rings and pendant ear ornaments with their gaudy dresses, and we have two as fine women and as characteristic as I have ever looked upon, be they gipsies, Jews, or Christians; and if one was the most grand, the other was the most beautiful. Their encampment is never seen now; there is no place left for them. There are no berths on the wayside for the wayfarers; there is no bellying curve on either hand, and the angles, if any, are sharp, and follow closely and at even distance the centre of the road. There are spared but few sunny banks for the primrose, nor star-lit terrace for the glow-worm, nor hawthorn shelter for the thrush, nor bosky cover for the nightingale; the hedges are narrow and thin and run in straight lines, enclosure (robbery) taking our rights, and better roads have bespoiled us of our old lanes. But though we regret the loss, we will not sigh over the change. The past is the past, and the god Necessity has conquered and must reign, and we mortals must submit; the picturesque must give place to the practical and the useful, and it is best to welcome what we cannot shun. So with one more look back we will say good-bye to our dear old lanes, and so, too, in a few words we will to the gipsies. I know nothing of their camp life, only I think I remember that in passing their encampment, beneath and around the old oak in Hempstead Lane, I saw that disorder reigned there slutty and supreme; that the lean dogs, like their masters, looked sly and suspicious; that the cocks and the hens, living a roaming life like their mistresses, had grown bold and careless of the presence of strangers.

The glory of the fair to the Hailshamer was the Town Band. The musicians were all men of mark, and residents. The leading clarionet, our house painter, plumber, and glazier, was the last representative of a decayed family who had been fortunate enough to keep himself above mere day labour. His father had been doctor in the place, but dying early in life, the son was apprenticed to an uncle to learn the art of mixing colours, making putty and using the soldering iron. To these he had added, by the force of his own genius, music, and well he played his part in all these acquirements. As leader of the Town Band he was considered to be next to faultless, time being well marked, forte and piano judiciously varied, and running into ad libitum, he would return to tempo with the ease and skill of a professional, and all around him felt and acted by the influence of his practised and unerring guidance. The least jar or discord caused him to lift his shaggy overhanging brow, and the reproving look was good-humouredly recognized by the defaulter. The discipline was complete, and few country bands could "hold a candle" to ours. Few leaders, too, were better supported. The bassoon was all that could be expected; in fact, a lead by itself. The flute, save at times a little husky and hissing, was always correct. The bugle, that most suggestive and telling of all musical instruments, calling one's thoughts to home sports and the long-gone-by day of battle, took the subject and played second according to requirement or copy The French horn (of the old type, and tuned in the bell by the player's hand), with its grand melancholy tone, and all other intermediate instruments, came down with the proper note at the proper instant; and, though last, not least, the trombone's awakening echo could be heard. If the player was a bit of an enthusiast his instrument was never out of time nor tune, and he would hit off solos with precision and taste. To some among the crowd this instrument was more than a puzzle, and upon one of these occasions an old man standing by watching the ups and downs of the slide was heard to say that the player "would never get that thing right."

The drummer upon rare occasions was a hired hand — a military man and pensioner. He lived away in the county town, where in all municipal and election matters requiring a demonstration his services, by the rival parties, were eagerly sought after; in fact, from the Liberal party he generally held a "retainer," as the drummer was considered, by his influence among a few old comrades, to carry their votes in his pocket. He was a jovial talker, a hearty drinker, and in all business matters where his duty and his conscience were engaged, if he could carry his point, the end justified the means. And so he had his place and value, and was not to be despised. He had been away to the wars, and had beaten his drum to the dying groans and cries of his fallen comrades. He too, had not escaped unhurt. He returned crippled for life, wounded in the left knee; but he was erect, and walked with a firm step, and looked, as he marched, daring and defiant.

Dancing on the green wound up the pleasures of the day, where, in front of the music stage, mingled all our beauty and chivalry. There were no grades; from the "doctor" to the dairymaid all were equal as they footed it together in the country dance. One among the many amusements was the fire balloon. This was under the management of our master printer, George Breads. He being an adept with the scissors and paste, manufactured these fiery messengers according to his fancy and pleasure. He, too, was chief at starting and sending them off on their airy voyages. It was a wonderful thing to Johnny Tompkins and Molly Brown, as the couple stood gaping, to see these balloons, rise into space and go off nobody could guess where; and to all parties they were a great attraction, and all eyes followed the fleeting speck of light as it drew away on its silent and trackless journey. Then there was the race. Exactly as the church clock had struck ten, three balloons were let off to contend; but as there was no winning-post, so there was no prize. They were named rather grandly, after the ancients, Mercury, Ariel, and Puck. This race was instituted by well-wishers as a warning to leave and go home, and boys and girls asked to stay, and it served as an excuse to many to linger until this hour before saying good night and good-bye to the fair for that year. Our June fair ultimately collapsed and died out, as almost all pleasure fairs have done. These assemblages of tag-rag and bob-tail have nearly gone into the limbo of forgetfulness. In some degree the anniversaries of benefit clubs have supplanted and kept alive the character and complexion of the defunct day, but the substitute is dwarfed and lame in comparison. There is not the "go" in the new that there was in the old. Coquetting between the Priest and the Prince of this World — the Brewer and the Parson; empty speechifying; heavy eating, beer drinking, toasting the top of the table or rather the top of the table toasting itself; one advocating thrift and self-help, the other descanting upon the moral virtues, each speaker complimenting the other, and both, as early as decency and good-manners permit, retiring from the thankless task, one satisfied, thinking he has attended to his own interest, the other that he has done his duty in the yearly, conventional, attendance and wishing all future anniversaries with Pharaoh and his chariots' wheels at the bottom of the Red Sea.

Like everything popular, this old fair of ours had a rival. In conversation with our poet, from whom I have received several hints and some information relating to "Our Sussex Parish," I suggested that as the Poet's task is to condense, he should put into rhyme and relate the nature of the amusements of this Cacklebury Fair, and thanking him, I here offer my readers his epitomized description, which, though I never was one of the company, I believe to be as truthful as it certainly is graphic:—

## CACKLEBURY FAIR

TUNE — *"There is no luck about the House."*

Oh I how degenerate are the times
From what they used to be,
When men, without the least disgrace,
Could have a jolly spree;
When women and young single girls,
Who had the time to spare,
Could go and have a randibooze
At Cacklebury Fair.

And how they did amuse themselves
Throughout the day was curious,
For jollity was all the go,
And fun was "fast and furious."
And many who attended then
For miles around would swear,
The "Fair up town" weren't half so good
As Cacklebury Fair.

Chaps blindfold'd driving wheelbarrows
Jumping in sacks for cheeses;
For mutton climbing the greasy poles;
Girls running for chemises.
And 'twas a jolly bit of fun
To see the little souls,
With hands tied round behind their backs,
Bobbing at treacled rolls.

And then another famous move
To keep the game alive —
The chaps all round a water-butt,
For oranges would dive.
Aunt Sally got well patronized,
And so did Captain Swing:
Others would run like lamplighters
Around the kissing-ring.

And when King Beer was on his throne,
And folks were getting tight,
So sure there'd be a row or two,
Which finished with a fight
And when the night was well set in,
For home most would be prancing:
Others would to the "King's Head" go,
To have a night of dancing.

And there they'd dance, and drink and smoke
(From Bobbies had no warning);
So they kept it up till broad daylight,
And went home with the girls in the morning.
Some few, there are, who are living now
Are ready to declare;
No Fair around weren't half so good
As Cacklebury Fair.

One great cause of the breakdown of this fair was the fate of one of its constant votaries. Thomas Harris, a labouring man, on his way home after the revels, stumbled into a pond, and the next morning was taken out dead. Alas, poor Tom! This, too, was a case of too much beer. There are yet a few of his companions who aver and declare that the fair never after that went on well. There was a cloud hanging over it that would not be dissipated. Neither beer, nor song, nor noise would blot out the recollection of the past. Looking back would not do; and so one by one the old hands fell off, slunk away, and the end came. Conscience made cowards of them all.

## WHEN GEORGE IV WAS KING

Our town has always been noted for its high tone in politics. This may have been anticipated by anyone who is, or has been, acquainted with the general character of the inhabitants. The preceding sketch of the tradesman may prepare one for such an announcement. Where there is no outside countervailing influence at work, no intimidation feared, where liberty of thought and speech can have free exercise, certain consequences will follow: the action taken will be of a decided character.

So it was in the year 1820 when that most exceptionally wicked man, George IV, persecuted his Queen, and caused her to be brought to trial, after years of the most cruel treatment on his part, upon charges which altogether failed and served only further to convict the profligate monarch and to convince the people of the worthless character they had to reign over them. Then it was, when the Queen triumphed, that Hailsham broke into a sudden blaze, and put itself into illumination as best it could with the means at hand. The demonstration had been premeditated and prepared for. A combination of forces was ready to act upon the anticipated victory of right over might, of virtue over vice, of innocence over unabashed wickedness; and our free men and free women did all their little means could do, and openly, to show their detestation of the ways of the tyrant. I well remember the exultation and the rejoicing among our fathers and mothers, and the busy consultations, and the unhurried partings, as they talked over and watched the progress of the trial; and I do not forget the denunciations of those who differed from them on the topic. Feeling ran very high on both sides. The two parties were known as the "King's men" and "Queen's men," the first-named being a very small minority — composed chiefly of a few old Tories, headed by the clergyman. The news of the victory arrived by stage coach — the "Safety" — then our telegraph, and as all things were prepared and ready — the clay candlesticks and the tallow candles — as soon as day was gone, and darkness deep enough to develop the sickly yellow light given out by a "cotton twelve," every little window became a protest and a proof of the exultation of the indweller, and there were no defaulters in all our little town. In this way we gave our verdict, and pronounced both our approbation and our disapprobation, appeased our conscience, and thanked God the wicked had not triumphed; and in many a house that night was the Queen toasted and the health of the worthy Alderman Wood, her Majesty's friend and protector, drunk in a bumper.

## FIFTY YEARS AGO

OUR social condition fifty years ago [1] may be written down as deplorable. There was this negative consolation: we were no worse off than our neighbours, the whole community being at that time under the darkest cloud of pauperism. Those were sad days, and not a few. Our political economists ascribed the state of things to over-population. There was a redundancy of labour, for which no employment could be found. The poor-rate had gone up to twenty-one shillings on the rateable value, and the law said, "No man shall starve." The unalienable right established by Elizabeth in 1601 was well understood and as severely tested. Men in the full vigour of life did not hesitate to "throw" themselves on the parish; relief in money or kind, or both, could not be refused. Self-help was not

---

[1] Circa 1830

understood among our labouring population, neither was the glorious privilege of being independent recognized; we were in an abyss of degradation and moral degeneracy. Groups of men were to be seen daily in our street hanging about having nothing whatever to do, but every man expected his daily pay. To entitle him to this he had to put in his appearance in the morning at the Workhouse, and if the Master, Bartholomew Osborn (*Hardjaws* was his nickname) had no order for the man, he was turned adrift into the street for the remainder of the day, there to remain. To while away the time the game of marbles was indulged in, and great proficiency was arrived at by some of the players. I have looked on with the envy of a boy at a shot that would strike one in the ring and kill an enemy with unerring aim at a long distance. To remedy in some degree this waste of time the parish hand-cart was introduced. To each cart six men were attached, and sent off to Langley or Wallsend. This for a time was a popular job. They were then under no control. They had perfect liberty for the day. Each set had to collect and drag home a few hundred weights of boulders. The men would go off, singing and joking, to the drudgery; but the return journey was no easy task, and ultimately the men revolted, and the carts were broken up by these rebels. Billeting was tried as a help. Here the farmer had the best of the bargain. The men could be made to earn some thing on the land, but the tradesman often could find no employment for the work-man forced upon him, but he must pay for the number of days named on the ticket notwithstanding. This system produced much dissatisfaction and jealousy among the ratepayers, but for a time it had to be borne; there appeared no way out of the difficulty.

Another and a last move, and one which proved to be the climax, was the introduction of the hand flour mills. These mills were erected in the Workhouse yard, and just within the gates, as they now stand, might be seen the men at the thankless task. The monotony and the exhaustion brought on by the cease less turning of the crank, so different from the games in the street, after a time caused murmurs, which by degrees grew into threats, and there was about this time a general upheaving in surrounding parishes.

100

Mobs had begun to collect, and agitators and would-be leaders sprang up. We were threatened with a visit, and to the time named the men appeared — our street was in their possession. Speeches were made — help was demanded — the Hard-hearted Overseer was denounced and threatened, but no personal violence ever occurred here. The men were demoralized by their condition as paupers, but not vicious. The cry was for help, for work, to be saved from starvation and nakedness. The cause of all this distress was not easily understood, especially by the class most afflicted. Individuals and the present were blamed, when the past should have been held accountable. The nation had sown the wind, and this consequently had followed.

In the midst of all this useless and wasted human force a horse thrashing-machine or two were set up. The use of any machinery was looked upon as an unjust interference with the rights of labour. Murmurs thickened and daily grew deeper. The tempest was heard howling in the distance. A second visit by the mob was threatened, and our authorities, after a hurried consultation, thought it advisable to take down the flour-mills. They were removed in the night, and secreted in the vestry of the church. It was none too soon. The day following our ragged regiment, headed by a fifer, arrived, and marched direct to the Workhouse yard. The gates were invitingly thrown open. The men entered. The mills were gone. The mob had triumphed, and hearty cheers, mingled with laughter, followed and proclaimed the victory; but we were as deep as ever in the abyss — almost in despair. We had had more than one farmyard incendiary fire; threatening letters were flying about, signed SWING, and the gallows had many a victim. I witnessed the conviction of one young fellow at the Assize at Lewes — the saddest sight I ever saw — for firing a barn in the neighbourhood of Hastings. As he turned to leave the dock he said, in trembling accents, to a man who was standing close behind him, "Jack, you have sworn my life away." In a few days the culprit was, as the Judge had told him he would be, hanging by the neck. There was less delay than now between sentence and execution — sanguinary law. Under the beam his last words were, "I am innocent." Ten years later remorse and the near approach of death made Jack exclaim, "*I fired the barn in Jim's shoes.*" These men had been fellow-workers, and both had lived together in the same house. It was the shoe-prints that had sent poor Jim to the hangman.

In the year 1834 the Poor Law Amendment Act came as a relief. Authority was re-established, having power to deal with the difficulties of the time. But all that relates to this is history, so well known and understood, and the result so satisfactory and well appreciated, that further mention of the subject here would be altogether out of place. The overseer before this had been the best-abused man in the parish. As tax collector and administrator of relief, he was a target shot at by all parties, and various, and some times grave, were the charges brought against him. A serio-comic song, which was very popular, will show how feeling was running about this time. It was sung to the tune of, and was a parody on, "The Mistletoe Bough." Here is the last stanza:—

> At length the soup copper repair did need;
> The copper-smith came and there he see'd
> A bundle of bones lie grizzling there,
> In the leg of the breeches the boy did wear.
> Ah I dreadful to tell, the boy gave a stoop;
> And fell in the copper, and was boiled in the soup,
> And they all of 'em said, and they said with a sneer,
> He was push'd in by the "Cruel Overseer."
> Oh, the poor Workhouse boy!

# SOME PERSONALITIES
# IN OUR PARISH

## OUR WITCH

The man is yet alive who can remember our witch. Yes, we have had our witch, and the cottage is now standing by the roadside where she and her married daughter and husband all lived together. Poor old soul! I have often seen her out sunning herself in front of the house, innocent and harmless as any other woman or man in the place; yet she was suspected and charged with having dealings with the devil. She was too decrepit when I knew her to be able to get away from her home, and was never at that time seen outside the wicket-gate of her cottage, where, on the grass-plat in summer, and among the wallflowers, double daisies, larkspurs, and many other old-fashioned flowers that make some of our cottage gardens so beautiful, she might be seen perambulating, leaning on her staff which she clutched, leaving about a third of its length above her bony hand. This staff we wicked ones used to say was the broom-stick on which she rode to the moon on her nightly errands of mischief.

In person our witch was small, and in her gait stooping, and, like all other witches I have ever heard of or read about, she was poor. She was not ignorant of the charge standing against her, and

*Our Witch's cottage*

in her poverty would say, "If I was a witch I would never want for snuff." This happened when the coppers ran short. The rich and the well-to-do escape this ban. The devil does not seek this class of his helpers in high places. It will be no parade of words to say that to *us* children she was a scare, and though, perhaps, unwittingly, a repellent thing that kept all that is lovely in child-life far away from her person. A glimpse of her gave a chill, and her presence was a terror — in short, she was, indeed, a very witch, an evildoer, and a friend of Satan. All this had come about (innocently, no doubt) by teaching, but whatever parents conjecture, speculate upon, or indulge in, children will believe, and so the imagination early, and perhaps for life, becomes clogged, and shackled with chilling fancies of ghosts and gabbling warlocks and witches, helps allow able enough to the dramatist, the poet, or the romancer, but toward children and weak-minded persons often cruel. We have years ago cleared ourselves of this incubus. We have now neither witches to trouble our hearths and homes, nor ghosts to cross our moonlight pathway. The faith in both has died out.

# Our Beadle

One important person must not be forgotten, John Holland, the parish beadle — *Old Dog's Fat*, as we boys wickedly called him. He lived in an old double cottage, where now stands the pretty little house built by the Rev. F. C. Harvey, the Vicar. The old place had only one sleeping room in each apartment, all being on the ground floor, our beadle and his wife occupying the end nearest the road. In the other part was reared a large family of boys and girls, the husband, wife, and children, cocks and hens, all sheltering beneath the same roof. The cocks and hens went upstairs and roosted on a few crossbars nailed to the naked rafters in the common living room, and often when the evening meal was on, the old bird was threatened with decapitation for not enforcing stricter habits of decency and good manners among his wives and their children; but circumstances go very far towards making us all what we are, and the owner, recognizing the difficulty, would forgive them again and again, and so long as the old man lived the poultry occupied their old quarters over the family supper table. Altogether it was a happy family. Would as much could be said for every other household. In confirmation, one of our poets, C. H., apostrophized at the time as follows:—

> Old rooster, mind your P's and Q's;
>     If at such tricks again I catch you,
> As such a practice I don't choose,
>     Down from your perch I'll surely fetch you.

But to return to our old beadle. During summer his office was a mere sinecure. The boys would delight and tire themselves at cricket on the common or with a ramble in the fields, but as winter drew on the street became the rendezvous, and the old man the butt. He had raised their ire by a tale he told about a dog he said he had once owned. It was a wonderful dog. It had died from repletion, and he said he had sold forty pounds of fat taken from the carcase. For this "crammer" our juveniles never forgave him, and they perpetually worried the old fellow by shouting, "Old Dog's Fat! Bow-wow-wow."

105

Our old friend was a man of good height, figure, and features, and when on duty, robed as he was to the heels in a dark blue coat, with ample cape to protect his shoulders, and cocked hat, both turned up with yellow, and staff about five feet long, he had somewhat of dignity. His orders were despotic. No three persons were allowed to stand together on the public footpath, and John was in no way loath to say, "Move on." Indeed, he was known to scatter the three kings of the place whom he detected thus breaking one of their own laws. To the boys of an evening his appearance had a similar effect as the red flag is reputed to have on the bull. They were soon all alive at the sight of him, and ready for a fray. "Bow-wow-wow" might be heard from the shelter of many a distant corner, but by degrees they would draw out and converge to the centre of attraction, and soon the attack would be simultaneous and furious, the boys generally getting all the fun, and the officer all the vexation.

Indeed, I do not remember, except on one occasion, the Fifth of November, that our beadle ever made a prisoner. This was his great day, or rather evening. Lord George Cavendish was passing through the place from London to Eastbourne. The squibs and the crackers rattled, the fire blazed in our market square, the horses shied and ran foul of the post and rail that then guarded "Hoad's Corner." The carriage pole broke and progress for a time was delayed. This was a great event for Hailsham. It was the first time a live lord had ever been seen in the place. It was like a juggernaut passing through our street, and of course there must be sacrifice. Authority, to be appeased, must have a victim. Law must be vindicated; the crime must be punished. So about a dozen young fellows were sent off to Lewes Gaol for a fortnight, and fussiness developed and prevailed, much, as we afterwards learned, to the chagrin and disgust of "my lord." With this we will say good-bye to the old beadle. The name of Hollands has died out in our parish.

## OUR NIMROD AND HIS TALKING HORSE

Richard King-Sampson is a name that must not be passed over in the annals of our parish. Would that I could satisfactorily describe

106

his person and dress. He was one of the sons of Anak, tall, upright, square shouldered, long-limbed, with head erect and firmly set on a well-formed neck, small twinkling eye, ridged nose, and a face altogether which a sculptor might covet for a model. He moved with an easy, gliding motion, without any apparent exertion, with small hands and cheeks which, without being ruddy, were ever tinged with a healthy glow that showed no variation. In short, Mr. King-Sampson was a handsome man. In his dress he affected the sportsman, and showed his passion for the fields and the chase on foot or on horseback. He rarely appeared out of the long green hunting-coat and vest, both, of course, set off with gilt buttons. His hat was made after a fashion of his own, and at our own manufactory — low-topped, broad-brimmed. "Bags" he rarely condescended to get into, but knee-breeches, tan-leather spats, laced boots were his general lower encasements, and giving a finish to all was the double-front frilled shirt and white necktie or cloth. I have a passion for the double frilled shirt, so white, so crisp, so adorning, so bespeaking the gentleman. Altogether, our friend had limbs, figure, and gait so to set off his clothes that his tailor might be thankful in more ways than one for his patronage.

Our Nimrod's residence was an old-fashioned brick-built house of two floors, with centre doorway and hall, double-windowed sitting-rooms on either side, standing where now stands the modern stuccoed house owned and occupied by Mr. Aires. The old place, I having no special name, stood end to the road, and facing the common, was surrounded by some fine old elms and loose wild-growing shrubs and garden hedge rows, wild and high, giving shelter and safety to numerous birds that lived and sang and reared their young, according to individual habit, all the year round; and a quiet, cosy, out-of-the-way place it was, altogether fitting for one fond of retirement and prone to country life. The roadway leading to Michelham left it, as now, close to the right hand. The garden wall, edging the road, was then in its dotage, old and shaky, and had become altogether out of the upright, looking, perhaps, like an attempt to rival Hogarth's line of beauty. Starved ivy crept up over the broken ridge from the north side, taking a peep to see what might be going on on the south, or sunny side. The wall was grey with moss and scurf, the mortar, from age, at sundry places shaken and fallen out, and the joints in possession of the rue-fern, which was stinted and shivering, looking as melancholy as a wreath of cypress in a death-chamber. The grassplat in front of the house was none of your trim, prim, close mown and well-rolled lawns. The borders surrounding were to match, not nicely kept; the shrubs, few in variety and mixed with the yellow broom and the prickly furze, helping to make up the show. Among the flowers the coy and gay daffodil shut up and sported itself at pleasure, and all growing about the place belonged to home and home nature. The residence was backed up on the north by apple, plum, and a few oak trees. In one of the latter a pair of magpies built their nest, and for years in succession carried out the behest of nature, the consummation of their love and the rearing of their young. The fruit trees showed age, and the effect of an uncongenial soil in a coating of grey moss and many a naked limb.

Such is somewhat a description of the abode of the owner, and here he lived for many a year in the full enjoyment of life, his great hobby being his hounds and his kennels. Mr. King-Sampson inherited this house, and succeeded as resident his paternal uncle, William King. My informant, who has seen eighty summers, tells me this William King was a benevolent man, and did many kind acts for the poor. "When I was a boy," he says, "I used to go regularly every morning to the house for milk, which was given away to the needy by the housekeeper, Mrs. Hart." Who now knows aught of Mrs. Hart? But as I have a good character of her, it may not be amiss to make record of her name by the side of her masters. This William King, as his initials will verify, if you kindly look up at the vane that surmounts our church tower, was in the year 1801 one of the churchwardens, W. K. and W. H. being the initials of William King and William Hilder.

It is in his more natural guise as huntsman and man of the field that we must study our hero, R. King-Sampson. As neighbour and friend, to those about him he was cold and phlegmatic, showing but little sympathy with change or improvement. His heart was with his hounds and his groom, his kennels and his stables. See him ready for the start in the life-like portrait in oils by Henwood, of Lewes, his favourite doghound "Druid," by his side, and the superannuated huntsman, John Press, in the background, and you see him at his best, and when his heart is fullest. He is looking towards the Downs where, at the foot of those soft and beautiful hills, he finds his chief hunting grounds. Folkington Common, now cultivated, oft resounded with his view-holloa and the clamp of his horse's hoofs; and the hinds of the hamlet nestling around the old church and the squire's mansion knew well the short, sharp note of the pack as they pursued the doomed hare to death, for the hounds were swift hunters and trained to kill. In breed they were unique, the pack being made up of dwarf foxhounds, bred by the owner with the greatest care. To the ordinary hunter this hare-hunting with foxhounds was not the proper thing, and many and grave were the objections raised against the "cry" by old-fashioned sportsmen, and the pack was never popular, nor, I believe, ever intended to be. "Stole away" might be echoed as you saw the master and the old-fashioned groom, Hide, jog off towards the hills on a wintry morning to enjoy alone the sport, for rarely any friends met them. Short and sharp were the runs, and issue was soon death or escape. There was needed none of the science and thought required in the wealden hunting through cover and over a variety of soil and surface. These conditions affect the scent, and cause many checks, and the hunts man is often obliged to exercise his wits, sharpened by practice and experience, to again pick up the lost trail.

Our friend rarely hunted at home. He did not like the clay of the "wild," [1] and I remember but one run with his hounds close at home. Then I was drawn away from my duty by the shrill music of their throats, and who that is alive to Nature and to instinct can withstand the call as you hear the crack of the huntsman's whip and his cheering "halloa"? On that occasion I bolted and left the workshop to take care of itself. I was soon up, and had a good run, and at the end found myself in a field about half a mile from the church called the "Lower Dens," then covered with brakes and

[1] The Weald

dotted here and there with furze, and, of course, not cultivated. It was in this field poor puss met her fate, and I witnessed the whole thing. How she struggled for the little life left in her! More than tired — she was beaten, and could not shift and double and baffle her pursuers as she could at the start. Poor hare! She passed close to me, with the hungry hounds in full view, panting, struggling, her ears back on her shoulders, her soft coat begrimed with mud, pressing forward to gain one more moment of life; but her chance was gone, and as she gave out her cry of despair she was within the grasp of the leading hound's mouth, and all was over. This was the first and last time I was ever "in at the death," and I have never sought to be; but I am neither envious nor censorious. Happy is the man who can secure to himself occupation and health by indulging in field sports. The glory of the huntsman is to draw blood, and his ambition to be in at the death. As the worthy knight Sir Roger de Coverley, and the good parson, Doctor Primrose, have both remarked, "There is something to be said on both sides."

Our hero had a considerable amount of humour, was always ready with a tale or anecdote, and was fond of a joke, even putting others in a dilemma. The public on one occasion were entertained at the "Crown Inn," by a wandering ventriloquist. The patronage and the wonderment were great, and Mr. R. King-Sampson ,being one of the audience, was so much delighted that he invited the wizard to his table to breakfast the next morning. The meal over, he was taken to the stables. The groom, an elderly man in blue gaberdine, was in attendance. The stranger stood in the stall, patting and praising the favourite hunter, speaking well of the glossy coat, and tickling the groom's conceit, when the master asked, "Have you fed him this morning, George?" "Yes, sir" — with a nasal twang — was the reply. "No, you have not," gloomily and very deliberately said the horse. "What!" said George; "tell you I have." "No, you have not," emphasized the horse. "What do you mean?" said George; "tell you I have." "No, you have not," said the horse again. "And what do you mean, George?" said his master. "The horse says plainly you have not fed him." "Tell you I have," again said George. "Tell you you have not." The dispute was running high, when the wizard, opening the mouth of the animal, said, "How old are you?" "Seven," said the sleek hunter. This was too much for the old groom who, rushing out of the stable, declared the devil must be in the place; and much did his master enjoy the chagrin of the poor old man. He was soon recalled and reasoned with, but George always declared that the horse did talk. He could never settle in his mind any other way. "'Twas done so naa-tur-el," he said. "But he lied though; I had fed him."

Over the marsh to the east, peeping out among trees and foliage, is to be seen the modest spire of Wartling Church. This spire stands sentinel over a grave, marked by a headstone telling the reader that there is the final resting-place of Richard King-Sampson, and that he died at the good old age of eighty-one. Time has already erased the family from the parish, there being no descendant left among us. Our present representative of the "mighty hunter" is Robert Overy. The family have been for more than one generation men of the fields. Years ago, and miles away, I was asked if I knew anything of Overy's blue mottled harriers. We have the same breed now, as beautifully painted, as well-modelled, and as mellow tongued as they were at that time. The family then lived at Marl Green, Heathfield; but that generation has passed away, the defunct being represented by our brewer, Robert. He is now enjoying the autumn of his days by hunting ten couple of the old breed, giving sport and healthful recreation to all who choose to join the chase. His is hunting in the good old fashion; hence the popularity among all classes. See him with his man, Bean, both whip in hand at the find. Off they go, and happy is he who runs fastest. With good scent no runner can keep pace with these hounds, but knowing the country, master or man is generally in at the death, or gets up to help over a bit of ground when a check occurs. The lot is now somewhat mixed with a touch of the foxhound and a large breed from the kennel of Bexhill. We all, in every matter, want to go faster — the old ways are too tame for the blood of this day; and besides, variety has a charm in any picture. Hence, among the present ten couple, you may see, perhaps, half the number made up

of the old family breed. Hear them on a strong scent, and you will
say—

A cry more tunable
Was never halloaed to, nor cheer'd with horn.

It is an invitation to shake sleep from your eyes and sloth from
your feet, to be up with the morn, to sweep the dew from the grass,
to beat the tangled brake and briar, to find poor puss in her seat, to
cry, "See ho! there she goes," and to hear the sudden burst of the
hounds and see them settle down to the work. This is an exciting
moment for all concerned, for 'tis ten to one in less than two hours
the hare will be lifeless and in the huntsman's hands. Then
heigh-ho! for another find. The sun is yet high above the western
hills, and the master says, "We must have a couple to-day." Depend
upon it some men are born hunters. Hunting is one of the fine arts,
and its votaries are filled with a passion that will accept of no
substitute. A born hunter must and will hunt; man must submit to
his fate.

We must not dismiss this notice of our friend without one word
for his song. He has but one, and in this he centres all his heart and
vocal talent. Of course the song is a hunter's song, dedicated to the
sylvan queen, the Goddess Diana. Nancy is the charmer; the stag
the game; "Hark forward!" the cry; "The hounds all after him go,"
the chorus; and with smiling faces all round the table, the picture
is completed and satisfying. As I am a bit of an enthusiast in
musical matters, let me, in conclusion, do homage to the leading
hound, "Ruler," who, at the challenge in the morning, or in the
fields with the trebles and counter-trebles, does the double bass to
perfection, and so say good bye.

## THE BARBER AND HIS SHOP

Reader, hast thou ever heard of Diego, the barber of Olmedo? Of
his history as told by Gil Blas, of his poverty and his gaiety, of his
industry and his thrift, of his loves, his temptations, his fortitude,
his triumphs, of his many gifts and accomplishments? If thou never

hast, be assured that for all these, and more, he deserves thy reverence and homage. A most diverting man was this barber of Olmedo — a genuine gossip, though in no way given to malice or gloom, bright, benevolent, ready to share his crust with his wayworn fellow-traveller, enlivening the journey with his merry conceits, ever ready to welcome Fortune, be she fair or be she foul. I confess his character moves me to admiration, and opens my heart toward all his latter day brethren and fellow-professors — most favoured of slaves, most trusted of men, most honoured of mortals! Patronized by the fair, in their *déshabillé*, hanging over their shoulders, breathing about their necks, arranging their locks, dallying with the ringlets, rivalling Zephyr, playing with the tangles of the hair, and making no creature envious. In childhood, too, one of our first professional attendants, and last, giving us a clean chin ere we are shrouded and made ready for the coffin.

So among the many notables of "Our Sussex Parish" the barber must not be forgotten. How subdued his tone, how civil his manner, how clean his napkin, in which he wraps you; how soft his fingers, how delicate his touch as he seizes your nose, and in five minutes rids you of your trouble. Listen to his razor as it travels beneath the snowy surface — white as Hecla, wann as Etna, soft as Venus. Do you hear the rattle of the bristles? — platoon firing right, left, and centre! The fight is soon over, the foe is vanquished, the victory is complete, and the man, shorn of his beard, is himself Let the unrazored deride; let him pride himself on his strength, vaunt in the street, gibe as he passes by, and, if he will, dip his beard in his cup or sail it in his soup-plate; let him be proud as he may be. My delight is in a recurring shave and a clean chin. And oh! that again my locks could be clustering and my pate well covered. Then, when seated in his chair and folded in the ample cloth, then had I pleasure. Closing my eyes, care fled from me, envy was banished, the whole world lay at my feet; then was I in a land flowing with milk and honey. Every moment was hallowed. This was my millennium, when sitting under the mesmeric touch of the barber, hearing and feeling the click of the scissors. It was then I sighed, when I had to make way for the next patron, and he, perhaps, hating the operation, cursing the barber if he dallied, and on some occasions rushing out of the shop — as our eccentric man, Mr. M. Slye, would do, with a half-cropped cranium, shouting, "I'll pay next time," and trotting away. Alack for the oddities of life! I am told that since Nature has resumed her rights and fashion fallen, vanquished — since man has discarded borrowed plumes and woman false curls, going to the necropolis for their dead brothers' and sisters' hair — since then I am told the golden days of the country barber have passed away, when he could before breakfast earn his guinea dressing wigs and glossing ringlets.

To catch a glimpse of our old and fashionable barber we must go a long way back. It will be like looking into the broad end of the telescope; distance reduces his person to almost an atom. Very few now among us can see him at all, and if his history be taken up and detailed, it would tie the two centuries together. Fifty years ago he died,[1] aged ninety-five. Fifty-seven he held his shop, but never during that long half-century tenancy, as I can learn, did he put out the pole, the basin, and the ribbon. No, he was not a quack, but stuck to the legitimate cutting and shaving, false curls and fashionable wigs. He in his bloom kept his horse — or, to be exact, his chestnut mare — and for miles round, with Eastbourne and Bexhill for the base of operations, swept the country, exacting his fees, and it was one of his boasts that he never rode out or home without a guinea in his pocket. In fact, as he told the tale, a prouder couple than he and his mare never set out together, as upon one occasion, he having "cleared out," being worsted by a party of friends over that now obsolete bantering game of cards called "Put," and miles away from his home, the old chestnut refused to budge a peg until her master had returned into the house and, with that excuse, borrowed a guinea from his friend the host.

Here let me relate that John Gibbs, like John Gilpin, was a citizen of fair London town, that Saint Giles' had the honour of his birth, and that until he fell in love, and sighed for his master's pretty daughter Kate, he was happy enough; but the fair one, after encouraging the apprentice, threw him off and accepted another

---

[1] 1834

one, who offered an earlier marriage (and who, I ask, can blame her?). Then it was that John lost heart, and determined once for all to abandon city life and the snares thereof; for how could he, as he said, lay his head upon his pillow, tired as he might be, and rest, knowing the girl he adored was in the next street, and in possession of another? So, on a summer morning, fitting himself out with razor, scissors, and other appliances to commence on his own account, he mounted the stage coach, and before the day was out found himself on his feet in front of the "Crown" in the old town of Hailsham, and here he soon grew into importance. His peculiar town dress, curly wig, his smooth, clean-shaved face and chin, and, above all, his polite manner, at once won him favour, especially with the ladies, and before the year was out our new man had ousted the old, home-spun barber, and had taken possession of his shop, and here, as has been related, he plied his art fifty-seven years. Let us settle another important point. He never wooed again. He died a bachelor.

Whether it was lacking the influence of a good wife and the comforts of a home, who can now tell? — but this we do know — John, though no drunkard, was convivial. He loved the tavern, rum punch, and a merry evening. Here is the refrain of his favourite song, and this tells the whole tale of his life. When he was in his cups, he would sing with great glee—

And all that Jack's father had gathered together
Jack spread all abroad with his fork.

Then, when old age had overtaken him, and as he could work no more, he soon found there was no friend like unto a friend in the pocket. He was stranded, left a wreck, and where he had sported he could sport no more; but, bad as it was, he was not forsaken. He was high-spirited; he had the reputation of having been a wit, a wag, and a swell; he held up his head, and a few of his old friends and companions, in his utmost need, did not forget him. He was no swell then, indeed. Little, and lean, and tottering was Barber Gibbs, receiving parish relief, had given up his tailor, and would accept any favour. Anything then fitted him. He made himself comfortable in the cast off breeches or trousers of a six-foot man, would wrap his shoulders in the coat and vest of another weighing over twenty stone, and by favour of the third he wore top-boots up to the last. This was one of his weaknesses: he would not be seen in the street out of top boots, and with the dingy wig, high, broken-topped hat, he was covered from head to heel, and better than all, he was blithe and gay as ever. He would stand a very Lazarus, at the churchyard gate on a Sunday, as the congregation left after service, ready to accept any gift. Even then his proud spirit was unsubdued. "Where are your calves, Barber Gibbs?" — the boots were hanging about his heels — said the eldest son of our Squire, as he dropped a coin into the extended hand. "Some men are all calf," was the tart reply, as the suppliant pocketed the coppers. His tongue had ever been as sharp as his razor. Upon one occasion a simpering swell of a bagman from the "George" opposite, walking into the shop, asked if he could have an easy shave. "Sit down, sir," said the indignant barber. "I shaved your master last month when you were at home behind the counter."

It was in somewhat such guise as described that I remember John Gibbs in his superannuation as he slouched past, going to the old shop for his weekly free shave, not daring as he walked to lift his feet from the ground, fearing he would uncase his little legs and leave his boots behind him in the street. There is yet a relic or two about the shop that once belonged to the old man, enough to revive his memory among us. A full, or nearly full-size plaster-cast bust, with very fair face, dark-brown eyelashes, vermilion lips, and lightly tinged cheeks — a swell of the period. It was upon the head of this dandy that our barber exhibited the work of his art, the wigs of his customers, when these had passed through his hands and received the final touch, This bust used to stand on the present table, and in the right-hand corner of the shop, in full view of all who entered; and further, there is yet one wig of the olden time on hand, and the present owner, sooth to say, finds a use for both. In summer, when the audacious cock sparrow sits high up in the apple tree, uneasy, flitting from bough to bough, looking anxiously at the rows of peas in the garden, there stands the figure with the worn-out wig on its head, sentinel; and the cock sparrow, be assured, old and hardened as he is, or may be, in crime, looks twice before he ventures once. "To what base uses do we come at last?"

Our old man retained, until death, one staunch friend, Mr. King-Sampson, who, playing the part of the "Barmecide" in the "Arabian Nights," gave him, for years, a substantial breakfast. The bargain was that the barber had to take the letters from the post office, deliver them at the house, and then sit down with the servants. This he did until he became almost one of the establishment. There is a touching episode in connection with this early daily visit. A favourite hound, turned out of the pack to live his life in freedom, was every morning on the look-out for the barber. The two high-mettled ones generally met at the gate, the dog giving out a howl of welcome, and licking the bony hand as the two moved off together towards the kitchen door.

Again, from all times and from all countries, are we not reminded of the barber? From Samson, as he lay with his head on the knee of Delilah, bewitched, and listening to her importunities, until his locks fell at her feet, and he sank helpless, to Absalom, the King's beloved son; from the chattering barber in the "Arabian Nights," surnamed the "Silent"; again to the famous Diego, and onward to the Sussex barber who, mounting his large signboard high up over his shop, at the angle leading into Market Street, in the ancient town of Lewes, sporting (impious man!) with one of the most touching tales of Scripture history. Who, I ask, that visited Lewes in those bygone days, did not stop to look up at Absalom, robed in purple and scarlet as he hung suspended by the hair of his head, wild with fright and agony, his mule dashing away, leaving the rider an easy mark for the pursuing enemy? Who then did not look up with an eye of pity at poor Absalom? Will the reader call to mind the trading, left-handed appeal to the public I Here runs the rhyme—

Oh, Absalom, unlucky prig,
Hads't thou but worn a periwig!
For had thy luckless head been shaved,
Thy life most surely had been saved.

And may we not infer from this that Mr. John Inkpen[1] was a man of resource and ready wit? Whether he acted as his own artist, designer, painter, and poet, cannot be settled here; but there was, in addition, this belonging to the work that told a tale as to the character of the owner. Thereon figured his name written in capitals, built up with copies of articles belonging to his trade — brushes, combs, razors, scissors, curling-tongs, etc. Altogether an elaborate and striking affair was the signboard of the Sussex barber.

But we will do our old friend no injustice. The country barber, especially one of the old pattern, is an exceptional character, exposed to many and varied influences, and in writing his history he demands our best consideration. Among his neighbours he is expected to know "everything." I remember one, who in his monthly visits to the farm house, where there was a large family of boys and girls, young men and women, was always called "The Gazette." The shop of the small country town barber, too, is the focus to which all news flies. Gossips of all colours congregate there. There are chairs for their accommodation — all are old customers — and each man among them is expected to tell his tale. The meetings and the news are perennial; the tongues never tire, the subjects are never exhausted — politics, the wars, fortunes and failures of trade, robberies, scandals, births, deaths and marriages, the loves of the village, breaches of promise, and elopements, should ever such an exciting affair have come off in the neighbourhood, and there, too, Rumour stations herself, and bloated with garbage. sends off into the thin and spongy air her messages, soon to become exaggerations, if not lies.

But who, with all this, will be censorious or say aught against the barber or his shop? Both are necessary to life as we live it, and we welcome both. To the idler and to the listener, to the worn-out tradesman and the independent man of small means, taking his regular round and shave, gathering up the news for home consumption and digestion, there is no place so inviting as the barber's shop; and the room, too, has other uses. Here are to be

[1] Another Sussex writer states that the Lewes barber's name was Cooley. (Arthur Beckett)

seen symbol lessons: the humorous and the serious are mingled, and the walls covered. There hangs (or used to hang) Kean, as "Shylock," with the hard, grim, calculating visage, the exacting scales in one hand and the ready knife in the other; Cruickshank's "Bottle" and its climax; the fate of the drunkards' children; the boy in the felon's dock, convicted and ,banished for life; the girl plunging from the bridge to cover her shame and quench out her miserable young life in the river-bed. There, too, goes the staggering sot under escort, just turned out of his drinking den at midnight; the devil, more ghastly than death, on one hand, and the constable on the other — the man weary with helping, the fiend waiting for his victim. And other picture lessons might be named, each telling some distinct tale. But this is noticeable, our barber has no written sermons, either in prose or rhyme. Perhaps he judges, and wisely too, that the brain and heart may be as readily reached and as truly acted upon through the eye as the ear.

And this brings us down to the present hour. For the last fifty years we have had no change of occupancy; and now, if one would know the pleasure of an easy shave, he will do well to seat himself in the chair of our barber's shop.

## OUR POET, JOHN HOLLAMBY

As the poet needs no pedigree by which to herald his name and fame onward to posterity, it will be enough to say that John Hollamby was a native of Frant, in Sussex, and that he all his life was a working man; that like almost all other working men he could trace his pedigree back only to the third generation. Does the reader know, does he recognize the fact, that this is the limit to which the working classes are tied? The family history, in almost all cases, allows us no peep at our great-grandfathers. We gather no fame from the past, and heralds tell our children no lies about their ancestors. Our virtues and our vices die with us, and as to fame, we have of this no hope but in the present: therein lives and lies our all. We leave no legacy for the future to deal with, and our children's children will not blush for the fourth generation, nor need we for our own characters by

119

*Our poet, John Hollamby*

anticipation. Our graves close over us and haply we are gone. History never records a poor man's vices: it is for those in high places this peculiar privilege is held in reservation. Oblivion is the poor man's compensation. It is that which adjusts and balances the future with the past, and there is this further gratification — no poor man ever becomes famous but by his virtues or his genius. The poor poet survives in spite of his adverse fate. If Homer had been the blind beggar only, his name would have rotted with his bones, and "like unto him in fate." Milton, ere now, had been forgotten but for his virtues and his never-dying melodies; and be they rich, or be they poor, 'tis men such as these that hold out in their immortal hands the lamps that never dim, and sing the songs to us that never tire. The poet is the ruling and the guiding spirit for all ages, knitting together the past, present, and future; the seer, teacher, and prophet, the one mortal we do homage to, and to the influence of whose mysteries we all bow, whose teacher is unknown, even to himself, and we in our ignorance and want of more perfect knowledge or light say he is inspired. He is of many grades, and of all complexions. There are the greater and the lesser lights, while some are as gods among their fellows.

It is a minor we have here to deal with. Our representative man was a minnow among the tritons; but he was a true poet nevertheless. Poetry was no studied art with him: he sang his simple lays from the overflow, or impulse, of his nature. He knew not why, but the gods visited him, and he obeyed. It was given him to speak, and he spoke in true rhyme and measure, and always to the point. He would be grave or gay, humorous or severe, and modestly and honestly. He was for thirty years grinder and leading man in Hailsham's oldest mill, and if his occupation was humble, so was his appearance. See him and you would say, Can there be any genius hidden beneath that dusty old smock-frock and broken-down old hat? His gait, too, was against him. As he went tumbling by, a stranger might say, He will be down in a minute! But make his acquaintance and engage his attention, and you would find him to be full of life, and no novice in human affairs. The cottage just by the mill held his all, a good wife and a large family of boys and girls. He was happy in his home. Reading and observation were his teachers, and you would find he had profited largely by both. The schoolmaster had never known him — he was purely THE UNLETTERED MUSE.

In the year 1827 issued from the Hailsham Press, then presided over by George Breads (as worthy a man as any among us), a small volume of poems, under this title, by John Hollamby. The following may be considered his apology for putting his thoughts into print. He said—

> I ne'er aspired to mount Pegasus,
> Nor climb the height of steep Parnassus;
> But often as my time would suit,
> To saunter near some mountain's foot,
> To crop some humble sprig or flower,
> Amusement for a leisure hour;
> And if for this I have permission,
> It is the height of my ambition.

His perception and discrimination, his force of thought and power of arriving at conclusions, the following sonnet will show:—

> That Love at random throws his darts,
>> And seems to make such odd mistakes;
> That he, in wounding of our hearts,
>> So many curious blunders makes;
> That some are doomed in love to mourn
>> And in their hearts endure the pain,
> Who for their love meet no return
>> But cold unkindness and disdain;
> That Fortune does not always give
>> Her favours to the most deserving;
> That some unsought her gifts receive,
>> While others seek and yet are starving;
> How can we cause for wonder find,
>> Since Love and Fortune both are blind?

The address to the wren will show the tenderness of the poet's heart and that his happiness is bound up and intensified by being able to add to the happiness of others:—

## TO A WREN WHO HAD BUILT HER NEST UNDER THE EAVES OF MY DWELLING

Fond, timid bird, why lookest thou so shy?
Why keepest thou aloof when I am nigh?
Why does my presence thus thy fears alarm?
Think'st thou I'll rob thy nest or do thee harm?
No I thou the shelter of my roof shalt share,
And undisturbed thy tender young shalt rear;
No schoolboy's ruthless hand shall e'er molest
Or tear thy unfledged offspring from thy nest,
For I will be thy guardian and thy friend,
Far as my power and humble means extend;
Thy nest from every prying eye I'll guard,
And in thy happiness find my reward.

Thomas Gooche, a Norfolk man, was at the time our poet went into print, our brewer. The following song, which was very popular, forms part of the volume:—

## GOOCHE'S STRONG BEER

"Fancy it Burgundy, only fancy it, and 'tis worth ten shillings a quart."

O, Gooche's beer your heart will cheer,
    And put you in condition:
The man that will but drink his fill,
    Has need of no physician.

'Twill fill your veins, and warm your brains,
    And drive out melancholy;

Your nerves 'twill brace, and paint your face,
    And make you fat and jolly.

The foreigners they praise their wines
    ('Tis only to deceive us):
Would they come here and taste this beer,
    I'm sure they'd never leave us.

The meagre French their thirst would quench,
    And find much good 'twould do them;
Keep them a year on Gooche's beer,
    Their county would not know them.

All you that have not tasted it,
    I'd have you set about it;
No man with pence and common sense
    Would ever be without it.


## ON THINKING

"Life is but thought; therefore I will think Youth and I are house-mates still."

    By some philosophers we're taught,
    That happiness consists in thought,
    That howsoever things may go,
    The man is blest who thinks but so.

    Oh I could I but that heart attain,
    I'd think away each care and pain,
    And on this philosophic plan,
    I'd think myself a happy man.

    I'd think my spare and homely board
    With every pleasant dainty stored,

And when my cup is fill'd with tea,
I'd think it port or Burgundy.

And when in homely garments dress'd,
I'd think those garments of the best;
With but one shirt I'd think I'd two,
And my old coat, I'd think it new.

And when the wind blew cold and chill,
'Tis then I'd think it warm and still,
Tho' snow and hail come down together,
I'd think it pleasant summer weather.

And tho' at times upon this plan
I cheat my senses all I can,
It little satisfaction brings,
For "facts," I find, "are stubborn things."

The following, showing the punning power of the writer, was written in the old mill forty years ago:—

### HAILSHAM

Of Hailsham sure I may presume
Some short account to give;
For in this place full thirty years
I've *made* a *shift to live*.

And oh! the changes in that time,
How many that have *come*:
How many born, how many, too,
Have *gone to their last home*.

As strangers coming to the place
Would wish to know, of course,
Where they may *entertainment* find
For man as well as horse.

First there's the "British Grenadier,"
Stands just above the town;
And when you get into the place,
You next will find the "Crown."

Go on, and turn round to the right,
The "George" will then be seen,
The "King's *Head*" that stands further *out*,
But that's not the *head inn*.

There is a place, the "Garretts" called
Lies just below the town;
Tho' most *up* to the garrets go,
We Hailshamers go *down*.

It is a pretty shady place,
Where *lovers love* to be;
But you must go on higher ground,
If you would *see* the *sea*.

Upon the church tower many go,
Because that place is higher,
And there upon a pleasant day,
You may *spy* many a *spire*.

There's *East*bourne bears about due *south*,
As near as can be guess'd,
And *West*ham that lies plain *south-east*,
And *East*hoathly *north-west*.

In looking round there you may see,
Full six-and-thirty mills!
And *flocks* of shepherds with their *flocks*,
Upon the Southdown hills.

Or in the Channel you may see
The *ships* pass to and fro,
And think upon the great hard*ships*
Which seamen undergo.

There are five bells hung in the tower
As good as any round,
For tho' they've always carried the *crack*,
That does not spoil the *sound*.

And tho' all five are excellent,
Were I oblig'd to tell
Which is the best, why I should say
The tenor *bears the bell*.

Look up, and you will see five vanes,
Which sometimes turn so true
That if the wind shifts but *one* point,
The vanes will all shift *too*.

And if upon a market day
You go *out in* the street,
You many farmers' calves may see,
And many butchers' *meet*.

Bullocks and sheep there you may see,
All *round* the market *square*;
And *whether* the *weather* be foul or fair,
You'll find some *wethers* there.

Of men and beast the town's so full,
Folks scarce know what to do;
I always think it *dangerous* when
The "*Safety*" coach comes through.

And when the market folks are dry,
And want a drop of beer,
Some carry their sixpence to the "*Crown*,"
Some march to the "*Grenadier.*"

A pot of beer is very well,
If people don't get more;
But some are not content with that,
For they will have a *score.*

Here parties going to the sea
Oft make a pleasant show;
For once a year to Langley *Point*
Some make a *point* to go.

Others will go to Eastbourne Bay.
(By roving fancy led);
A body then may go on *foot*
Round under Beachy *Head.*

Mr. Wenham, auctioneer,
Long at this place has been,
And *busy* at his *business*,
He every day is seen.

And if he can a trifle *gain*,
He'll either sell or buy;
But when there anything is *lost*,
We often *hear him cry.*

"Mr. Wenham, in addition to his numerous other avocations, acts as Town Crier. He also lets Post Horses. N.B. — Not wooden ones.
"JOHN HOLLAMBY."

*Old cattle market, High Street, Hailsham*

In the snug north-west corner of our churchyard, together with his wife, lie the remains of the old miller; one mound of earth covers both graves. As in life they were meet companions, so in death they were not separated. The old lady was of a superstitious, confiding turn, quite unlettered, but like her husband, had a taste for painting, and there are yet to be seen specimens of their skill in oils. The wife, too, had great faith in charms, ghosts, and tokens, and in the case of young women and their early loves she used to declare that her husband was "lotted" to her, and she knew it before he had ever spoken a word to her. She had consulted the oracle at the bottom

129

of a basin of cold spring water in this wise:— The initial letters of
the names of three young men written on three separate slips of
paper were wrapped in three balls of paste made of wheaten flour
and dropped into the water, and as she stood watching up came
first "J. H." This is the test — so says the legend — the first up
from the bottom of the bowl to be the lucky man; and so it came to
pass, as the old lady has said, "After fifty years of wedded life, we
never once repented. What the gods did for us they did well,"

## MR. JAMES HENRY CAPPER
## AND THE WRECK OF *THE THAMES*

OUR art representative was J. H. Capper, of Ersham Lodge. He
was son of the Vicar of Wilmington, and uncle of the twin
brothers, Vidal, one of the first Bishops of Sierra Leone, the other
Vicar of Chiddingly, two men of more than average character. As
it is no degradation to the Church clergyman to be poor. I need not
in the elder Capper's case hesitate to say that he was in his early
married life one of those unfortunate people. I name the fact to give
an opportunity to show the way in which he became rich. It is a
splendid feature in the character of our national Church, that the
clergyman loses no cast by being poor — so unlike any other of
Her Majesty's subjects — and they have this for their reward for
their days of self-denial. The gown is an introduction to the very
best society, and every lady's drawing-room becomes open to the
wearer of the sacred vestment. In this life there is perhaps no
unmitigated evil; every inconvenience has its compensation. There
are two sides to every question, and in nearly all a remedy, and a
way out of a difficulty; especially so in the case of the poor
clergyman, should be he a widower or bachelor. Perhaps a
commercial value may be discovered in this privilege of the gown
giving the needy and the aspiring a chance of bettering their
condition. That poverty is a great inconvenience, even when no
social degradation is the penalty, cannot be denied, and escape

from its hungry fangs is laudable and worthy a great effort and venture.

In the case of the Rev. Mr. Capper, the widower, the opportunity did offer. He made the venture; was successful, and he triumphed. He banished poverty from his own and his children's homes for life, and his and their happiness was not damaged by the change of circumstances. Fortune shone doubly upon him: he married a wealthy woman and secured a good wife at the same time. The way in which this match was brought about gives it the novelty. The lady was the widow of a rich Manchester man. She, again sighing for the bonds of Hymen, advertised for a husband — a clergyman. Mr. Capper negotiated, was accepted, and the lady became Mrs. Capper, wife of the Vicar of Wilmington — a blessing to her husband, his family, and the neighbourhood.

Much of the latter part of the Vicar's life was spent in visits to Ersham Lodge, and after his death the widow took up her permanent residence in the home of her son-in-law. Here she kept up her establishment of servants, horses and carriage, with its dishing wheels; the body swinging on straps and springs (with footboard behind for the footman) was of the old pattern and colour, yellow or straw. There was, too, in attendance, the plum-pudding dog. The coachman, Overy, was a little, lean old man, swallowed up in his top-boots and box-coat of drab, in winter of many capes. He drove a pair of good horses, and when seated, looked all he was intended to be. He was a good whip and proud of his profession and his position. He had the reputation of being a first-rate story-teller, and marvellous adventures would he relate of his own experiences, many, the envious would say, too good to  true. One such story may be ventured. He called "The Flying Leap." "Being well mounted," he said "and well up, the hare sinking, the hounds in full cry, we came suddenly upon one of those deep-cut, narrow roads among our downs, and full of go, both myself and horse, we had neither time nor desire to turn about. My rule was to ride straight, and the horse never swerved. The road was deep, and the opposite bank a long distance ahead. However, at it we went, and cleared the opening in good style. Nothing very particular in the leap after all," he would say; "but the amusing part was, that in our flight we had shot over a farmer's team of four horses and a waggon-load of straw, on which lay the boy fast asleep, his mouth wide open." This the fellow would chuckle over and declare to be true. The appearance of the carriage in our street was a cause for pride and rejoicing. The brougham had not been invented, neither had the stuccoed villa put in its appearance. Esquires were few, and life was more real among us. Now squires are as plentiful and of a like character to mushrooms in the autumn. I have a reverence for these old times, these visions of the past.

But let us return to our painter, Mr. James Henry Capper. I regret we have but little record of his art life. With us he was looked upon as a genius, and great expectations were gathered around him. His future was credited with honour, if not with renown. He was a ready sketcher, and in an open competition and exhibition at Southampton carried off first prize, his subject being a home scene — "The Quarry Pond by Moonlight." He also very successfully painted the *Thames* East Indiaman, aground at Langley, which painting was engraved by J. Clark, and published.

Shall I attempt to resuscitate the wreck of the *Thames*? It was an event that caused for miles round considerable stir and commotion. It happened on Sunday, February 3, 1822. I have by me a slip cut from the "Lewes Journal" of that date, giving an extract from the captain's log:— "Sunday, Feb. 3, at ten minutes past 2 a.m., while in the act of steering, weather very thick, ship struck upon a reef a short distance east of Beach-Head, called the Boulder bank, at 3 a.m. There being no chance of getting her off till flood-tide made, nor then to sea, lowered down cutter from the quarter, and attempted to hoist our launch, which attempt (on account of the sea running too high to risk the lives of the men, as well as the cutter having swamped in veering in a storm, by which misfortune six men were drowned), was abandoned. At half-past 3 a.m. began to fire signal guns and show lights, and cut away mast to ease ship. At 6 a.m., ship, by violence of the surf, was forced upon the beach near 72 tower in Eastbourne bay. At 10 a.m., sea having left ship, opened communication with shore, and ship's company landed with safety;

began to make preparations to land cargo:" The narrative goes on to state that great praise is due to the officials of Eastbourne for their exertions to save the lives and protect the property of the ship wrecked crew, the whole of the immense cargo having been discharged without being plundered to the amount of a single shilling — a rare instance, it is added, in case of a shipwreck on any part of the coast of England. The dimensions of the *Thames*, the paper says, are — length of keel, 175 feet; width of beam, 40 feet; burden, 1,350tons register. On Wednesday evening eighteen shipwrights arrived with caulkers to stop her leaks, and she was eventually got off and towed to London, whence she sailed the same season for her original destination, giving Eastbourne a salute as she passed down channel. Mr. James Breads, of Hastings, contracted with the underwriters to convey the cargo to London by land at 3s. 4d. the cwt., or by water at 1s. Manley's apparatus is referred to, but being incomplete, was not brought into use. A lady, Mrs. MacInnis, was saved by means of a grating or open hatch, slung by gammets to a hawser, and not by Manley as reported.

At that time I was a tiny elf of eight and a half, and I walked out and home (an old woman being my companion and protector) to visit the scene, I wishing to put my inquisitive eyes into the case, and to see for myself something of the wonders I heard so much talk about. The bulk of the cargo had been removed, and was stacked away in the most regular order on the beach. What struck me as a marvel was, how the quantity could by any contrivance be stowed away in the hold of the stranded vessel. Like Tom Bowling, she was a sheer hulk, lying high and dry, without mast or rigging — nothing left to give her life and beauty, hopeless and helpless; driven by the elements she was intended to master, conquered and thrown a victim on the unpitying shore, a sport for the waves, if not a prize for unprincipled men. A stranded vessel, showing her riven sides, ribs and framework, her nakedness within and without, is a touching thing to look upon. The sight teaches many a lesson, and points many a moral, as broken hopes, ruined exchequers, grand ventures, noble doing, heroic death. The wreck was visited by thousands of country people, coming from all parts many miles round. It was the event and the talk of the time. There had been no such disaster on the coast many years preceding.

## THE OLD DRUGGIST: HER SHOP AND HER LODGER

Captain Barclay, the celebrated pedestrian, with the 23rd Foot, in which regiment he held his commission, was, about the year 1804-5, stationed, if not in our barracks, in the neighbourhood, he having apartments in the house of Mrs. Gearing, druggist. The druggist's son, James, who had been barrack-sergeant, in after life delighted to gossip away an hour detailing many of the doughty Captain's habits while in quarters here — that he was constantly training himself, both in bodily exercises and in diet, to fit him for endurance; that he would, when off duty, be walking out and home many a mile, taking in his satchel half-cooked meat for food to sustain him on these journeys.

From a narrative detailing many of the Captain's exploits, published by Smeaton, 139, Saint Martin's Lane, we will select a few particulars of his parentage and his sporting career. First, that on Thursday, August 16, 1804, Mr. Barclay, who had become Lieutenant in the 23rd Regiment of Foot, then quartered at Eastbourne, in Sussex, engaged to run two miles in twelve minutes. He accomplished the undertaking with ease. Again, that he was for years engaged in walking contests, either against time or against some rival who disputed his prowess; that large sums of money were ventured, won, and lost on the results, ventures which nearly always ended in the advantage of our hero. He came of a family remarkable for athletic exercises. His father, who represented Kincardine, used to walk every session of Parliament from Scotland to London, and could run the journey as fast as the stage-coach; "but frequently," the memoir says, "he deviated from the direct road in order to attend some fair which happened to be held at the time. Dressed like a plain farmer, he mixed freely in all rural sports usual at these meetings, particularly cudgel-playing and wrestling, and won many a prize hat in his progress to Saint Stephen's Chapel." The grandfather of Captain Barclay was still more powerful; his muscular strength was such that he had been seen to fling a horse which had been impounded, at Elric, over the wall. "To this gentleman also," says the narrative, "Scotland is indebted for setting the example of improved husbandry."

The Captain inherited from his family estate four thousand per annum; he also inherited the great muscular strength of his ancestors. My authority says that while he was in garrison at Norwich he offered (but it was not accepted) a bet of a thousand guineas that he would lift a ton, and in order to try the experiment, he obtained a number of weights, which were fastened together by a rope, through the rings, when he lifted twenty-one half-hundredweights. He afterwards, with a straight arm, threw half a hundredweight a distance of eight yards, and over his head the same weight a distance of five yards. In the mess-room a gentleman, who weighed eighteen stone, stood upon the Captain's right hand, and being steadied by the left, he took him up and set him on the table. Some of his friends say that he was as nimble a feeder as he was a walker, and that on his way down from Newcastle he ordered a leg of mutton, weighing eight pounds, to be but little roasted, the whole of which he picked clean to the bone within the short space of ten minutes. This exactly agrees with what my old friend the barrack-sergeant has told me of the Captain's feeding ability when he was living in Hailsham. The crowning exploit of his sporting life, his walk of a thousand miles in a thousand hours, in October 1808, is well known. At that time it was an unparalleled performance, by which, it was said, he netted £16,000, and money to the amount of £100,000 in bets changed hands. Posts were erected at regular intervals, on which were hung lamps to light the track during the night. Smeaton, on his front page, has given a sketch of his hero walking in costume, so full of life that the Captain appears to be actually on the move, easily and jauntily, with the right hand in his jacket pocket, while in the left he carries his handkerchief.

Our old druggist's shop, with the small front sitting room which the Captain occupied, has now for the last fifteen years been turned into a bookseller's shop, and the place altogether has undergone a complete transformation. New windows, fittings, counters, etc., have replaced the very old ones, and the alterations have brought to light a piece of deal board which evidently once formed part of the lid of a box, with the Captain's name and his Hailsham address upon it while he was residing here with the old lady druggist. The writing, a fine, large, clear hand, is as follows:—

"BARCLAY, ALLERDICE,
    "23rd reg.,
        "R. W. F.,
            "Haylsham,
                "Sussx.
                    Oct. I/9."

This piece of board had been used to repair a hole in the counter, and the workman of the time, to bring it to the required length, had cut, as the sailors say, the handle off the name. "Captain" is missing, and "Barclay" but barely escaped the saw. Now, this discovery puts before us the fact of the power of association. Here we have a relic that carries us back to the early part of this century — a thing that has been looked upon, handled, and owned by a man who had made himself notable throughout the kingdom, a man who had lived where our fathers had lived, who had walked in our streets, who had sat in our church, and who, years after he had left, was spoken well of by those with whom he had resided. And by this simple circumstance of the bit of old board our interest is revived in him, and we summon our recollection and our knowledge to bring together some events of his life. We make some claims to his history — he in some degrees belongs to us — and no apology will be needed for having introduced him as one of our notables.

This power of force of association is one of degree, and depends much upon circumstances. We will suppose a piece of old board found under similar conditions at Stratford, addressed to "William Shakespeare, Poet, Playwriter, Stratford-on-Avon — 1/9." The world of letters would be up in arms; conjectures, inferences, proofs even would abound. The length and depth of the box, and the inventory of the contents would be made out; the address, photographed, would be in every shop window; the relic would be enshrined; and perhaps, by its aid questions of disputed authorship would be settled for a generation or two to come. This, of course, is exaggeration, but the power of association involves and gives colour to the whole of our lives; it brings together and places in order things and times, circumstances and character, that yield us our history. It is the medium through which we look back upon the past, a help for the future; it is, in the main, the father of our joys and the mother of our sorrows; of things we cannot forget, of love and honourable pride, of sorrow and scathing shame, of friendships pure and lasting, of deceits, dastardly and cruel.

But enough of this rhapsody! Let me give a parting word or two to our old-fashioned maiden druggist, Miss Nancy Gearing. I remember her mother, a little dark-eyed, precise, shrivelled-up old dame. Her fame rested chiefly upon salves and ointments, and to the daughter, Nancy, devolved the honour of continuing to our town and neighbourhood these two blessings. Patent medicines in those days were few in comparison with the present. The virtues of Larwell's Pills for the benefit of our lives, and "Mann's Approved Medicine, " a *sure cure* for consumption, met nearly all our wants. To Lewes belongs the honour of inventing the first, and to Horsham the second; and we did pretty well in our simple way. Now, as we all know, nostrums are legion, and alas! our ailments increase in proportion with the remedies. Bating the tortoise, the stuffed alligator, and the skins of ill-shaped fishes, our old shop might be taken as a counterpart to the apothecary's of Mantua. If not poor, it was meagre to a degree, pots, jars, and bottles all being of the plainest pattern. There was a good array for number, but I have always supposed many to have been dummies. There was also a department for dolls and wooden horses, and the house of the cruel, weather-wise old man who would turn his wife out of her door when it rained and keep in himself, had a place on her shelves. One small bottle of blue liquid was the only show in the window, across which, reaching about half-way up, stretched a faded green blind, which also added to the melancholy of the interior. POISON might be read in plain English on a few bottles and jars, to impress her visitors, we will suppose, with a dread of her power; while "Paregoric" and "Soothing Syrup" show in faded gold, to give confidence and to show all was not lost, nor hope entirely fled. The majority of the labels were covered with a mysterious combination of letters, too learned for the general public, but which served to strengthen our faith and to give reverence and confidence to the one, and the only one, person who could unravel their meaning. At the window end of the counter were three slots, or slits, into which dipped the three ointment and plaster knives, which knives were of varying sizes and lengths, to suit the work to be done. The front of the house was shut off from the public road by a brick wall, and a gate had to be opened to gain admittance to the shop door. The door creaked on its hinges, and the floor beneath the feet yielded to the weight as one entered, showing cracks and holes which led one's thoughts to the cellar; but our dear old lady regarded none of these as blotches. She, her shop, and the contents had all grown old together. Where she drew her first breath, there in the same chamber she breathed her last, and like her creaking old door, she hung on for many a year, always attending to her business duties, and glad to the last to take a shilling over the counter. This was her great delight, and if ever gratification and satisfaction could be seen dominant in one's features, then these were in hers when a customer had entered the shop and she had fingered the money. But the joy could be intensified by a gossip about her celebrated lodger; it was then her dark eyes sparkled as she recounted her recollections of his manly presence, and his kind, gentle, manly demeanour.

There are yet a few memories floating among us relating to this hero, some much too broad for the general public and the ears and nerves of this generation. One among the many may be told. The Captain and our eccentric man, Mr. M. Slye, were great cronies. The two, in a ramble in the fields, were passing a pond. The Captain, on an impulse, said to his friend, "For a guinea I jump over and land in the adjoining field." "Done," said his companion, and a spring being taken, in a moment in the water up to his neck stood our gallant vaulter who, proud as he might be, did not refuse the helping hand to regain the turf of the meadow. For once he had overrated himself, and came out loser.

Our old druggist lived on to be eighty-one, and a very short period of her long life became subject to decrepitude and mortal decay. The old shop has altogether changed its character; the medical has given place to the mental, books have taken the place of boluses, mind has become triumphant over matter; literature, from "Punch" to the "Christian World," and that most diverting of all Sussex histories, "Tom Cladpole's Journey to Lunnon," can be had at the current prices, and many a good modern author is to be met with on the packed shelves. The bookseller being well read, and having a good gauge of his customers' minds and tastes, can help a reader out of a difficulty by placing the proper book in his hand. So the old gives place to the new; and with this we will say good-bye to both.

## OUR ECCENTRIC MAN

Moody and boisterous, scornful and mirthful, bashful or bold, is the eccentric man. He follows no rule; he is out at elbows with the world; he knows no method. Chance is his mother, and Mischance his companion and his guide. He neither calculates nor considers. What is opinion to him? He lives to himself, and not for his fellows. He is "off the line," and can afford to be so. Meet him in the street, and he rushes past: he has not seen you. He neither raises his head nor his eye, and you are not offended. You expected he would behave so, and he is gone. You say in excuse that he is shy. Again, next day, he clutches you by the hand; he shakes you by the shoulder, he is boisterous among many passing by. He is loquacious, talking oddly, it may be sensibly; and we say he is eccentric. But we do not dislike him nor his ways. He sees not as other men see; he is oblivious to surroundings, though his eye is upon you seeking an occasion. It may be he has neither wit nor humour, yet when he does speak he is expected to say something extravagant; but he is natural, and his manner is not put on for the occasion. 'Tis thus we look for it, this strange demeanour, and we welcome his presence. He has always been so, and is to the manner born. He helps to diversify life, causing us to think and to laugh. If he rides, he sits loosely, and the reins fall about the steed's shoulders; he is careless of consequences, and the horse has more than once returned home without the rider.

Our friend is a great walker; he is fond of the fields, and he rushes over gates and stiles faster than would a king's messenger. Having nothing to do, he is in great haste. If you meet him, he may not lift his head nor speak, or he may hold you for an hour; he has much to tell, or nothing! His political as well as his religious opinions are not for the public. His talk is of the parish, though his knowledge is not confined to that local boundary. He is of good height and presence, but stooping, dwarfs himself, and becomes a character of mark, and he may be recognized at a distance. In dress, more than in any other feature, he is uniform. He resents familiarity, but will talk to a beggar. We meet him carrying a basket; probably it contains a present for some cottager's child, or farmer's daughter. It may be he is hurrying up the street; he has a parcel in his hand — old boots tied up in a coloured handkerchief. He knows not when the heels or soles are worn through until his stockings are gone and his feet suffer from the gravel of the roads. The shoemaker and he are friends, and to him he is confidential. He has no pride, save the pride of self-respect, yet he does his own shopping, and will not hesitate to ask the first boy he meets to run an errand for him, though the grocer or the post office be close at hand.

In correspondence he is often unreadable, and should an explanation be required, he cannot decipher his own letters; he apologizes, and offers to write again. He is parsimonious, but has been known to return £50 to one who had paid a doubtful debt of £150. Though he knows every turn in the roads, he has more than once, on his way home by moonlight, walked into a pond, and left his sugar, tea, and other articles at the bottom. When on a journey he makes himself safe against the caprice of friends, or the chances of the wayside inn, by carrying with him food for the day. The satchel, or bag, is strapped round the loins, and hangs behind. This appendage is covered by the flaps of his coat, and he pushes on, defying fortune and the gibes of passers-by. The winter is severe; he rushes from the morning service at church, enters your home without ceremony, takes the best seat in the room, and stirs up your fire, declaring that he has seen a hundred Christmas Days, but never one so cold. He is at home in every family, making himself welcome, and finding it to be so. When alone, he holds converse with the angels — or himself; talks aloud, laughs, but has never been known to sing. To music he has an aversion; a concord of sweet sounds tends only to melancholy, though the sound of the big drum or the drone of the bagpipes light up his enthusiasm. Among the divines Swift and Sterrie are his favourites, and his library, like its owner, is a mixture of extremes. In his charity he occasionally writes sermons for his friend the Curate of Pevensey, whose stipend will not allow his reverence the expense of purchasing that weekly necessary. In his case, as in so many others, the child was the father of the man. He is fond of telling the tale of his arrival in the parish, as a boy of eleven, with his widowed mother and her numerous family, and of the tunic or coat he then wore, made of light blue cloth ornamented with gilt buttons and further set off with a red collar. This individuality sticks to him through life In short, he was our "unique," and with him we had nothing to compare.

Upon occasion our friend is social, and even jovial. He peoples his home and surrounds his table with friends; he calls them by name, but they reply not. It is he who answers, for they are not there to do so. He talks, laughs, and keeps up a merry conversation, but he is alone. He is not fond of company, neither does he relish the expense of entertaining friends. If he makes a feast he eats and drinks by himself, and it is upon this principle he gives tea and other parties, when the cups and the chairs are placed and every seat is occupied. He is polite, and all are freely invited to partake, but no ladies ever grace his table; towards the sex he is hostile. The company is gay, and the room filled. Each man is called by name. The friends laugh and converse — one gives a toast, another a song, and the host is all alive; but he is alone. No stranger intermeddleth with his joys. Each supposed visitor has his glass and his chair, and the entertainer drinks in succession to all his friends; even so, that before the party breaks up he becomes "glorious." But through all this mirth with the cup that cheers and the cup that inebriates he has had no companions. His brain has peopled his room with his "good fellows." He has had no disputes — he is at peace with the world —and he is satisfied. His old housekeeper, who occupies the house while the master lives in two detached rooms, knows his habit and the consequences. She enters the chamber, lights the candle, and the master retires to his lone bed, for he is a bachelor, and past all hope.

This picture, which is but a drop in the bucket among the many peculiarities, truly portrays our eccentric man, Mr. Matthias Slye. He died August, 1855, aged seventy-four. He is buried in our churchyard close to the chancel facing the rising sun, where the birds, flitting from tower to tree and shrub in the Vicarage garden, sing, and ever will sing, his requiem. Peace be with him!

We had a reverence for Mr. Slye; he stood out from among the common herd. He was a gentleman, and this includes all that belongs to mind, manners, and income; for though the latter was small, yet by his frugal habits it was enough to meet his requirements. He was kind and considerate to the poor; he openly avowed his love for an honest man; and when he died the children mourned him. He was our friend and philosopher, and we all loved to hear him babble. "Summer Hill," so long known as his home, has almost faded out of sight and recollection. The bright name now falls flat on the ear; the spirit that once gave life and ascendency to the place has fled. What have "Starve Crow," or the "Butter-wedges," or other suggestive names and places surrounding it, to equal Summer Hill in attractions? In my young days, after creeping up the hilly roadway, made pleasant by overhanging, towering elms, waving larches, and orchard laden with fruit or in promise, we boys in passing spoke in whispers and turned the eye and head askance, hoping to catch a glimpse of the peculiar man who had chosen that lone spot wherein to dwell and to die. But with his life the glory has departed. The elms, the larches, and the apple trees are gone; the hedges are narrowed; the place is naked; and the nightingale no more sings in at the open door.

## A "CHARACTER"

Beneath the shadow of a drooping stone to the north of the church tower lie the remains of William Long. The memorial, like all earthly memorials, is passing away, falling out of the upright, to follow to the earth the bones of him whose name it so far perpetuates. The inscription is faultless, there being no mention of character, qualities, or virtues. The stone is not defaced "with lying verse." Every reader may draw his own conclusions. Silence on the grave stone is golden.

William Long died in June, 1833, aged sixty-five. I have a perfect recollection of his person, and remember somewhat of his life and habits. He was for many years our leading surgeon; he stood high, had a considerable practice, and was popular with all classes, from the county squire and his lady to the labouring man and his wife. In manners he was a gentleman, ease and independence being combined with the suavity of the courtier. In social life he was the wit, the humorist, and the convivialist; in emergencies at the table he was equal to all things. In short, he was, fifty years ago,[1] our leading convivial character. For miles round "everybody" knew Doctor Long, and if on the one hand some among his friends blamed and looked sad, there were others who laughed and excused. He was not fortunate in his married life. While his wife was serious, good, religious, he was gay, licentious, and fond of midnight revelling. The match was unequal, and the yoke became unbearable. For many years they lived apart, until the final separation came in the death of her he should have loved and cherished to the end. In person he was bulky, more than grand, and his dress was peculiar, and after a fashion of his own — top-boots hanging about his legs and ankles in many a wrinkle; long, square-tailed coat with outside flapped pockets; long vest, covering a "capacious paunch"; double frilled

[1] Circa 1830

143

shirt, with high, upstanding collar and white neckerchief, well-tied up to the chin, topped with a somewhat broad-brimmed hat. The hat and the boots never varied, nor did his walking-stick — a heavy bamboo or cane — silver-mounted, with key hole shaped for the tassel or ribbon, iron shod, of which now I can hear the clang as the owner trotted up or down our street on his morning calls to his many patients. His gait was shuffling, though not void of dignity. His address on meeting you was in character with his profession — assuming and profound — putting you at a distance, rather than drawing by too great familiarity. There was no appeal from his aye or nay. He was dogmatic and final. Add to all this the silver headed cane before mentioned, and you have a tolerable picture of Doctor Long.

Long was the son of a Romney Marsh farmer, and brought with him his fortune of £7,000. How he came to settle here I cannot tell. Whether there were friends who attracted him, or whether he succeeded to an established practice, I do not know, nor would I stop to enquire if the £7,000 had not been in the way; but it does seem strange that a young man with that sum in his hand, and a profession to boot, should bury himself and his money in such a poor place as Hailsham must have been in the year 1800. And here arises another question: why should I take up and pursue the subject at all? What has Doctor Long to do with the present time and its people? His patients are all dead, his servants are all gone, and the memory of him has almost died out. The record of his good deeds was written in the sand, and is dead also. Then why, I ask again, should I raise his ghost to trouble the glimpses of the moon of our day? Is it to be accounted for by any law of affinity? Since I first troubled his bones and wrote my heading — "A Character" — his presence has grown upon me. I see him as he was yesterday, and I cannot forbear, as I think of him, from laughing at the follies of his life, which were comic and grotesque rather than vicious and hurtful; and as I delight in contrast and the comical, I am attracted towards him, and the more I see the more I am disposed to excuse than condemn.

In economies Dr. Long had no method: he could never make the two ends of expenditure and income meet. The former always overlapped the latter. Both in his house and stable the inmates felt the pinch. On the other hand, he adored the sex, and was lavish. Upon one occasion, when asked by his creditors to account for his insolvency, he exclaimed, "The ladies, the ladies, and the juice of the grape!" He was not afraid of port; the liquor of the ruby fruit inspired him. 'Twas then you'd see him. He would sing, give a toast, or improvise a speech at call. He was patriotic and despised the French. Dibdin was his poet, and " The sweet little cherub that sits up aloft," together with " Poor Jack," were his constant and unfailing themes. In his revels, when others thought of going, he thought of staying. Then he would say, "Shall I give you another of Charley Dibdin's?" When he thus volunteered, things had become serious, and his companions knew well what they had to expect. The doctor meant, "We won't go home till morning"; and he would keep his word, too. Though the guests had all departed, and the host had retired to bed, the man of science kept singing. Company or no company, it was all one to him, till sleep overtook him, and next morning he was found upon the floor. Our hero was soon himself again. He had great recuperative powers, and though he had spent the night "down among the dead men," he would early next day be bustling about visiting his patients and friends, feeling the pulse, bleeding and sending out his medicines.

Our town at that time maintained its social, though exclusive, institution. It was a privilege to be a member of the "Crown" Smoking Club. There the elite met weekly, and none but the elite were admitted. The front parlour was known as the club-room, and on meeting nights it was a privileged chamber. You should see the neatness, and, in winter evenings, the comfort, of the room, the bright shining fire — there was no stint of coals; the sanded floor set off in waves with artistic touch by the broom of the house maid; the table garnished with tobacco-pipes — regular churchwardens — ready waxed for the lips. What memories does not the mention of those tobacco pipes awaken!

> Little tube of mighty power,
> Charmer of an idle hour.

Past joys, and yet anticipated delights! Thou mighty weed and magician! What struggles for the mastery do we votaries endure I and yet you conquer again and again! The members comprised men on the retired list, professional men, the schoolmaster, the church warden (then a post of honour, as may be seen in many a church-yard), the farmer and the respectable trader, in their way all wits and humorists, and each as fond of a joke as of the pipe and grog. Over this and these Doctor Long presided for many years, "The best chairman," said a brother doctor, and one who had outlived him forty years, "I ever sat beside"; and he too had had great experience in dining out.

Doctor Long's eccentricities and misfortunes followed him through life. In his character and habit he was timid and suspicious. He had a great dread of fire and housebreakers, and always kept his pistols loaded and sword drawn in his bedroom ready for action. He was easily excited to anger, and then he vociferated and became as wild as a tiger; but the subsidence soon came, and he was then as gentle and harmless as a lamb. He was vainglorious of his skill and position as a doctor, but was so dissatisfied with his lot that he used to say he wished his father had " 'prenticed him to a chimney-sweep." His manner of life gave licence to boys and idle fellows to practise jokes upon him. It has happened that he would be roused in the night to find a donkey tied by the tail to the knocker of the door or to the knob. At another time a bundle of straw would be lighted close up to the house front, to alarm him in the night. All this I know is prosy and plain, but it was a phase of our parish life at that time. Then we had no police to look after us, and the dreamy old watchman, by his presence, only added to the fun.

Our doctor returned from Horsham Gaol, then the county town, whither he had been sent to wipe off his debts, cheerful and unabashed, saying he would "begin life afresh." His household bill of fare was simple and inexpensive enough, the dinner every day throughout the year being beefsteak pudding, and no side dishes nor extras. I have by me a leaf taken from the butcher's ledger of the time, James Kennett. The entries run thus:— "To one pound and half beef, no bone," 365 days in succession! Our butchers' and bakers'

146

shops were then opened on Sundays till the bells began to chime for church, and the doctor's groom might be seen, among other customers, going with dish and cloth for his unvarying allowance. The doctor retired from active service and lived a few years in the old cottage where the Curate before him had found a quiet home. Here he prepared his last will, and settled down for the last struggle — to meet death — and here the end came. His executors found the devisor liberal to many of his old friends. There were numerous legacies, but the legatees were never the richer, there being no estate to administer; and if his last debts were not paid, I have never heard of a creditor who bore him a grudge. His eccentricities rubbed out with his fellow-men the balance of his life standing against him. It was one of his last requests to be buried at the head of the grave of his old friend, George Carey, the substantial yeoman who had offended William Long. The whim was carried out, their bones almost touching, mingling in the common earth, awaiting the day of general resurrection, then and there to meet again, and, as the doughty doctor put the case, "have their quarrel out," after which, as he said, he had no doubt the farmer and he should again become friends. In religion he was not without a creed, and he solved for himself the important problem of man's moral responsibility by saying every night, drunk or sober, his prayers at his bedside. Upon one occasion his servant, as was her wont, on calling him, received no answer, and opening the door, discovered her poor old master at the foot of the bed in his night-shirt, on his knees, fast asleep. He had retired to his chamber too full; he had taken just one glass too much. His hands were clasped, his head sunk on the bed; he had prayed, he had slumbered through the night on his knees.

Here we will leave him. He is not the first penitent who has been overtaken as he prayed, and has been forgiven.

## OUR ANTIQUARY

I confess that from the day I first read of "Bill Stumps, his Mark" in the early days of the first edition of the immortal "Pickwick" I have occasionally been scared by the doings of the antiquary, at times looking upon him as one born out of due season — perhaps a little crazed, a meddler, a busybody, a man who will not be at rest, who cannot let bygones be bygones; one ever on the rack to raise the ghosts of our fathers and mothers, showing off to his own and all succeeding generations their faults and failings, when all might be quiet in their graves and be forgotten. To what better purpose, may I ask, can a man live than to oblivion? Did not holy Job say, "Let the day perish wherein I was born, and darkness seize upon it"? And is it lightly to be endured that one has lived only to be the sport of to-morrow? If our fathers have been convivial, are they to be called sots? if good at a tale, to be dubbed liars? if imaginative, not to be trusted? And so run up the gamut of their lives with conjecture for the dominant and suspicion for the top note.

Even now I hold the antiquary to belong to a doubtful fraternity. Time and experience have not reconciled me to all his doings. If I read of his exploits, he rarely satisfies me. His conclusions are too often no clearer than the misty moon on a dark November morning. It is true he may be far-seeing and profound, grasping for the highest and delving for the lowest. He is found in the charnel-house, and like the mole, works on in the dark, or nibbles as the rat in the garret, seeking hidden treasures. He follows the pick of the workman in a newly-made trench as earnestly as a crow seeking a grub in a gutter. His eye is ever on the stretch, his fancy beguiling him. There is nothing too small nor too large for his longings. He feeds upon the lightest, and will digest the hardest of morsels; in short, he is omnivorous. For individualism and character, with the antiquary none escape his searching eye. He is the resurrection-man of the neighbourhood. The good and the bad are all alike, and wherever he sets foot the dead are not safe in their graves. He is ever seeking, ever devouring. No man can stay his hand, nor say, "Thus far shalt thou go and no farther." He will do a pilgrimage to a distant shrine, and next lift his hand against his idol, to spoil it by restoration, attempting to do what man yet never did do — to make the old young again. He revels among nicknames, making an inventory of those unblessed cognomens of his parish, or writing off the inscriptions from tombs in the churchyard, puts both into print, and

148

perchance calls it history. Without defining, he may tell you that the mark of Noah's wife's patten, when she stepped from the door sill of the ark on to the soft ground, was neither round nor square, and that the umbrella was perfected in those damp days and first used. He will remove a mountain to discover the first home of a surname, and trace back a pedigree to the overflowing of the waters. Whenever we meet him he is a man of mark, ever learning, but never full or satisfied. The past is his goal, and, like Lot's wife, he ever looks behind him. The gibbet — strange man I — has greater attraction than the cradle, an old iron fiddle than the latest musical improvement. But who can name his fancies, or catalogue his accumulated relics? "Of Eve's first fire he has a cinder," and from creation he has been collecting, and ever will be.

In our parish we are poor in relics. Our own antiquary, who has been dead many years, has left behind him little or no record of his life and successes. Nearly all we know is traditional, and, of course, must be taken according to individual taste and humour. But this may be said for certain, he was a good churchman, the Vicar's churchwarden, and a man held in great reverence in all matters relating to home affairs. He was social, fond of an outing, of a good dinner, and a glass or more of good wine; could make a neat off-hand speech, and was ready with an apt quotation. He was of good presence and voice, wore a flowing beard (at one time as glossy as a raven's back), which beard, in his day being exceptional, added much to his dignity. He had a dark, flashing eye, and by those who knew him best, was much esteemed. In his dress he was very precise and characteristic, and copied the past in this matter so strictly that, after a long absence, when he returned and was last seen among us he appeared to be arrayed in the same vestments which he had worn years before. In this matter time took no hold on him nor his belongings. Fashion he defied and scorned, and he held his own against all change. He was our philosopher, and the parish looked to him, and not in vain, for the solution of many a difficulty.

And who now-a-days, let me ask, since fate has taken him away, can measure the depth of the loss to his generation ? He, too, was the patient man, and like unto his fellow-professor, the great Pickwick, ever took his disappointments as would a martyr. Gibes and jeers he scorned, and he looked upon a doubter with pity. From the weakest premises he would define and draw the most profound conclusions; and when fact, as fact did at times, proved too hard for him and his surmises, he would shake himself up with laughter, saying, "The wisest of men some times do err." The tale relating to the old handbill may be cited in proof. Among the many incidents attached to his long life and profession as our antiquary, the discovery of this old-fashioned implement stands prominent. The maker and the original owner had been dead many a year when the relic was brought again to the light of day, during the pulling down of an old brick-built house in our street that had formerly belonged to the blacksmith. This house, and two others of like build, had at an early date formed part of the estate of King Charles I. We have writings among us to prove thus much relating to the house property. Now, this handbill, having the initials "C. S." surmounted by the Royal Crown, stamped upon it, led the intelligent and curious men of our village to many conjectures and much reflection. Of course, the one man who had made antiquities his special study was called in, and, moreover, being churchwarden, his opinions were held in high esteem in all matters parochial. The implement was handed over to his keeping, with sundry hints connecting the initials with the royal name, and the once owner of the brick-built houses. Here was a serious matter for our man of business and science, who, being in all preliminaries a man of caution, pleaded for time and consultation. He had a trio of friends whom he could at all times command — the hatter, the shoemaker, and the cooper — whose united opinions agreeing with his own, would settle any matter relating to home affairs. These four, meeting in consultation, at length gave their united opinion that under all the circumstances, and knowing the town to have been partly owned by King Charles, the "C. S." could be nothing of less import than Charles Stuart; and, humble as the tie might be, it certainly connected their own time and history with the Royal Stuart of blessed memory. The relic should, in their opinion, be treasured up and valued accordingly. The case was thus settled, and another wreath was twined round the brow of our professor and churchwarden. The very next week a meeting was called for the "Crown" Inn, and attended by the ratepayers generally, when a vote of thanks was tendered to the quartette — the four wise men who had made this interesting discovery, and settled so important a point. With an extra glass all round, and one cheer more for the leading man, our antiquary, the company were upon breaking up, when the owner of the handbill, a labouring man, who had been invited, and who was a little out of his usual companionship, saluted the chairman with, "I say, zur, I think, perhaps, you have been a little too fast to-night. I have heard my old grandfather say that Charley Standing, the old blacksmith of the place, made, in his day, as good a tool as any man, and that he would give as much for Standing's make as he would for any." Here was fire among gunpowder — the whirlwind among the chaff! The pigmy had slain the giant who, thinking with Sidrophel "it was no part of prudence to cry down an art," stalked out of the room, and, paying his score at the bar, quitted the house, giving vent to one of his peculiar laughs, and hurried off home.

There is a counter tale, a story current when I was a boy, showing the usefulness of the antiquary. It was said that in a certain churchyard there had been a tombstone, having the following inscription:— "To the Memory of," etc., concluding with, "He was one of the IVRATS of the Corporation." The exact meaning of this, and the nature of the office, had been for years subjects of dispute among the towns folk, the largest party declaring the deceased to have been one of the *four*, and the lesser set saying he had been one of the *five rats of the Corporation.* The dispute was continually on, and ran high, when a gentleman who made antiquities his study, and who was out touring, arrived, and soon made the case clear, and put the matter right by showing that the defunct townsman had been one of the jurats of their far-famed town and port of Pevensey.

To the most industrious collector our parish yields archaeologically but a poor complement of facts. Our past is almost a blank. We have not been a romantic people, and as we sow, so we must reap. We cannot gather figs from thistles, nor grapes from thorns, and to invent in these matters would be insulting to, and beneath the notice of, the antiquary. We have, however, one little fact that may be adverted to. This relates to a remarkable stone that gives a name to the northern boundary of our parish, namely, Amberstone, which stone, unlike the stones of Mount Sinai, the Moabitish stone, Delphic or Memnon, has no history, no inscription. It gives out no musical cadence or articulation. If ever it had formed one of a Druidical circle, like unto the tribe of Judah, it has lost all its ancient companions. It is a lone, deserted thing, moss-covered, cushion-shaped, lying on a hedge bank that surrounds the cottage, orchard, and garden of the hoary old pedlar and his maiden daughter (a weird and neglected place), a relic of the past, rarely, if ever, seen, save when the hedger periodically sweeps over it with his handbill, and lets sunlight into its damp dwelling, a thing of no pretence what ever, which, but for its name and one tradition, would have died and rotted out of memory long ago. The question, and not unreasonably, has been asked over and over again — Why is the stone called Amberstone? But no reply has come from the man of science. No goddess from the Baltic, or any other amber-bearing zone or circle, claims it. The present generation is in no wit wiser than the last. We can testify to its identity and the situation, but of its origin, nature, or purpose we know nothing, and we are waiting for the man who will enlighten us. All we do know is, that the story has been handed down from our forefathers that the Amberstone at every new moon, and every time the parish church clock is heard to strike at midnight, turns round on its bed. And but for this story, whatever it may mean, the deserted thing would have been forgotten ages ago; and so long as the conditions do not change, so long as the moon waxes and wanes, and the clock strikes the witching hour of midnight, so long must the weary thing lie on its moss-covered bed, and obey the behest of Cynthia and the ghostly power of the parish church clock, so long will the Amberstone turn on its bed. It may be added that there is floating among us the faintest echo of a whisper that in Charles's days the stone was the trysting-place of the outcast, the plague-smitten of the parish and neighbour-hood.

Again, near Polegate, we have another stone, which, if neglected in this narrative, may cry out. Almost close to the high road, and within a few minutes' walk of the railway station, lies a mass of conglomerate made up of yellow flint, very compact and hard, marking the western boundary of the ancient Corporation of Pevensey. It is told, and has been from my boyhood, that an old woman brought this huge lump from a neighbouring field as her contribution towards the foundations of Pevensey Castle. She had carried her load thus far on her way in her apron, and at this spot her apron-string broke, and down went her precious burden. If we may assume her height and her bulk to have been in proportion to her strength, would it be an impertinence, in the interest of archaeology, to infer that this lady was the wife of the far-famed Wilmington Giant?

## THE LAST OF THE MYNNS

In these my mental perambulations through the parish, one thing that had not been recognized has now become strikingly apparent, and that is the number of our families who have within the last fifty years died out, the name clean gone, the flesh and blood vanished, leaving no trace or mark of his or her generation; no representative of either sex to recall to our memory their grandfathers or grandmothers, and these lapses, too, generally occurring among our better-to-do people. Our doctors, lawyers, and par sons, with one exception, are gone, leaving no trace behind them, none to follow and keep alive the profession or name of the family. Our old-fashioned farmers, too, have gone, their old houses being occupied by strangers. Our yeomen have given way to a stronger force, and yielded their acres to all-absorbing landlordism, and our solitary squire, and his children, have given up their estate and homes to other owners. The changes time has wrought among us are such that if we would build up a genealogical tree, starting from some present living subject, we must go to the poor and the needy for our material — that is, if we except the Mynn family and our lawyer, and these in either case hang upon a single life.

Time was, when I was a boy, when the family of Mynn stood at the head of the notables of our parish. Socially or otherwise the position was nothing remarkable; it was chiefly this — the Mynns occupied their own house, and lived on their own estate, the father, John Mynn, holding a commission of the peace from King George III. The magistrate was our only squire, and this of course gave him individuality and consequence among us. He was a plain, unassuming man, having no special trait of character, was easy to approach, free in conversation, and well-known to all his neighbours from the highest to the lowest, from the youngest to the oldest; and when he appeared in our street, dressed in full cut blue cloth coat adorned with gilt buttons, frilled shirt, drab kersey breeches, white gaiters and stout high-lows, all grades approached him respectfully.

The family have a written pedigree running back to the time of Henry II. I have in my possession, by favour, the parchment roll, enclosed in a wooden tube (sarcophagus may I call it?), the record taking us through many generations. There is age hanging about this relic that gives it character and demands our reverence. The edges are tattered and torn by the frequent withdrawals from the solemn hiding-place by bygone men and women. There is a mustiness that tells of centuries, the touch of delicate hands and noble digits, marks of thumbs and fingers that have been dead and buried years long gone by. One may fancy, too, ancient faces and peering eyes looking out from emblazoned arms and from beneath the family coronets that bedeck this record of genealogical facts. Not having the faculty of research (looking back to the fourth generation wearies me), I am indebted to a friend who revels in all such out-of-the way work for the following transcript. The record runs in a direct line on the mother's side for seventeen generations, from Sir Robert Parker, Knight (to whom King Henry II, as a reward for his good services to the Empress Maud, gave the Lordship of Foord, in Hertfordshire, about the year 1160), down through Knights of the Bath and marriages with celebrated heiresses, including a daughter of Sir E. Harley, the ancestor of the Earl of Oxford, who has perpetuated his name as the collector of the famous Harleian manuscripts. William Parker, Standard Bearer to Richard III, married Alice, sister and sole heiress of Henry Lovel, Lord Morley, whose son in right of his mother became Lord Morley. His great grandson, Lord Morley,

154

married the daughter and sole heiress of William Stanley, Lord Monteagle. One ancestor married a granddaughter of the Lord Chancellor More, the pedigree running on to the present generation. The family of Mynn is said to be of German origin, to have sprung from a line of giants, and to have been particularly handsome in form and feature. Fifty years ago the name was well-known in the county of Kent, the two brothers, Alfred and Walter, nephews of Mr. John Mynn, being two famous cricketers, who by their exploits in the field sent their name and fame through the length and breadth of the land. Their burial-place is the churchyard of Goudhurst, where are many tombs and inscriptions to the memory of the family. Our family, made up of four daughters and two sons, have all with one exception followed their father and mother to their final resting place in our churchyard—a long-lived race. According to the order of nature or birth the youngest survives a well-known man among us.

Who is he or she who does not know Mr. William Samuel Parker Mynn, and has not had a gossip with him? And though, as he says, "I'm as deaf as a post," he is ever ready to listen and to talk. Indeed, this faculty of talking is his strong point, and he is never at a loss for a subject. His store of tales is exhaustless, never-ending, and his memory never fails him. He will vouch from his own recollection for things that have happened, as he says, "a hundred years ago"; and so artless and earnest is his manner, as you listen, that you will not charge him with an untruth, for though he would scorn to tell a lie, he is fond of a good-natured exaggeration. "Forty times" is his common measure, but upon occasion when he would be impressive he will declare for forty thousand with no unmistakable emphasis. Octogenarian though he be, meet him when or where you may, he is full to overflowing of fun and anecdote; and though his locks may have become grey, and his limbs are failing, his tongue never tires, nor do his eyes grow dim. He is spontaneous in his mirth, and may be he can yet sing a song. He is ever full of good-humour, and, as has been said of the typical satirist, that "he hissed as soon as he saw light," so it may be written of our humorist that he laughed when he opened his eyes and first looked on his mother; and though the face cannot be trusted as an index to the mind, few men, I must think, have enjoyed life more, or sighed less, than our old friend William Parker Mynn. But the heart only knows its own sorrows. Though now alone in the world, he has a friend or two left. The weed divine is his solace, and a moderate measure of the glass that cheers the evening accompaniment. Conservative by nature, he is an enemy to all "fads," and that Radical innovation upon last century's habits, teetotalism, he denounces in earnest language; but he is ever warm in his praises of the few things which time has left him capable of enjoying.

Occasionally, years ago, when in company, he has been prevailed upon to sing. His only song is "The Carrion Crow and the Tailor." This, our friend declares, he has heard sung at Searland (the family home) by Master Pankhurst, an old workman, at a hundred harvest suppers, and it was upon these occasions that he learned it. Here is a copy from Mr. Mynn's own memory, this very month of May, 1884:—

## SONG — THE CARRION CROW AND THE TAILOR.

As I went out one May morning,
It was all for to hear the little birds sing.
With heigh ho! The carrion crow
Went Croak, croak, fal de ral de rido!

The old carrion crow sat perched on an oak,
And spied the old tailor cutting out a cloak.
With heigh ho! The carrion crow
Went Croak, croak, etc.

"Boy, boy, bring me my arrow and my bow,
For I be hang'd if I don't shoot that old carrion crow."
With heigh ho! The carrion crow
Went Croak, croak, etc.

The tailor he shot, and nursed his wrath,
And shot the old sow right through the heart.

With heigh ho! The carrion crow
Went Croak, croak, etc.

"Boy, boy, bring me a little treacle in a spoon,
For I have given the old sow a most lamentable wound."
With heigh ho! The carrion crow
Went Croak, croak, etc.

The old sow ran back against the wall,
And she swallowed treacle, spoon and all.
With heigh ho! The carrion crow
Went Croak, croak, etc.

The tailor's wife said, "What do you mean
By killing the old sow now she is so lean?"
With heigh ho! The carrion crow
Went Croak, croak, etc.

The tailor, says he, "I don't care a louse,
For we shall have pig's pudding, chidlings, and souse."
With heigh ho! The carrion crow
Went Croak, croak, etc.

The bells began to ring and the bells began to toll,
And the little pigs cried for the old pig's soul.
With heigh ho! The carrion crow
Went Croak, croak, etc.

While this quaint old ditty was being sung by our humorist, the
Squire's son; half the audience had their eyes fixed upon a friend in
the room who was sharing the applause with the singer, and who, if
present, was invariably called upon to give the croaks. Samuel
Rickman, second son of our Quaker, Nathaniel Rickman, of
Amberstone House, was, according to the requirements of the part
he had undertaken, well fitted to give the two characteristic
utterances belonging to each verse, Samuel's croak being so

crow-like that the company all burst into a roar the moment he opened his mouth. He was unconsciously comic in his gravity, and had not mistaken his line of character. No smile lit up his cheek nor wrinkle knit his brow; his long face was then at its longest. Through all the fun and mirth he was as solemn as a priest at Matins or a Friend at his meeting-house. Nature had doubtless designed him for a Quaker. The moment of his conception must have been a solemn one with his parents, but instead of following the sober profession of his father and mother, Fate, or adverse fortune, had drifted him into a public-house, where he made a good landlord, doing the duties at the "George and Dragon," until, in mid-life, the "Dragon" conquered the landlord, and laid him low in the grave.

Mr. Mynn's laugh is now, as it ever has been, as rich and as full as an argosy. In his merry moments he gives out no uncertain sound; there is honesty in his chuckle, which satisfies all who hear him. It is no mere pastime; his heart is bursting with his pent-up jests — he means it. When in the woods, as has been his wont, sporting with his old friend "The Colonel," his deep-toned voice would rend the morning air; and many a time his cheer to the favourite beagle, "Rattler," has been heard a mile away. His shout has been likened to the war-whoop of the Red Indian. He is strong in his prejudices, and stentorian in argument or controversy. Nature did not intend him for labour, and he has ever taken Fortune's favour or her refusals alike with good cheer. He has not been without his trials, but over and above all he has reasoned and laughed, and mentally sung—

> Away with melancholy,
> Nor doleful changes ring.

He was fortunate in his early friendships. As he grew into manhood, our humorist and our eccentric man coalesced. In their intercourse their dormant faculties lit up and mingled, the two became one; and never had a knight a better squire or a more faithful companion than had our Don Quixote of Summer Hill (Mr. Matthias Slye) when the two, as they often did, rode out together tilting at windmills.

The father, Mr. John Mynn, belonged to the medical profession, and wrote "M.D." after his name. He was practising at Eastbourne, when one fine day, riding past Searland, he was caught by the hazel eyes and dark-brown tresses of Miss Sarah Crowhurst, heiress to her father's estate. She was looking (unconcernedly enough, no doubt) out of one of the dormer windows of the old house. (The present garish windows have since been added.) The young doctor was at once in love with the comely country maiden, and, pressing his suit, they eventually became man and wife. The doctor soon after was honoured with his commission. Here the couple lived happily enough all their married lives, the Squire dying in 1851, aged eighty-seven; and the wife in 1850, aged eighty-one.

The following episode in connection with our friend may be interesting. We have in our church an inscription on a marble tablet to the memory of *Richard Plumer, Esq., of the South Sea House, London.* He married a daughter of Abraham Laugham, of our parish, and both are buried in our churchyard. The wife died December 16, 1798, aged forty-one; the husband May 3, 1813, aged fifty-eight. Now is this he of whom Charles Lamb has said incidentally, "Not so sweetly sang Plumer as thou sangest, mild, child-like. pastoral M., son of the unapproachable churchwarden of Bishopsgate." Again, "A little less facetious, and a great deal more obstreperous, was fine, rattling, rattle-headed Plumer;" and further, "But besides his family pretentions, Plumer was an engaging fellow, and sang gloriously." The essay on the South Sea House was written by Lamb about 1820, seven years after the death of Richard Plumer. Now, if we may surmise this Richard Plumer, of whom Mr. Mynn says, "I remember him well," to be a grandson or son of the Walter Plumer who flourished in George II's time, and who, as Lamb tells us, "was a bit of a rake, and who had seen much of the world," may we not cherish the conceit that our clay about the church holds the bones of one whose name will be handed down age after age as one of the worthies belonging to that gigantic bubble, the South Sea House, immortalized by the gentle Elia? For Lamb will, as humorist, outlive many a greater genius and many a harder nature.

Mr. William Parker Mynn's life has been spent in the country, and his adventures and his tales belong to rustic life. He has now for a few years retired to the old farm-house occupying the southern corner of the Searland estate, close to the high road and to the mill field, where the mound is yet to be made out on which stood — though not in living memory — the windmill; and here is Mill Lane, leading on to the old family home, where, eighty years ago, our friend first opened his eyes; and here may he end his days, and may they yet be many ere we finally bid adieu to the last of the Mynns of our parish.

# SKETCHES AND TALES
# OF OUR PARISH

## THE LEG OF MUTTON,
## AND OUR OLD CARRIERS' WAGONS

On a summer morning, somewhere about the year 1805, there was seen walking up our street a tall, well-made man, having a prong hanging over his left shoulder, from which dangled a leg of mutton. He had purchased the joint at the old shop close to the churchyard gate, then kept by his friend and neighbour, James Kennett. The tradesman, according to custom, was about to send the joint home, but the purchaser said, "No, I will take it myself;" and thrusting the fork into the hock, off he started.

This defier of the rule of the trade and the rule of society was William Hilder, the parish churchwarden — he whose initials figure on the topmost vane of our church tower. He, too, was our London carrier, and owner of the old-fashioned covered wagons. What a democrat the man must have been! how defiant of his fellow-townsmen's opinions! how careless as to character for appearances and gloss! He must surely have been a Radical; but perhaps he was eccentric only. Be this as it may, the office he held is a guarantee that William Hilder was a respectable man, and that he had the confidence of his fellow-townsmen; but, taking the present time as our rule for the past, it does seem strange that the guardian of the church should so demean himself as to be seen in the full glare of day, in the High Street, carrying his uncooked dinner in the manner described. But so it was, and he felt not abashed, neither that he had done anything unseemly.

Since 1800 Hailsham life has somewhat changed. If not more sincere and virtuous, we certainly are more precise, perhaps more polite. We now demand that our parish officers shall, in behaviour, be men of probity, those who will pay due regard to appearances, and not do as W. Hilder did when he purchased the leg of mutton. How strange, how grotesque, are many things in social life to look back upon! Usage so changes in a century that, to do as our forefathers did, we shudder at the thought. But we are no better men than they were. Neither man nor mutton was any the worse for what happened in our street that summer morning. Perhaps the church-warden thought he was giving a salutary lesson to husbands and wives, to housekeepers and maid-servants. If he did so think, the lesson has been lost or laid aside long ago and forgotten; the veneer of civilization has so crept over the old lines of propriety. Some among us now may blush in our pride, looking back and seeing what our mothers and fathers used to do. It has been no uncommon thing for the wives of respectable tradesmen to turn out in the early morning to wash the "front bricks," as the street path was called, in pattens, and fetch the water required with their own hands from the "parsonage" pond — a thing no maid-servant would now think of doing. Well, in the year 1884 we do not wish the wives to do the one nor the men the other.

It was on W. Hilder the old-fashioned Hailsham depended for the supply of many of the necessities of life; our bacon and cheese, our sugar and salt, our linen and woollen fabrics, all came by grace of Hilder and Easton, the firm doing, as before related, all the goods traffic between Eastbourne and London, our town being head-quarters and the home of the partners. Both families have now quite died out. The only record to recall the name is on a gravestone opposite the chancel door to the memory of a daughter — Sarah Hilder, wife of John Sinnock, she dying in 1797, at the age of nineteen, a wife and a mother. Has the old home of the family, since it has gone into the trade, grown bold and barefaced? Can it be nearer the roadway, and has it drawn itself on in its desire to tempt the passer-by with the variety of its contents — with bluebottles and bullaces on one hand, and Berlin wools and wooden hoops on the other?

In my earliest recollection the house bore a very demure face, standing back almost gloomily. The front was then protected by a green palisade fence; there was a gate opposite the central front door, and being the home of our lawyer, it was considered to be one of our few genteel residences. On either hand of the gate grew a purple lilac, and a few hollyhocks hung their weary-looking heads over the fence. The approach was by a raised brickway, beneath which crept sluggishly towards the north the surface drainage. Where Belle Vue Terrace now stands was the garden, with a roadside hedge fencing; then came the horsepond, flowing from the stable to the road, the stable, now standing, being turned into a warehouse. The pond was surrounded by pollard willows, casting their shadows into the turbid waters. This was tenanted by a few sleepy tench and the croaking frog, singing to his mistresses in early spring time his mysterious love-song. Melancholy music!

In this preliminary my chief object is to introduce to the reader's notice our old-fashioned carriers' wagons, that, for I don't know how many years, had dragged their wearying journeys to and from London. It was on a Monday morning, after two nights' and one day's rest, that the horses were most lively and the men fresh and gay. The Sabbath had been a welcome interval from toil and drudgery. The effect was to be seen in the extra glossy coats of the horses and the newly shaved chins and clean shirts of the men. All hands and feet were again ready for the start. The employ was marked, being out of the ordinary routine of labour. There was ever some incitement to be away again. The chief wagoner and his black dog, "Boxer," were both characters. The men often bore small commissions from thrifty housewives — some small article that could not be procured at home, and which the "Boro'" could supply, was needed. A little trading of this sort (the men's wages were twelve shillings weekly) was winked at by the masters. A small fund for extras on the road was required; wayside inns must be attended to and propitiated. "Beer and bait" were among the things that must be had; and thus a small sum was netted that satisfied the owners and gratified the men. These covered wagons were our argosies, our vessels of trade, and the men our inland sailors. Then we cheered their outgoing and welcomed their incoming, full of all manner of good things and life-necessaries. We knew nought of iron horses nor iron roads, and if we ever heard of steam, we neither believed the power nor feared the consequences. At that time it took our travellers five days and nights out and home, their carriage being their bed; now we go to the great city in two hours, and that by a more circuitous route.

The autumn was the carriers' harvest time. Our parish, being the extreme west of the Sussex hop plantation, was a focus for the London market. The teams from the north and east arriving with their scented burdens, the fragrance was delightful. Who has been known to "turn up his nose" but in approbation at the scent of the hop? The loading was a task as well for the head as for bone and muscle. The heavy men were then alert and active; then there was bustle, and even excitement, the master's eye scanning as his voice and hand directed. The load must be put on square. It was no small matter to place a hundred and thirty, and perhaps a few more of these "pockets," so that they would ride fifty-five miles free from accident. The pile, to our young eyes, was prodigious; the middle rows, hanging out before and behind, being secured by ropes lengthways. It was a feat few men could perform to mount the crowning pocket. There was one man who, bred to the task, and having followed the wagons from his boyhood, was famous for this. It was said of him he would carry a hogshead of sugar if he could get it to lie on his back. The weight of a bag of hops was a "flea-bite" to him, and he would traverse the ladder and complete the load as easily as the professional "labourer" would mount the scaffold with the old-fashioned hod of mortar.

The roads of Sussex figure badly in history. Part of our London road belonged, especially to the bad ere the "Dicker" was enclosed, at the time when the Hanoverian Legion encamped for one night on the heathy and barren surface, on its flying march to the metropolis to gladden the eyes, and as some said at the time, to protect the person of their King, George III of England. At that date every traveller chose his own way over the spongy and rotten surface. Horsebridge back-lane, as it is now called, was one entrance, and at the present day is a sample of what a part of the high road to London then was. Broad wheels were absolutely necessary, and these wagons had three tires, or nine inches, to travel on and to keep them afloat, and sometimes eight fine heavy horses to drag the load along. These horses, with the gay head-toppings, and each with a couple of jingling ear-bells, were the wagoner's pride and the village boy's delight.

On Monday morning there was a general assemblage of eyes to witness the start. The crack of the whip was the signal, and watching, we listened to the dying sound of the twelve or sixteen tiny bells — *snag-shells* we called them — as they drew away on the raad, the good dog "Boxer," as he stood looking out from the front of the wagon, wagging his short tail, as if saying, as well as he could, "Good-bye." All the year round two of these wagons were on the road, Wednesday and Saturday being the Eastbourne days; and it was to these wagons and the six or eight horses each that the old seaside town, then a watering-place and a resort of pleasure, had to look for a supply of most, if not all, of its merchandise, there being no other public conveyance, excepting the stage-coach. Look at Eastbourne now, in 1884, and the many wants of its fixed population, of from twenty to thirty thousand, and the old mode of supply, and we can have no better or more fitting contrast of the tale of the rise and progress of the beautiful town more vividly told.

The hop-grower of those old-fashioned days was not without his troubles. When he was fortunate enough to secure a crop a market must be found, and as agents could not at all times be trusted, to London the farmer must go. This journey was an event; in fact, the event of the year. First came the question of conveyance — should it be by coach, the wagon, the nag, or the old chaise-cart, with the old horse so steady and safe for church or the fortnightly market? Either of these might have the preferencc each man according to his likes or his dislikes. The pleasure of the journey weighed but little with the farmer; it was necessary, and that was enough. He would prefer being at home in his old arm-chair in the chimney corner, catching, it might be, a glimpse of the stars as they twinkled, looking down the open chimney upon his head on a clear, frosty night. Here he could puff his pipe in peace, and chat to his wife and the grown-up daughters. They could talk of yesterday and to-morrow — and that would be enough — and be happy. By and by comes a lull of the tongues; the master becomes drowsy, he sleeps, and the clay pipe drops from his lips and glides through his hands, and is smashed on the floor, and the laugh is turned on the good man. There had been a wager with the youngest daughter that the pipe would not be broken on that particular evening. The bet is lost, and the coin is demanded. The fire on the hearth, backed up by the iron stock plate, embellished with the well-known six starlings, throws out a great heat, and the maid is called to place the oven's door in front of the master's legs to prevent blisters; and while the wife sits sewing, and the daughter darning, how free from care would all be but for this visit to London.

But it must be done; the crop must be sold, the money is needed, and the decision as to locomotion cannot be further put off. Well, which ever way, the journey will not be undertaken with a light heart. The dread of the London pickpocket and of the country highwayman looms in the distance. Ashdown Forest is considered to be an unsafe place for a lone man to cross. Does not the gibbet stand by the roadside, and do not the irons rattle, and the bleached bones glisten of the man who robbed the mail-cart and had died for it? What! If the traveller on his return journey, with his pockets filled with gold, should be attacked, little worth does he think his life or his money would then be. These terrors, if not spoken of for pride, pass through his mind, and his heart quails within him.

Well, all this may be somewhat imaginary, but the tale is yet told that the Sussex farmer, in the early part of the century, before he ventured to the great metropolis, thought it to be his duty to make his will. This settled, and trusting in God, he failed not to do his duty. However, I have never known a misadventure follow. All my old acquaintances have returned with the bank notes in their pockets. The journeys have been minus of adventure, though one of my old friends used to relate, with considerable glee, that in the evening, sauntering from the "George," in the Borough, towards the foot of the bridge, on more than one occasion a lady had welcomed him to London, calling him "my dear," and inviting him to extend his walk, but as he exultingly said, "I was not to be had."

The return from the hop market was a time of rejoicing. The wife expected a new silk gown, and the daughters minor presents — remembrances of their father's successful trip to town. All this done, the family settled down again to work for another year. Let others, if any choose, draw the contrast between the past and the present; I will not be the critic. But this I will say, that as friends, and for genuine hospitality at their homes, I have not met the farmers' equals.

## THE PAPER GHOST

Our parish is not rich in ghost lore nor haunted houses; there is no evidence of any place in particular being troubled by a ghostly tenant of any individuality. One old place near the foot of the marsh was, years ago, under suspicion of being in possession, and there was good authority as to noises that could not be accounted for; but that a real ghost was ever seen on the premises there was no proof. Our ghosts have been sylvan, and two only have been recognizable. One was known as the "Ghost of the Garrets," the other as the "Salt Marsh Ghost."

First let me tell you what the Garrets were. The present three naked meadows, with the footpath running through (to Magham Down), need no notice here; it is the past we have to do with — when these fields were garnished round with fine old oaks, which, alas! Necessity, or that less excusable impulse, Avarice, full forty years ago laid low. Then, at the bottom of the field where the pond now is, we had to pass through a grove of these trees; the pond being about the centre of a copse of hazel, bramble, and other like scrub that could maintain life under the shade and shelter of the finest lot of oaks we had in the parish.

Here, then, was the home of the "Paper Ghost." It was said to be white, shadowy, misty, and had often been seen to tear itself as it fled away and vanished among the trees. Once, for certain, it was thought to have been caught napping by an arrant gunner who, one wintry day, searching the cover for a shot, fell upon an exhausted fire-balloon that had the previous night chanced to fall there. This fact tended for a time to weaken the belief that the place had ever been haunted; but ghosts die hard, and the following spring there was again proof positive of the ghost's vitality and activity. A young fellow of an imaginative and gossipy turn of mind had exceeded his evening hour. The mother and the children had gone off to bed; the father was up waiting, and getting rather out of temper, when our hero arrived, all huffing and puffing, and trying to look pale and frightened. The boy said he had come home through the Garrets —which was the fact — and that he had seen the Paper Ghost leaning against a post; that the thing kept opening and shutting its mouth so sharply that he had heard its teeth rattle, and the long beard rustle in the wind. "Upon this," said our young friend, "I became terribly frightened, and shouting aloud, cried, 'Father, father,' and ran off home as fast as my legs could carry me." The parent, upon this explanation, became mollified, and quietly ordered William off to bed. Before retiring himself, the father, being a ready rhymer, made the following entry in his diary:—

> As poor Will went past a post,
> There he saw a paper ghost —
> His great long teeth and rusty beard
> Made poor Will quite afeared.

Next morning at the breakfast table this was read to the family, as a warning and a deterrent against late hours.

The sequel to the story of the Ghost of the Garrets shall be given in Will's own words. It is best to clear up any ghost story. Will had grown to man's estate; had learnt a few facts connected with married life and a large family; knew what it was to work hard, and many of the illusions of his youth had vanished with his experience. He had given up all belief in ghosts, when on one very moonlight summer night, as he bent his weary way homeward coming from Pevensey through the Marsh, his eyes intent looking downward tracking the narrow footpath leading through the rich pastures, where the cattle were stretched upon the turf, cudding the stored food of the day, scenting the air with their unpolluted breathings, where all around was peace and quiet, of a sudden he was confronted by the ghostly figure of his young days, moving steadily onward, and coming direct upon his plodding steps. As he told me his tale he said:— "I stopped suddenly at the sight. A shiver ran over me, and lifting my eyes heavenward, perhaps at the moment hoping for help, when lo! and behold! there, above my head, was the marsh owl, out on her nightly ramble, seeking her mousy meal. It was the shadow of this bird that had so suddenly disturbed me, and I saw in an instant that it was my old friend of the Garrets who had discovered herself to me, there being no trees this time to cut off her floating image from the ground, and so this mystery of my youth was solved."

## SALT-MARSH BARN AND ITS GHOST

It had never been settled to what order this visitor belonged. It had shapes as various as one's fancy bred; some would say it had but two legs, while others declared it had four, and the colours were as many as the viewer's eyes; so that in passing the old barn one never knew what to expect. This uncertainty tended to make the case more dreadful, and led, of course, to much exaggeration. It was given out at one time for certain that our old enemy had been seen there. Be that as it may, all agreed that, whatever its nature or shape, the thing always vanished at one particular spot, that it passed beneath the boughs of an old oak stand ing close to the barn, and went plump into the building through the folding doors, whether they were open or shut. The following account is given in explanation. It is called —

## THE BUTCHER BOY'S STORY

He says:— "I was nearly out of my time as an apprentice, and was romantically in love with a pretty girl who lived with her parents in

169

the neighbourhood of Pevensey. Her witching eye was always following me wherever I went. I often walked on that happy day that comes ' 'twixt Saturday and Monday' to get a deep look into the blue of her living eye, and to lose myself in admiring her lovely form and great beauty. Then I was happy. I had no need to say with Burns, 'O, Mary, at thy window be.' My Mary would come out to meet me, and the father and mother made no objection to the attention I was paying their daughter. I may say I was respectable, and it was well known that, when opportunity offered, I could have the means of starting in life with the chance of a comfortable home.

" Time wore on, and on a Sunday, when I could get away, I never failed in my visit. On my return in the evening I had always to pass the old barn, and although my thoughts would be with 'the girl I had left behind me,' I never passed the haunted place without thinking about the ghost, and wondering if I should see it. However, I never caught a glimpse of the strange figure, and Salt-marsh became as common and free as any other part of the journey. But my assurance was hardening me for a catastrophe which, when it happened, was very alarming, and ultimately turned out to be a source of great annoyance to me.

"It was in the autumn of 1840 I had the opportunity of having a horse, and resolved to ride out on my usual Sunday afternoon visit. The animal was aged, but well-bred and spirited, and I knew his temper and habit. I thought he was as safe on his legs as a snake is on her belly. I had ridden him over two years on my rounds, and he and I were well acquainted with all the roads in the neighbourhood. On my return that night there was no moon. It was dark, and a fog came creeping over the marsh; the wind was gusty and moaning. I was nearing the 'Bridges,' when, I cannot tell why, a sudden thrill of terror ran over me; the horse snorted, threw his head, and refused to go on at his accustomed pace. He swerved from the road; there was something stirring his blood or his brain, and having a very unfortunate effect on him. As I have said, I knew his temper well, and that gentle means to soothe him must first be tried. I spoke to and patted him, endeavouring to bring him round to a sense of his duty and submission to my will. We were getting on better, and approaching the haunted place, when my old friend pulled up and refused altogether. Quiet means had failed. I knew now he had made up his mind, and accordingly I had to make up mine, which was, at any cost, to go on; so at once I thrust the spurs into his sides, and round we went again and again. Getting his head once more in the direction of home, I gave him the steel with all my might — a continued application and a topper between the ears with a slight bit of oak I always had in my hand when riding, as a help in time of trouble, sent him forward at full speed.

"We were close upon the barn; I thought of the ghost, and felt my horse tremble under me. We were going madly, and in the dark and fog — he was scared, and so was I — when all of a sudden headlong we went together, the rider coming to the ground several yards in advance. My poor old nag groaned; but behind and above all came a roar that caused the hair on my head to rise and stand on end. At this moment I thought all was over with me; but I did not die on the spot, neither was I carried away. A succeeding roar or bray restored me to reason. I found I had done nothing either romantic or really dangerous. I had only ridden over a poor harmless donkey that had taken up his quarters for the night in the middle of the road!"

Soon after this the rail ran close past the spot, and the steam whistle has since banished the ghosts from our parish. The idea of laying ghosts had not died out when I was a boy. Often I visited an old lady at her farm in Hellingly, who would make me shudder with fear as we sat on a winter's evening at the fireside, the old-fashioned family clock all the while tick, tick, ticking away the solemn moments. I was ever a ready listener to her marvellous tales, as she told me how ghosts, or evil spirits, were laid in the Red Sea, and the wonderful overthrow of the Egyptian host in those miraculous waters appeared to give character fitting the place to be the receptacle of intruding spirits here on earth. The priest must be sent for, and he had to remain until the ghost made its appearance. Then the exorcising ritual would be gone through. The holy man would say:— "In the name of the Father, and of the Son, and of the Holy Ghost, why troublest thou me?" The spirit then departed, and would have rest in the Red Sea, perhaps for ever. The old lady had faith in the efficacy of the ritual, and of course in ghosts and witches.

The old lady's husband, in his young days, had walked to Heathfield to witness a witch-proving. I have heard him, more than once, relate the tale — how the victim, being almost drowned in the horse-pond, through which the people dragged the poor old woman, barely escaped with her life.

## BEER: THE POOR MAN'S BEVERAGE

"Beer," said a talkative old man in reply to an enthusiastic abstainer, who had called his favourite liquor poison, "Beer," he exclaimed, "will outlive the British Constitution, the Monarchy, the Lords, and the Church as by law established. Beer is stronger than faith, and as everlasting as the hills. It is the one thing needful; man cannot do without it. If bread is the staff of life, beer is life itself, and rather than give it up and put on the blue ribbon, I would die first."

Thus our old and experienced friend, in all honesty, gave a finality to his outspoken exordium. Well, now I am not about to find fault with any man on account of his opinions or his conclusions. If he choose to die for his faith, so let him! I will not dispute about his wisdom. He may be fanatic; he may be superstitious; he may have many wild ideas concerning the potency of his favourite liquor; and if so, all argument will be lost upon him; and should he drink and die for his god, his method certainly will be considered by the majority of people to be more respectable than by the use of the rope or the razor.

But I am not to be cynical. I have set out only to chronicle a few comical phases and facts belonging to beer among our common people. I am free to confess to the witchery of the liquor upon my own senses. I have drank and enjoyed it. The influence of the aroma as the cork is drawn is still strong upon me. The combination is perfect. Nature and art working together have triumphed, and man's most fastidious organ is satisfied. The sweet and the bitter have met. John Barleycorn has married his mistress, the Hop, and the nostril is invited after so amorous a fashion that few who catch a sniff of the vapour can say "No." But Bass or Allsop, those aristocrats of the

172

trade, and their bewitching bottles, we will pass by. It is the "common brewer," and his friend the working man, we have to do with here. The first "mashes" for the million, and provides the poor man with his favourite liquor, and the second turns his coppers in his pocket as he labours on during the day, hoping to find enough for a pint and a "screw" to make him happy with his friends at the beerhouse in the evening. These two, the brewer and the free-drinker, are twain, and if not familiar, the one lives for the other.

Let us distinguish and draw a line betwixt the various devotees of the beer barrel — between the man who drinks in faith, believing the liquor really does him good and adds to his strength, to his bone and muscle, and he who drinks for the pleasure of the thing, and becomes drunk. The sot and the man of faith are two distinct characters. To the latter — that is, the men of faith — belong nearly the whole of our farm labourers. The habits of this class have undoubtedly improved. Better wages have made them better people, and few now among our fixed field cottagers who are found to be drunkards. It is among the odds and ends of our working men we must look for the careless professional drinker — the man who goes "on the spree," who sits down to enjoy himself, regardless of consequences or of character, who will sing, and, but for the law, would not go home till morning; who is not very particular as to the flavour of his beer, so that it will, as he says, "touch a nerve." I knew one old toper who had a great contempt for a particular brewing, because, as he said, the liquor would not, after a night's debauch, make his head ache in the morning. Among such men beer has a mighty power. A quart of sixpenny has more influence than a shilling coin. If you offer one of this class beer, you sympathize with him; you move his heart; you are his friend, and he is ready to serve you. You may draw tears from his eyes if you taLk quietly to him about his last "drunk," but you must not remonstrate. This touches his pride, and you loose all hold on him. But, talk to him as you will, he gets drunk again the next opportunity. "I like it, I do," he says; "and I will." But he is half-ashamed, and says again, "I know what a fool I am; I wish I could give it up." The poor fellow is a victim to a tyrannical habit, and though he must be blamed, as he blames himself, he must be borne with, and should be pitied. He is a great transgressor, and he knows it. Use and habit, we say, are second nature.

Here is a case. There was sitting, within the last two years, in our barber's chair, a fine, tall young fellow of the navvy class, whose chin was ready for the razor. The lather had been applied, and in another minute the beard would have been taken off, when "Stop!" cried the fellow; "I must have a drink." The barber, of course, remonstrated, and approached, whetting the razor on his hand, ready to begin the operation. "It is no use," said the man; "my time is come, and I must have a pint. Here goes!" "If you do," said Mr. Tonsor, "I will charge double." "All right," shouted the man; and off he bolted with his whited chin to the nearest public-house, swallowed a quart, returned quickly, seated himself, paid double fee, and civilly quitted the shop.

The ability to imbibe is quickened by practice. I have stood by and seen a beer-drinker turn off a quart at a guzzle, the liquor running down the neck as freely as water through a culvert. On another occasion, one of our publicans was somewhat astonished by the action of a well-known customer. The man had ordered a quart at the bar; this he drank off. He then ordered a second, which at a gulp followed the same road, and then a third. "What do you mean?" said the landlord. "Mean!" said the man, drawling out the word; "I was rather dry, and now I mean to sit down and enjoy myself."

We cannot bury our dead without the aid of beer. The navvy's widow could not, as she said, "bury her deceased husband respectably with less than eighteen gallons." "And let it be the best," she continued, as she gave the brewer the order; "for Alick," she added, amidst her sobs and her tears, "has been a good husband to me." So the day of funeral must submit to the tyranny of beer, and even in after years we are driven to weep over the graves of our dead relations under its influence. Our well-nigh forgotten parents, and our dormant love for them, are both revived and made alive again by the magic power of malt, hops, and fermentation. We weep as we would not if we did not drink. Then the soul is stirred as no words could stir us. We acknowledge the paternal rule to have been just, and the maternal love beyond the expression of thought or word. We rave, we blubber; in fact, beer has found us out. We are at times, under its influence, verily asses!

A striking instance of this happened a short time ago in our churchyard. Years after the interment, when the green turf had become the only winding-sheet, a son and grandson, both inebriate, were standing over the mother's and sister's graves — the father sobbing, and muttering out their dead relations' praises; the grand son taking up the theme, and mingling his tears with the father's — when suddenly the elder shouted, "Cheer up, boy; we will go and have another pint." And off the two started to the nearest beershop, to wash away with their favourite liquor the short-lived and falsely made-up sorrow.

In pleasing contrast to our deep, we have had our delicate drinker — the man who would not upon any occasion, exceed the half-pint; that is, a half-pint at a draught or at a time. This moderate measure was upon all occasions his limit; he was never known to order a pint. He did not countenance deep drinking. It may be, he drank in this way for example's sake. He rarely, if ever, sat down in the tavern, or formed one of a noisy crew. He was of a retiring character, and as soon as he had emptied the pewter off he trotted to the next bar, and the quartern was repeated; and this would continue throughout the day, or as long as the coppers or his credit held out. It has been said that thirty-two chalk marks were added to his score at his favourite house during one particular day. But these half-pints, as was his custom, he took at separate calls. He was then in his glory; he was "on the run." Thus he made his mark among us, and dying at a good old age, left behind him a harmless character, as has been sung by our own poet in his punning rhyme —

> A pint of beer is very well,
> If people don't get more;
> But some are not content with that,
> For they will have a score.

Again, what can be more characteristic of English country life than the wayside inn on a summer's evening? Passing, you see the rustics seated, probably with the fixed bench or table in front of them, well stored with liquor, that, at such times, makes the heart glad. The week's toil is over; the well-earned coin is in the pocket. The men are talking about their "jobs," their wages, their master, and how good a thing a drop of good beer is after the work of the week is over. They know but little of politics, or about the Church, or of taxes, of the Post Office Savings Bank; and as for the Blue Ribbon movement or teetotalism, they think less. They are generous, inviting anyone, stranger or no stranger, to drink at their expense, and be happy. Care for the time is banished. The quart measure and its contents are the ruling powers for that afternoon or evening. And who, let me ask, can totally object to this rustic mode of enjoyment? Look at the hard hands of these toilers! The flesh is turned almost to bone by the constant grasping of their rude tools. Think of their many hours, their meagre pay, their poor homes, and can you begrudge them the hearty laugh over their beer and the pipes in front of the old-fashioned way-side inn? Here they are kings, and it may be, some few of them queens too — in bygone times it would be so — maidens or wife, will be among them, kissing with their pouting cherry lips, though not wantonly or in excess, the liquor of their rural god, John Barleycorn. I confess that such a sight has not displeased me. When care has put off her coil, and left the labour-bound free, it may be but for one short hour. Tell me, if you must, there will be excess. I know there may be, the more's the pity. I know it is too often the "one pint more before we part" that does the mischief. We warm to the work, and dropping the reins of moderation, the steeds of evil run off with us, and then it is that we are capsized, and left in the mire to moan over our own follies.

But I am moralizing, when I intended to tell the tale of the twelve wise men who one evening sat at the long table of one of our beer-houses. Each man, in a fit of defiance as to the consequences, had ordered his quart, and twelve measures stood full before them, each fellow inviting his neighbour to drink, but not one of the party attempted to lift the pot to his mouth. They had not meted the extent of their capacity. They were all drunk and incapable. They babbled one to the other impatiently, "Drink! drink!" They invited the absent toper to drink, but he came not. They were alone and helpless, left to the tender mercies of the power that had vanquished them, and they became miserable. Joy had fled; they sat mute; their eyes dimmed; they slept; strange figures and sounds passed before them. One among the party dreamed. He saw the brewer with his liveried servant pass by, and these both cried, "Drink! drink!" The landlord cried, "Drink!" Then the man's wife entered the room, and she cried, "Drink! For here," she said, "you have more than enough, while at home the cupboard is empty, the rent is unpaid, and the children's feet are bare." Then the pots put on human visages, with gummy eyes, swollen noses, and bloated cheeks, and these all cried, "Drink! drink! for we are full and must be emptied; we are wanted for other drinkers." But not one among the sad party could lift the liquor to his mouth. Then the man's wife, who had been standing by silent, shrieked again, "Drink! drink!" and darted out of the room. At what hour the party broke up, and how the men got home that night, is not known. But this result followed, the man who dreamed the dream and saw the vision, never from that hour has tasted a drop of the publican's liquor, and he declares that since he has given it up the cupboard has not been empty, the children's feet have not been bare, the rent is always paid to the day, and Want, with his haggard cheek and self accusing eye, has not entered his dwelling.

How many a tale, too, has been told, and will continue to be told, of the absurd situations and temper men have been found in under the influence of liquor. Some we see merry, some sulky, some unconscious of the ridicule, and even oftentimes the danger they expose themselves to. Well may we sing with Burns —

> O, wad some power the giftie gie us,
> To see oursels as ithers see us.

I know one poor fellow who, being turned out of the drinking shop on a wet, wintry night, and being a mile or two away from his home, took up his quarters in an angle of a house on the roadside, where he stood shivering and shouting in happy ignorance that the water was rushing down upon his shoulders, issuing from the broken stack-pipe above his head. He was so "glorious" in his lone corner, through the effects of the beer within him, that one of the disturbed family of the house, venturing out, found the noisy brawler, who excused himself by saying, "I have only got here for shelter; pray don't turn me out in the rain."

Again, there was the old-fashioned farmer, one of an evening party at a brother farmer's house. He had ridden the grey gelding. The fun had gone on fast and furious, that is the ale and gin were passed round so freely, that the gentleman, thinking he had had enough, said good night to his friends, adding to the host, "I can get my horse, don't trouble yourself," when soon after the whole party breaking up, and seeking their steeds in the stable, found their old friend safely mounted and "wiring" away on the newly white painted water-butt, standing on its wheels in the wagon-lodge, the rider not doubting he was on his way home upon the back of his old grey horse.

Beer is a sovereign remedy also for a variety of ills that flesh is heir to. I have known it taken for bile and diseased liver, also as a sure cure for corns, the sufferer declaring a good dose to be effectual, at least for a season, against those troublesome companions of ours who will accompany us whene'er we take our walks abroad. And now to wind up with the jovial and devotional note of our bygone brick-layer's labourer and returned soldier, "Tom Lincoln." Who remembers Tom Lincoln? He sang —

> O, brown beer, thou art so dear,
> Thou art my darling night and morning.

And the refrain of the old song was Tom's last prayer —

> Write on my tombstone, a jug of this.

## HIGHWAY ROBBERY

This was a somewhat romantic affair. The spot the robbers chose for the fray was the hollow on the road leading to Polegate, and less than a mile beyond what was then known as Pinner's Hill, where there lived in a cottage by the roadside a noted smuggler — William Sayers — great-uncle to the celebrated pugilist Tom Sayers. The old man, who had his stable by his house side, kept a couple of horses, and was known as "Rubbigy Pinner." Hence the name of the hill, which is now known as the Jew's Hill. The highway then, as now, was flanked by Alfrey's Wood, a lonely, solemn place, "fit for murder, plot, or stratagem." The day chosen was our market day, and the game selected a gentleman farmer — Mr. James Pagden, of Willingdon. Men of his class then, for the most part, were their own bankers, and payments were generally made in notes and coin. Money taken at the market for corn or cattle was pocketed and taken home. Confidence in banks and cheques has been a thing of slow growth, one pound notes and gold in our purses or drawers at home being preferred to a balance at the bank; and so a bait was offered to the highwayman or the house breaker.

I have in my keeping a memorandum as follows, written on the cover of an old book by Mr. Matthias Slye, which at the time belonged to that eccentric gentleman: "1826, February 8: Mr. and Mrs. James Pagden stopped by three footpads." The lady and her husband had that evening supped with Mr. and Mrs. King Sampson at Hailsham, and had left their friends' residence about 10 p.m. to drive home in their single horse chaise. The singular feature is this: Mr. Sampson had a misgiving about his friends' safety on the road that evening. Something told him, as he said at the time, that mischief was brewing, and he strongly urged his friends to stay the night, and so be in safe keeping. But Mr. Pagden, pooh-poohing all such advice, determined to start, but in the end was prevailed on to take with him a stout oak-faggot "bat" as a means of defence, and this "bat," as we shall soon see, proved a true friend.

The start was made, and all went well with a good horse and bold driver until they had arrived at the hollow, when "Stop for your life!" was shouted by a husky voice, and the reins at the same instant were violently dragged from the driver's hands, the lady at the same moment being partly drawn over the back of the gig and so roughly handled that the rings were torn from her ears. It was at this bewildering moment that the oak bat fell crushing upon the villain's head, and down he went headlong, senseless upon the road, and down, too, went Mr. Pagden on his feet, as he leaped from his gig, and the fight commenced that soon ended in the rout and total defeat of the three cowards. They escaped for that night, but soon were ferreted out, their wounds telling against them. At that time Horsham was the county town, whither these men were taken away to gaol, and when the assize came round were tried, convicted, and sent away to join their fellow-roughs in that dreaded island, Botany Bay. The men were all natives of Hailsham, and were then living away, but knowing the habits of the time, and also Mr. Pagden, they had calculated upon a successful venture; but luckily they found their mistake. Mr. and Mrs. Pagden arrived home, save the earrings, safe and sound. Ever after Mr. P. was looked upon as a hero. He fought against three and prevailed. The spot is known to this day as "Cowards' Den."

## FOX HALL AND THE EMPTY CHURCH

One of the greatest charms of country life is the sight of the rustic cottage — the old thatched house standing in the fields far away from the busy haunts of men, surrounded by the orchard and garden it is in, in summer the "Arcady" of the parish. The inmates are reduced to two. The boys and girls are gone; the bantlings have fledged and flown, and are battling with life away in other homes on their own account. The "gaffer" and his dame only remain, and these represent the third or fourth generation that have slept beneath the old roof. Their wants are few and sufficiently supplied, and their happiness is great. The cat and the cow are the whole of their live-stock. They keep only one of each, save for a few weeks during babyhood, when the kitten frolics on the hearth, and the calf, as the day wears on, bellows in the shed behind the house for its mother's milk. The orchard is in full glow of beauty, hung with wreaths, circles, and bunches of blossom that promise the fruit of the coming autumn. Old-fashioned flowers paint the edges and borders, and send their mingled scent in at the cottage door. There may be a hive of bees standing away in the shelter of the northern hedge, but modern bee culture is not understood by the cottager, and the destruction of the swarm to secure the honey is yet the rule. The water supply is from a pond or open spring. The surface is half-covered with weed and grass, leaving only the dipping-place naked; the liquid, clear as a pebble, is peeping out at the visitor like a dark-eyed beauty in her *déshabillé* at the festooned window on a summer morning. Granny values her "gar'n stuff" above pearls. She has taken a second prize at the neighbouring Vegetable and Flower Show for her beans and potatoes, and avers she ought to have had the first — at least, so said one of the three judges.

There are about half a dozen old elms close to the south-west — a shade in summer and a shelter from rain and wind in winter — and a deep, dry ditch — the boundary of the parish. The ditch looks innocent enough now, but if it could it might tell many a tale. Years ago it was well known to the smugglers, who, under the guardian-ship of the old woodman, the then occupier of the house, made the place the safe receptacle of many a cargo of brandy and other contraband articles.

Can the home reader point out the old cottage? My object in noticing the place is to introduce an episode of parish life — a contrast to the present time — that happened perhaps a century ago. Mind, I do not vouch for the details to be facts, but what matter? Half our facts are founded upon legend, and if we will believe, we must do so on trust. Happily, the majority can do so. But to my tale. Close to the roadside leading from Cacklebury to the Hide, in its own garden, looking eastward, stands an old thatched cottage. In the north-east corner of the garden, years ago, stood a hut or dwelling owned by the occupiers, two brothers and two sisters. They bore the familiar and significant name of "Fox." They were sly, artful, retiring people, living apart from general intercourse, disliking to be interfered with, fond of night work, making money when other people were sleeping, rarely seen in the day time; in short, they were smugglers all, and lived for themselves. Their home was their castle, and they allowed no stranger to open the door, or to attempt to enter without challenge.

The women, as well as the men, worked hard at the traffic. The sisters were coarse and repulsive in manner, habit, and costume. With unkempt hair hanging loose about the shoulders, they would take their part in an inland fray, or many a mile away help to work the lugger on the coast, and take their share of the burden on the shoulder, or ride the pack-horse to the appointed rendezvous. They would brook no opposition, and rather than give way, use the blunder buss or the horse-pistol. They were known as the "Whistling Sisters," and their shrill call was a familiar sound and warning to the fraternity. The Revenue officers had no liking to these two syrens. The ladies had hardened their hearts, and preferred being feared rather than loved. Over the low fire-place in their home hung the defiant and death-dealing weapons. There was no disguise of their method in meeting and dealing with their visitors. "Your name and your business," was the rule, and woe be to the person who opened the door unbidden.

It happened on a Sunday afternoon in the early autumn, when the shadows were daily lengthening, that their home was rashly invaded by an unauthorized intruder, a man named Inskip. (I remember his son George, an old man when I was a boy; he used to walk about the street with a staff, instead of a stick, which at every move forward he threw off to the right hand, describing about half a circle. I know not the father's name, so we will call him George also.) He, wishing to see these defiant people, stepped over the stile, and walking boldly up to the door of their den, lifted the latch and looked in; but ere he had time to state his business, the Foxes' blood was in a ferment. One seized a pistol, another a cutlass, and in a moment down came the latter straight across the right-hand wrist of the man who had dared to break their law, severing a tendon and causing the third finger to fall useless into the palm of the hand. There were no questions asked, the whole family shouting defiance and cursing the intruder. Master Inskip was a man not easily cowed, but looking at the bleeding and useless hand, he deemed it discreet to retire from the unsought and unexplained strife; but he shouted as he retired to the road that before the day was gone they should see him again, and with company. The Foxes growled, "Shut the door," and all became quiet again in the Hide Lane.

The wounded man hastened home, but ere he arrived there he had resolved on his revenge. He was a native and well known, and he knew those who would help him. He said to himself, "The Foxes have slept in their house for the last time. To-day down comes their castle, and out they go, dead or alive." Master Inskip's blood was up. The red blood flowed and covered his fingers. The gash was becoming painful, and he ceased to reason about consequences. He would be avenged, cost what it might; but he made a semblance of abiding by the law. He called first upon the parish constable, for he knew he would sympathize and give assistance. The constable at that time was one of the people, and summary justice had been known to be winked at. It happened that the man of law and order was at church, where, perhaps, it had been better if Master Inskip had been engaged. However, he was not to be hindered. He would have no moment of delay; so boldly walking in, he called for the officer, at the same time holding up his bleeding hand. The Curate was in the sermon, preaching peace and forgiveness for injuries received. His deep-toned voice had just uttered, "Cursed is he who seeketh his brother's blood, or coveteth anything that is his." The constable at that moment left his seat in answer to the call. Then began a flutter all over the church; the people rose and looked towards the porch, where stood the two in consultation. The children mounted the seats and stared over the high pews; the minister paused, and was seen folding his sermon, keeping one finger between the leaves, in case he should resume the homily, but he saw he had lost all hold of his hearers. Some had followed the officer and his client into the vestibule. One was heard to mutter, "Murder." This, of course, caused a sensation and a thrill, when the Curate, foreseeing the end, raised his hands and pronounced the Benediction, and all the people fled, the place being emptied in a few minutes.

The official, staff in hand (that magic emblem of power and authority, surmounted by the crown, emblazoned with the Royal Arms, and inscribed in an oblong circle "The Hundred of Dill"), was soon on the march, surrounded by his volunteers. Particulars were inquired into, the facts learned, and the mode of punishment was discussed. The injured man did not reveal his whole resolve. He was calculating and working out his way to obtain his wished-for result. He did not tell his adherents he intended to pull the hut down about the owners' ears, cost what it might. He talked of murder, of wayside robbery, and danger to the public, especially to women and children, in allowing such people as the Foxes to live in a lone house close by the highway. He advised his followers to be prepared for rough work, to be armed in self-defence, to take a bludgeon, prong, spade, or mattock; and a motley party, mixed with boys and girls, his followers became as he passed through Cacklebury. Here the number became strengthened. The Foxes had no friends that day: the women and girls, especially, denounced them. Their house lay in the highway to the old mill at Michelham, and many times had the husbands and fathers heard complaints from their spouses, who had passed homeward with the grist on their shoulders or on the ass's back of the behaviour of these rough, forbidding people. The past rose luridly, and ere the force had arrived at the point of action one woman, especially, was heard to say, "Pull the place down, and turn them out." This hint exactly suited George. He quietly and stealthily fanned the spark, and soon it burst into a flame. "Better," said he to himself, "have a lion for your neighbour than a woman for your enemy." The suggestion soon found an echo, and "Pull it down" said a second, and a third "Turn out the varmint; they will some day do murder."

The leader of the mob had no difficulty when the party came in sight of the dwelling in urging them to do his work. It was said the sisters had money. This idea, and the probabilities, whetted the greedy tooth of many among the party. There were unscrupulous men, and women too, ready for any treasure, let who might suffer, that they could grasp. The clamour of their voices preceded them, and the cloud of rising dust betokened the approach of the banded foe. The Foxes had taken several peeps out, and had turned their eyes and ears townward, wisting and listing as in anticipation of a storm. The storm was fast approaching, the cloud of dust drew nearer, the muttering voices became more distinct, and the brothers and sisters pretty accurately guessed their fate. The sisters were the first to fly. Their large stout pockets, one on either side, tied round their waist, secured their gold and other treasures, and, each with a pistol in hand, they fled southward to the shelter of the woods at the back of their house, and there among the trees awaited the issue of the day. Their foes had not observed them in their retreat. So far they and their gold were safe. The younger brother at that time was an invalid and unable to move; the elder had slipped over the road into the cover of the neighbouring wood. There he stood armed with the rusty and blood-begrimed cutlass, listening and awaiting the end of the fray.

When the constable and his party arrived the door of the family home was standing invitingly open. There was no parleying; a rush was at once made at the entrance, and no one, save the invalid, was within to receive the visitors. The sight of the helpless sick man in some degree moderated their passion, but the sick man would give no reply to the question, "Where are Arthur, Moll, and Bett." He sat stolid and would-be speechless. He did not know. This behaviour served only to inflame the anger of the mob, and to hasten the end. They were gone for help, was the ready thought of all The sick man was sitting in his chair, partly dressed. His blouse was taken from the peg on the wall and thrown to him, and in an instant he and his chair went over the garden hedge into the field adjoining. There he sat helpless, and looked on at the destruction. In less than an hour the house was razed to the ground. Enough brandy was found to give the party a drink. A bray of triumph resounded, and told the brothers, the elder of the two not being far away, the fate of their dwelling — that they had no more a home in the Hide Lane. The den of the Foxes, in our parish, was gone for ever. Fox Hall, as the place was called, had ceased to be.

The same evening Arthur was discovered by one of the party in the wood. He had become cowed and penitent, and offered compensation to the injured man. But Inskip's idea of justice was satisfied; the hurt was condoned in the destruction of the cottage. The wound soon healed, though the finger was never restored to use. The constable escaped censure, the hubbub quieted down, and there remained only the lump of the ruin to tell the tale. Every helper kept his own counsel, and all was soon over. The family after this sold the plot and materials to Mr. Mason, who at once built the present cottage, where, if you enter, standing on the brick floor, you may rub the crown of your head against the joist of the room above. After this the old owners retired over the border to Arlington — still the strong hold of the Foxes, both biped and quadruped.

## ILLICIT DISTILLING

As smuggling died out local and illicit distillation began, grew up, and became quite a trade among us. The leading men were well known. They belonged chiefly to the labouring class, broken-down smugglers, and others of lazy habits, men who would chance detection for the large profit of the traffic and avoidance of regular work. There was here and there a wise man among them; that is, wise enough to take care of his money. One especially I knew, who told me that the first £100 he saw he had earned and put by from illicit distilling, and he became in after-life a successful and an honourable man. The country carriers were deeply compromised in the trade — carrying in their carts the liquor to the various towns in the neighbourhood, where the publicans and the merchants became ready purchasers.

For some years the Excise officers made but few captures. But, as usual, boldness grew with success; then followed detection, conviction, heavy fines, and imprisonment without limit. So the traffic collapsed and died out.

The spirit was a vile liquid, easily detected by taste or smell. It had a slang name —"Dicker Flint." Why, I never could learn. The detection and capture, at times, of a party at full work has been somewhat exciting, and the various places chosen to put the "still" odd and romantic. It might be in the hollow of a wood, near some running stream; sometimes in a cottage or an out-house, close to the roadside; and one place of all others the most droll and daring was an old-fashioned wayside inn. The publican having more rooms in his house than his legitimate trade required, let two off for two such opposite purposes that the thought almost makes one laugh. The parish, which is large and scattered, has the church quite at the eastern end, so that the north and west were considered to be suffering from want of spiritual teaching and influence. There being no other accommodation to be had but at the inn, the good clergyman, making the best he could of the situation, hired of the publican a front room on the ground floor for weekly evening service, and here those who felt inclined met and worshipped, and the minister experienced great satisfaction in being able to administer to the spiritual wants of the people, and the landlord had the double gratification of pocketing the rent and supplying a local need. But the publican had another tenant just through the wall and on the same floor. There was the distiller at full work, and while one was offering spiritual advice and a prospect of heaven, without money and without price, the other, all silent and alone, was watching the drops trickling from the worm of the "still" that was making him the money — the publican taking rent from both parties, and all concerned working on together in perfect harmony; the clergyman, of course, in utter ignorance of his neighbour, the distiller. I have heard the publican and the distiller laugh over the affair, and tell with great glee how nicely they had managed to dish the parson and the Exciseman.

## The Fighting Age

A striking feature in our society fifty years ago [1] was that we were then in the midst of the fighting age. Scarce a week passed without a street row or fight, There were three distinct classes of combatants — first, those who fought to settle their differences, to avenge some fancied or real injury; second, those who were bemuddled with beer, and for no other reason but because they had fought together before; and third, the man who would throw up his hat in the fair, and thus give an all-round challenge and fight the man who would come forward for the love of the fray, and, as he thought, for his own honour and distinction. These last-named affairs were generally hard-contested battles, character for courage and endurance both being at stake, and he who won the fight was, ever after, looked upon

[1] Circa 1830

as a brave man and a hero, though often the conqueror was terribly punished. One of our octogenarians, at present alive, and well known to us all, carries to this day in his scarred face and broken nose the result of such a battle. He came out winner, but disfigured for life — a witness and a picture of bygone practice and character. He was one who would sing with Jack Scroggins —

> Oh, for the fighting days of old,
> When men were neither bought nor sold;
> When victory was the aim alone,
> And fighting crosses all unknown.

The one famous pugilist referred to in the introduction is John Gully, who, about the year 1805, fought his first prize battle on our common, and gives us claim to make capital of the event. His opponent was Pierce, who proved to be the victor, and won the stakes. Gully fought twice after this, and in both instances was the winner, and might have claimed the champion's belt, but he declined the blood-begrimed badge, and, quietly retiring from the ring, took to the turf for a profession. Here, as is well known, he managed matters so well that he soon won the confidence of the upper circle, made money, and ultimately became M.P. for the borough of Pontefract, and died an honourable and an honoured man.

Since those rough times customs and manners among us have much improved. If we have now no farmer and tradesman sots, the habit of drinking has not died out; we still drink too much. One little incident showing the power of beer, relating to the past, shall be given. Our barber, long since dead, was a drunkard — a sot. Poor fellow! he did not see, perhaps, his degradation, or, if he did, he endeavoured to delude others into the belief that he thought himself respectable by putting on an air of consequence and dignity. He wished to be called Mr. Duke, and would altogether repudiate barber. Tonsor, or hairdresser, it must be, if reference should be made to his trade and his services were required, but to ask for the barber was a high offence and misdemeanour, and one he would be certain to rebuke you for; but taking him altogether — and we had no choice in a second — he was a man one could not readily dislike. He was easy and polite, civil and obliging enough to satisfy the most fastidious, and, when his hand did not shake too much, a good shaver and hair-cutter; but as the refrain of the old song has it, "He must have his minnits." When the time came round who or what could prevent him? Many a time when a customer has been in the chair, his face lathered, and perhaps half-shaved, down would go the razor and out of the shop would bolt Mr. Duke, saying, "I'll be back in a moment"; and over to the "George" would he fly. His time had come round, and, let the moment be ever so inopportune or unseemly, the half-pint must be had.

## THE WOOD NYMPHS

The tale relating to our wood nymphs has ever been told as a true one. Our satyrs, fauns, and fairies, in the year 1814, were not mere phantoms of the brain, but beings made up of flesh and blood, bones and marrow — real living souls and bodies, laughing and sighing as the mental barometer moved up or down, languishing when hope failed, bright when desire was satisfied, angels of light and joy or of darkness and sorrow. In short, our nymphs were women, and belonged to a merry band of housemaids, milkmaids, chambermaids, and housewives, such as, in our changed condition of life, we shall never look upon again.

We will take one instance. Maidens or mothers, of whatever rank, do not now, as they would fifty years ago, put on a smock-frock, and, drawing a cord or belt round the waist, hie off to the woods for a day's nutting, carrying on the arm a bag wherein to shift the spoils plucked from the hazel boughs, these filled bags to be deposited in a chosen spot in the corner of the wood, where all the party would assemble ere they departed for home, each with the burden poised upon her shoulder, laughing, cracking, merry and munching, as they pass in single file along the narrow pathway. Among the many peculiarities and characters of those bygone days we could tell of our witch, and of our cunning man — he who would cast our nativity and foreshadow life by the aid of figures — of our ghosts and our

189

haunted houses. But we shall not raise a shadow of either to stand between us and this romance relating to our wood nymphs.

We will at once introduce our authority for all that belongs to the following narrative. It is to Will the Woodman, if any, that the credit is due, and we hold him responsible. But who that knew Will could doubt him? He was a man of fact. What he did see he did see, and what he believed he was certain about. He told his tales with no limping tongue nor wavering mind. When he had once settled a case, who or what could turn him? And various are the tales he has left floating about in the parish. This of the wood nymphs he delighted in, and many a laugh has he indulged in as he led his listeners on to the catastrophe — how the devil had been seen in human form, black as ebony, greasy as a tallow bag, sitting, unharmed, among the hissing flames, grinning and stirring up the embers that formed his throne, erected and made ready by unseen hands in the shady hollow of Tilehurst Wood. The situation and the circumference of these covers, being within a mile of our homes, are well known to us all.

From east to west the wood is intersected by a public footpath, and many a "ride" beside, to accommodate the foxhunter and the gunner, winds about the eighty acres. Fit place, it may be thought, for lovers to roam, to clasp hands, to sigh, to vow, if not to swear life-long fealty; but let us not be led away by fancy. This is to be no love-tale, no romance, neither of the head nor the heart. The woodman was no romancer. He, it has been stated, was a man of fact. He knew every rood of his ground — every crook and corner, every turn in the narrow ways, every hollow and every gorged pit; every oak, and all the varieties of undergrowth, and that among all these the silver birch, he had been heard to say, was his favourite — that she, with her fair skin and her tawny love-knots, was the queen of the woods. He could relate a variety of incidents belonging to animal life that had come to his knowledge by his familiarity with the woods. Here, as he was fond of saying, he was born; here he had lived, and here, it may be added, he died in old age, in the cottage sheltered by the ash and the oak, dose to a gateway that opened into his covers; and he had loved all that belonged to them, and, having an eye, he had noted many things. His head was his repository; it was in the folds of his mental cabinet that he stowed away his facts. Like many others of his time, he could neither read nor write. The "rogester" of his birth, as he called the document, could never be found; but for all these drawbacks, he was certain about a few things. He would declare, in spite of all doubters and unbelievers to the contrary, that he had seen young adders run, when suddenly alarmed, into their mother's mouth, and on one special occasion he had had the corroborated evidence of a fellow-workman to sustain him. The old viper, with a brood of six, lay basking on the level base of an oak which the previous year had been sawn down, dreaming, perhaps of the pleasures of viper-life, when lo! being disturbed by the woodman and his companion, the lady opened her jaws, and in glided the whole family, and the next moment all were safe beneath the root of the tree. In justice to Will's doubting friends, it must be added that, during his long life, though he had killed many an adder at this critical moment, he never could be brought to remember having opened one and taken out the young. This may, perhaps, be unfortunate for science, but in no jot did it abate the fact in Will's mind. He was certain the viper swallowed her young brood to protect them from danger.

The hedgehog, too, he denounced as an enemy to all game. He had "seen with his own eyes," as he phrased it, the partridge's nest poor piggy had destroyed, and right or wrong, he always put his heavy heel upon the prickly outcast. He knew all the birds, and declared they knew him, and that they and he were friends; all except the solitary crow he had an affection for. William was an affectionate man, and he loved a little nature. He had a strange tale about the cuckoo, or rather a story relating to an old grey parrot that had been for years (the bird, it was said, lived to be seventy) an inmate of the cottage, and a great favourite with his wife. That this bird should imitate the cuckoo living dose to the wood no one used to tame parrot life will be surprised at; but the curious part of the case is the bird sang "Cuckoo" in early spring, resuming the note before the real bird had made her appearance, and before that woodland sound, which all country people wait and watch for, had been heard. Here is an item for those hypercritical people calling themselves "naturalists"; those who are ever on the look out for something wonderful, and rarely satisfied with anything common people can testify to and under stand. But the woodman was as certain about the cuckoo, or parrot, as about the adders.

Then he had another tale about a man suspected to be a thief, who by Will's aid was captured in Tilehurst Wood by our parish constable, the master tailor. There had been ducks stolen from a neighbouring homestead. The lazy fellow was pounced upon lying on the ground fast asleep, with a duck beneath him, and though he protested he knew nothing whatever about the bird, was quickly handcuffed and taken before the nearest magistrate and charged with the robbery, the stolen property, as the constable triumphantly said, being found upon him. But his Worship soon decided that, as he must be ruled by the evidence, the case could not go before a jury. "You see, Mr. Constable, in your charge you said the duck was found upon the prisoner, and now you tell me the man was found upon the duck. He must be set at liberty, and the property restored to him"; and, swelling with pride and delight, his Worship cautioned the officer to be more careful in future. This case, too, William declared to be a true one.

But the story which most delighted him was that of the wood nymphs. It was a common saying in those days, if not an accepted fact, that should a party of girls go into the woods nutting on a Sunday, the devil would be there to befriend them by pulling down the boughs and otherwise helping. In what shape, form, or colour he appeared it had never been settled. These were points belonging to the spiritual, and to this day they have been left an open question, believed or not believed, involving no penalty; but that some had faith in the pretentious tale there can be no doubt, as Satan was often conjured into a sweetheart, met and welcomed. But be that as it may, in this case no such thing happened. Our party of five, two married and three unmarried, had upon this occasion worked on unprotected, and had more than once repaired to the place of final meeting and piled their bags, nearly filled with the nuts, in a heap, and had taken the last round for the day, and joining company at the gateway leading from the lane into the wood, marched thence towards the place of rendezvous in the hollow centre of the wood, laughing and singing, thoughtless of evil or of the sight that soon would discover itself, and wondering how it had happened that no hero had arrived to give them a kiss among the leafy branches and to help home with their burdens. But so it was; no helper came nigh. The unmarried grew testy and the married sneering. The last circle of the ride had been taken, when lo! in full blaze, there sat Satan upon the precious bags, looking happy and as if enjoying himself, the fire blazing up and lapping about his bare legs and loins. He was laughing and beckoning the party to come on. But this familiarity was more than the ladies could endure; they were, perhaps, conscience-smitten — it was Sunday. The next thought was about their lovers, who had failed to meet them, and next their own safety, and turning about quickly, they gave out a simultaneous screech that rang the wood over, the frightened penitents running off faster than their feet could safely carry them.

The woodman, who ever after was fond of telling this tale, declared he found them all together down in a heap, paralysed with fright, each having striven to outrun the other. He soon learned the cause of the dilemma, every woman pointing in the same direction, and declaring they had seen the father of all evil, and that they had left their nuts behind them in his possession. William, in recounting this part of the tale, declared he was at the moment rather bothered how to act. However, his advice was, "Go home and leave your nuts and Satan to me to deal with." He knew the spot, and was soon there, but the de'il a bag or cinder or old Nick could he see; a few dangling twigs broken by the wanton fingers of the girls as they had sat munching a crust, or an apple, and the trampled herbage, was all the appearance the place had of having been in possession of mortal or immortal. This, as Will phrased it, was to him "unaccountable." Had the devil visited the parish to turn rogue only? However, this point was soon settled, as the very next morning the bags, nuts and all, were found inside the garden gate of one of the cottages, restored, evidently, by human hands. But this did not satisfy. One poor girl declared she had heard her own name called out as they were running away, and in a familiar voice. This, of course, added to the general bewilderment, and soon it came to be a settled belief that the devil had been seen in Tilehurst Wood.

The solution of the mystery came in about two years. The Berkshire Militia had been quartered in our barracks, and had marched westward, and with the colours a tall, fat, stout negro, well known as Dan the Drummer, a fellow as full of fun as of good-nature. He had sauntered that afternoon into the wood, purposely to help the girls home with their burdens, and had discovered their store before he had met the owners. Seeing the opportunity, the bright idea flashed upon him of having a lark. He would frighten them and then help them home. He heard the approaching voices. So off came his clothes, and placing his scarlet tunic upon the pile, down he sat, naked, when he was instantly greeted with their cries and screeches, and seeing their sudden plight, he, reproaching himself, called upon them to stop. But this caused the lot to run all the faster, and to follow up, naked as he was, he saw would be adding to their terror. So, cursing his folly, he, quickly covering his bare limbs, decamped, taking the bags with him, and before he went to bed placed them, with their contents, over the cottage gate belonging to one of the party. This is the confession the drummer made a day only before the regiment marched. He had unwittingly played the part of the devil, and not caring to be his representative, was heartily ashamed of what he had done. It need not be said that all the flame and fire the women had seen was the scarlet regimentals upon which Dan had seated himself, and the devil upon that occasion was the good natured black drummer.

## THE PILLION AND THE HARVEST SUPPER

Among other things that have passed away in our parish is the pillion. Sixty years ago, we had our pillion in use. Then the old farmer, dressed in his white smock-frock, with his wife behind him, rode up to church on the back of the old horse, "Dobbin." The owner was Henry Hicks, yeoman, living on his own small estate near Otham-Quarter. The highway leading to his house was known as "Hicks's Drove," and the drove in summer was one of our sweetest

194

and prettiest old lanes, with a wide marsh ditch on either side. The way was garnished the whole distance with hawthorns of every shape, height, and bulk. There was no trimming nor training; Nature had formed them after her own fashion. They had grown high out of reach of the lowing cattle who sought shade beneath the clustering branches from the rays of the summer sun. The painted blossoms pleased the eye and pleasantly scented the air as you passed on a May morning between their thorny ranks. Grass to the ankle bedded your feet, and the walk was clean and pleasant. The saucy blackbird, chirping as he flew from bush to bush, with the more modest thrush, found here a home all the year round. There was beauty and security in summer and plenty with the hips and haws in winter. The sly magpie and the shy pigeon deigned to make the place the abode of love, and nested here. The moorhen and the water rat among the flags, the water-lilies, the rushes, and beneath the shelter of the over-hanging bushes, held undisputed sway and possession. Such was, and is now, somewhat the Drove in summer.

But see the place in winter, after a frost! For pedestrians it is impassable; the wheel-ruts are up to the axle; no cart, save the heavy-horsed miller's cart, ventures that way. The butcher's boy, with basket on his arm, makes the journey once a week on the old pony, picking and choosing as he goes the best footing. The mud is more than ankle deep; the flats are covered with water; the herbage is swept off; the bramble to the hardest tree is leafless; the decaying ash has no shelter for its naked limbs; the few stunted oaks moan as you pass by, drooping their heads eastward. All is desolate and chilling save the shining haws, tempting the fieldfare and redwing to join our home birds in their repast. If you venture up the lane, a snipe may spring up at your feet, and the heron will be watching as he thrusts his head only just enough above the bank of the watercourse in which he is fishing for his cold meal.

Such is no exaggerated description of the lane, as it was fifty years ago, whence Master and Mrs. Hicks emerged on the saddle and pillion on their errands to town shopping, or on their journey to church. I saw them but once as they dismounted on the block in the "George" yard on a Sunday afternoon; and this, too, was the only time I ever saw the pillion. It was said, perhaps maliciously, that upon one journey, when the old gentleman had arrived in the inn yard and was about to dismount, very much to his surprise and chagrin he found himself alone on the horse. He and his wife had started together properly seated, but at the end of the journey the pillion was naked and bare. The lady was not in her place behind her husband; she had been, by a lurch of the horse, thrown from her seat and left in the lane in the mud. The old man being deaf, had not heard her cry for help. He held on his way, little dreaming that his dear old partner was floundering about in the mire of the Drove. Luckily no serious damage was done. The surface of the ground was softer than her pillion, and if her dignity had been offended and her Sunday clothes spoiled, no bones were broken. The lady outlived the misadventure many a year.

The old-fashioned harvest supper, too, is an institution belonging to the past, when masters and men sat down at the same table, and soaked in nut-brown ale, brewed in the house in March or October, and carefully stowed away in the cellar until the following autumn. These meetings were merry ones. From the visitor down to the servant of the house, all was frolic and expectation — mistress and daughters, maids and plough boys sitting by, waiting to hear the men sing and toast the "founder of the feast." These suppers, save for the clatter of the knives and forks, were dull affairs, every man doing his best to demolish the puddings and the round of beef that steamed at the head of the table. There was little time, inclination, or breath for "table talk" — all were devout and earnest, thinking only of the present moment. There was "cut and come again" for all; but the heavy fare soon vanished, and considering the amount of work done, the feast was quickly over. Further pleasures of fines and extra glasses, of toasts and songs, of beer and tobacco glinted through the reek that rose from the burdened table, and the witching twinkle of the maids' eyes moved the young men to be echoing back some song or love-strain in reply.

But it is not until the cloth is removed that the real business of the evening begins. Beef may support and sustain, but ale charms and inspires; and though the juice of the grape touch not the rustic lip,

Bacchus reigns — John Barleycorn is supreme. More than once, years ago, have I had a seat with the rustics and the good-natured master at the long table in the large kitchen at the old farm-house at Otham Court.

Among farm labourers there is ever some speciality of character, some droll, or dolt, some grave, some I gay, one who is the great talker, another the chief singer; the hero, proud that he has been a militiaman, and once upon a time had, with his comrades, been complimented by the Lord Lieutenant of the County as a fine body of men, and fit to serve their King and Country in any land; and the returned warrior, too, the pensioner home from the wars, minus an arm, battling now with the hedges and in the harvest field, calm and as obedient to fate and fortune as when he faced the foe in a distant land.

These were all to be found around the old oak table, but chief among them was the singer. He who has, or he who has not, heard him sing —

> Lord Bateman was a noble lord,
> A noble lord of high degree,

may bless himself. It was a trial for the nerve, a subject for the eye, and a study for the mind. "Come Simmonds," says the master, "now we must have your song." The singer was waiting the call, and had swung himself round in the chair better to face the company. It was an accepted rule in those bygone days that no Sussex man could sing a song with his eyes open, and to this rule Master Simmonds was no exception. His preparation never varied. First he had twisted himself away from the table, the next to pull with both hands his somewhat long and new round-frock well above his knees, throw the left leg over the right, stroke the hair straight as he could down over the forehead, put his pipe between the middle fingers of the left hand, give vent to two or three ahems and haws, to clear, as he said, the passage of the wine-pipe, and off he would go, his strong lungs pulling his husky voice through all difficulties of rhyme or rhythm. His memory never failed him, and he was insistent upon the

*Otham*

recurring chorus; his eyes were shut, and never once looked out for light. He was then in his glory: his light shone full within him. Good Master Simmonds long ago now sang his last song. He has passed to his fathers, and the farm-house singer of his class has almost died out. When I knew him he was a thin, spare man, of short stature, high cheeks, hollow eye, straight lank hair, very angular in body, and with that characteristic of all Sussex ploughman, he was innocent of calves to his legs — so different from the sleek, well-fed footman. One never sees a labouring man who is in middle life that has "a leg to stand upon." These would-be ornaments, upon which a man may justifiably pride himself, are reduced to mere shanks. When Master Simmonds led off the catch or round —

> The miller's mill dog
> Lay at the mill door,
> And Bango was his name, O,

all the company standing, sang the theme thrice over. The leader then, turning to the man on his right-hand, said "B," the next would say "A," the third "N," the fourth "G," the fifth "O." Then the whole party broke out in chorus, "And Bango was his name, O." In this order the word worked round the table, and whenever there was a lapse in naming the proper letter the culprit, as a fine, had to toss off an extra glass of beer, and then very boisterous was the mirth. Drinking the health of the master and mistress was a serious part of the business of the evening. Here was involved duty — an expression of gratitude for the past and a promise of devotion for the future; and great was the effort of the guests to properly acquit themselves. There was one song above songs fitted for the occasion, and as the carter stood up and gave the call, visitors and servants were waiting and willing. From the silver-headed old man to the smooth, unfledged youth this was a time of honest pride. Another year had passed. They had sung, as the last load of sheaves had reached the barn —

> We have ploughed, we have sowed,
> We have reaped, we have mowed,
> We have carried the last load,
> And never overthrowed.

And here they stood again altogether in the grand old kitchen of the Court House, which, if not their dwelling place, they looked upon as next to their home; and the only change since last year's harvest was that they were all a year older. There had been no shifts from the carter to the cowboy; they were earnest servants all, and ready to sing in their master's praise. Their song opened like a trumpet-call—

> Come, come, come, ye sons of hearts,
> Come, come away:
> Tune up your voices, let your instruments play,
> For to celebrate this happy day.

And no troopers ever charged more heartily than did these devoted men and boys, their voices mingling in one shout to the founder of the feast and his good wife, the mistress. Then followed the health of the visitors, and then, of course, more beer, and-they sang —

> Then we all agree
> To spend this night most joyfully.

Whatever prudes may think or say about these old fashioned carnivals, these annual gatherings of rustic life, to those who have witnessed them and sat side by side with these hard-working men, there can be no doubt about the satisfaction to all concerned being great — to the ploughman and his boy, that the cultivation and the seed-sowing has not been in vain; also to the master, that the harvest is over and the barns are full, and that hope for the future is justified and in the ascendant.

> The farmer then to his full bowls invites his friends,
> And what he gets with toil with pleasure spends.

Depend upon it, there is no more genuine hospitality to be found nowadays than was to be met with in those old farm-houses.

## HORNE'S PATENT SAFETY

Horne's stage-coach — four-in-hand, licensed to carry four inside and twelve out — passed through our town from Eastbourne to London, up one day and down the next. The place of call was "The Crown." On the return journey, about four p.m., might be seen a few old cronies gathered together to greet the coachman, Samuel Rasan, their object being to learn the latest news from town, to crack a joke or two with the old whip, and to adjust watches and house clocks with London time, the driver being expected to give Horse Guards' time to a minute to any inquirer. The pulsation of this grand clock was then felt far and near, it being the chronometer for the whole country, and it was a privilege to be able to obtain the hour from this important authority.

What a pretty sight was the four-in-hand running at a gentle trot

*Horne's "Patent Safety"*

down the slight declivity into our old-fashioned street and pulling up at the old inn! It was a spectacle we shall see no more. Where is the man now who can handle the ribbons and guide and stop his team to an inch at the inn door as of yore? The professional whip is gone, and his art must be numbered with the defunct and lost ones. See him as of old, mount the box and take up his position, half-standing, half-sitting, and prepare for the start; mark how he gathers the reins in his hand and assigns to each finger its proper section, and then puts his horses together before he gives the final word to be off. Notice, too, the folds and coils of the whip as he raises it and gives a flourish over the heads of the animals, and takes, or pretends to take, a fly from the ear of the off leader. I remember her well — a flea bitten, skittish jade, lapping down first one ear and then the other, her behaviour appearing very suspicious; but the master valued her, and said her pranks were all in fun. With a peculiar chirpy whistle from the driver, off go the team, and the coach with its living cargo glides round "The Corner" — an awkward point — as easily and smoothly as would a stream of running water, and all are out of sight.

We considered Samuel Rasan a whip *par excellence*. All thought he need fear no rival, not even the "spendthrift son" in the "Road to Ruin," as he had been seen by one of our townsmen in a visit to London, at Sadler's Wells, to put his imaginary team through its facings; and our friend came home so much enchanted with the performance that he declared he had heard the rattle of the hoofs of the horses on the boards of the stage. Samuel Rasan was one of a well-known family belonging to Eastbourne. He was peculiarly fitted to do credit to his profession. Nature had dealt bountifully with him. With a good constitution and the hardening effects of out-door life, he had developed into a man who looked defiance to all weathers. See him in winter when wrapped in his box-cloth coat. Then he was a thoroughly representative man. The style of his hat had never varied, being made to pattern, with extra wide brim that stood out on a level all round. His broad face, from the effects of summer scorching and winter's blast, was highly tinged, and his deep flowing under-lip reminded one, for colour, and often times for cracks, of an over-roasted chestnut. Though naturally bluff, yet from continual intercourse with his numerous and varying patrons he was one of the politest and civilest of men. He was finally driven off the road by the uncompromising "iron horse," and we shall never look upon his like again. His occupation is gone, and he is gathered to his fathers.

Occasionally a passenger — a novelty — would be travelling up or down — a live turtle put on shore from some homeward-bound vessel, and sent on "express" by coach to London, sprawling on his back, strapped down to the crown of the "Safety." If the weather were hot, the ostler would treat his majesty of the soup-kitchen to a douche from the stable-yard bucket, reminding him that he was not altogether forgotten, and sending him on his way refreshed, if not rejoicing. Certainly we lookers-on thought that in a day or two he would be gliding down, pellucidly, into the gullet of some fat alderman. Sometimes going south would be the bare-headed, self-reliant blue-coat boy, escaped from the high walls of Newgate Street, out on a visit to his lone mother, who would be watching the arrival of her fair-haired, laughing urchin. His quaint dress made him to all other boys a wonder and a mystery. Poor laddie, with no hat or cap to cover his brows, how much we pitied him. But he was quite equal to a sixty mile journey, and we could see the old coachman and his independent fare were on very easy terms. I have often wondered if Charles Lamb ever visited Eastbourne in that guise, as all his readers know that in after-life, when he had outgrown the yellow stockings and thrown away the brown leather belt, that in vacation he made "Seaside" his place of refuge. What does he think now, turning his eye from Elysium on to his old quarters about Splash point, of all the crash and din of the last twenty years, and of the present grandeur and mockery of pleasure-seeking? We will await his reply rather than attempt to answer for him.

The old coachman has been heard to say that driving down the most interesting spot on the road was "Pinner's Hill," a point about half-way between our church and Polegate. There it was the sight of the sea broke upon those travelling outside the "Safety." To many it was the first sight of their lives. The blue waters of Langley Point and Pevensey Bay, bedecked with many a silvery sail, suddenly caught the eye, the effect upon the passengers being as various as their moods and natures, some sitting subdued in silence and wonder, while others sprang upon their feet and became enthusiastic in their exclamations of admiration at the first sight of the mighty ocean. What a change of conditions and circumstances we may now note, when at that time the coach was the only conveyance for passengers between Eastbourne and London.

A little affair in connection with this time may be recorded. As the coach, on one of the down journeys well laden with passengers, was gliding round "The Corner" a little girl, apparently unconscious of the danger, ran off the pavement on to the road, and at right angles with the leaders, and was all but under their hoofs, when a young man rushed at the child, and, catching hold of her clothes, rescued her. But so narrow was the escape, that the off-leader's head struck the young fellow on the cheek, and, as he said, "helped to drive him back out of harm's way." The mother of the child, petrified with fright for the moment, seeing the escape, sprang forward, and embracing the rescuer, kissed him heartily in the street. The passengers gave a simultaneous cheer, and the old coachman, nervously twirling his whip, shouted out, "Bravo! Bravo!" And this was the last time I ever heard the sound of his deep-toned voice.

## THE COOPER'S SIGN

Even in the smallest communities there is often to be found some eccentricity of character that marks the trade, profession, or time to which the individual belongs. The writer of this would rejoice in an odd fellow or two who had wit and humour — one given to jest — who could be referred to as the Merry Andrew of the place — a funny fellow who could, by chance even, say a good thing. But we have never had such an ornament to our society; we have never had a fool of the witty class.

This little rigmarole is to serve as an apology for introducing a rhyming sign which some few years ago hailed the passer-by, in black and white, on a board fixed to the front of our cooper's shop. At the time it attracted considerable notice, and the traveller often pulled up to read and to be amused, much to the gratification of owner and author. He said:—

> As other people have a sign,
> I say — just stop and look at mine!
>
> Here, Wratten, cooper, lives and makes
> Ox-bows, trug-baskets, and hay-rakes.
> Sells shovels, both for flour and corn
> And shauls, and makes a good box-churn
> Ladles, dishes, spoons, and skimmers,
> Trenchers, too, for use at dinners.
> I make and mend both tub and cask,
> And hoop 'em strong to make them last.
> Here's butter prints, and butter scales,
> And butter boards, and milking pails.
> N'on this my friends may safely rest —

In serving them I'll do my best;
Then all that buy, I'll use them well,
Because I make my goods to sell.

Our poverty in novelties must be the excuse for introducing this rhyming sign. The occasion, however, will serve to show off another rhyme — an answer to a request from a friend at a distance, who, passing through our place, had read the cooper's sign. Perhaps it would have been as well, or better, had the writer not capped his verses with Scripture; but for that he must be accountable.

"AND THEY ASKED OF HIM A SIGN."
The Jews, we read, required a sign,
For which they asked the Saviour;
A sign they got, well suited to
Their impudent behaviour.

About poor Jonah, who was made
A bait for a great fish —
The whale, we're told — who carried him
Contrary to his wish.

But you, dear sir, ask for the sign,
Truly transcribed on paper,
Of our good cooper, which I know
Is free from boast or vapour.

For should you want a pail, or tub,
Or cask, or hoop, or pattern,
You've only just your orders to
Give to the cooper, Wratten.

A cooper good as ever stood
Beside a pail or tub, sir I
He'll hoop 'em fast and make 'em last;
He does it for his grub, sir!

205

Here is another trade joke. A facetious cobbler, who had been a soldier, and settling down in one of our small towns in the neighbourhood, put on his board over his shop-door following his name, "F. R. S." Soon after he was visited by a stranger, a gentleman, who, offering his hand, feelingly inquired how it happened that a Fellow of the Royal Society should be found in so humble a position; but the man readily explained that he knew nothing of the Royal Society nor its letters. He had only, he said, initialed his last profession as Fifer in the Royal Surrey, and as he hoped the letters would attract attention and bring him customers, he did not feel disposed to alter the sign.

## AN ADVENTURE, SHOWING HOW I WENT OUT TO SHOOT A CROCODILE

It was in the spring of 1850, and it happened one morning while I was engaged in my business occupation that a neighbour, who lived opposite, called upon me, and, in rather a suppressed tone of voice, told me his errand, and requested me to accompany him to a certain field not far away. My friend was a well-known man in our town — jovial, hearty, and honest. He stood six feet one or two out of his shoes, was of heavy weight, fearless in countenance, with a voice that would make the house ring, the welkin rattle, and echo repeat herself — a brave companion to go abroad with upon any adventure. I was to him, if not a pigmy, a very light weight indeed. When he had told me his tale, I looked up to him with a considerable amount of confidence. I said to myself, "Here is Goliath, and if only I can be as brave as David, surely we shall do!" For the venture I thought rather a bold one.

First, let me confess to a certain weakness or hobby I had, and it still clings to me. I am very fond of the gun; I was always ready to go out to kill something. It is a strange feature in many an Englishman's character. I know many a good man now who likes going out to kill something. Do you require an excuse for such a man? Well, all I will say is, it gives him exercise and health, and I have yet faith in the gun. My friend and neighbour, in an undertone, said, "Have you your gun handy?" "Yes," I said; " what is the matter?" "Well," was his reply, "you know the six acre meadow, 'The Tutts,' don't you?" "Yes," said I; "go on," feeling a little fidgety as the gun had been named, and I wanted to be off. "Well," said he again, "you know the post and rail fence and the bar way leading into the lower field?" "Yes," I said; "and what of that?" "Well, just as you get through, and on the right hand, and close under the hedge, there is a little bank covered with scrub, and brake, and brier" — and stirring himself up a bit as he continued, "There among the stuff lies a large crocodile, and I want you to go with me to shoot him."

Of course I was somewhat staggered, and before consenting to his request, asked him to consider. "First," I said, "are you sure that what you have seen is a crocodile? You will remember it is rather a funny fish to be found in a field in the South of England." However, nothing I said moved my companion in his opinion. He was sure he had seen the monster's eyes "and all that"; so I was fain to be satisfied, and wanted to be off. I had a prospect before me of having something to shoot at, and that was enough to urge me on to any adventure.

But a few moments' reflection caused me again to pause. I remembered that I had read that the crocodile is impervious to gun shot. I had seen the passive and repulsive creatures in the Regent's Zoo, and I had a very vivid recollection of the narrative of the intrepid and eccentric Waterton and his ride upon the cayman's back in America, with his shirt-sleeves tucked up to his shoulders, tugging away at the creature's fore-legs to keep it from skidding, while his naked companions were hauling them both high and dry from the river, where the monster had been taken by the bait laid for him.

But having said that I was ready, I made all haste to be off. I had a great pride in my gun — almost an affection for "her." I believed I owned one of the best — a regular sharp-shooter. I have known many a man who has had the best gun. It is well we should think so; it gives confidence when a long shot offers, and helps oftentimes to fill the bag. Well, down came the gun from the rack; the largest shot to be had in the town was purchased; click, click went the triggers, flash went both barrels, that there might be no mistake when the critical moment arrived, and off we started.

We had a full half-mile before us ere we reached the fields, and one may be sure during the walk no other subject engaged our thoughts or conversation. I had not quite made up my mind as to the creature we were about to see. A crocodile, I thought, was a most unlikely animal to be found in a green or any other field. "Are you sure," I said, by way of stirring my friend up, "are you sure the creature you have seen is not a lion? And then, if it should be, what will become of us?" At this challenge he fired up, and settled the point by declaring that he had had a full view of the brute's head and his eyes, and the scales upon his shoulders, and that the body was drawn out of the hedge, and was as big and as long as one of the sheep feeding in the adjoining field. Well, after this I gave up all opposition, and became (though against my will) convinced; but the climax was arrived at when he suddenly stopped and, searching his pockets, declared he had forgotten to take his long-bladed spring back Spanish knife, as he earnestly said, "to hamstring the rascal."

We were now approaching,the gate leading into the field, and my heart was beating quicker — in fact, I believed in the crocodile, and had made up my mind for a fray with him. We were soon within a few minutes' walk of the spot where the game lay. A gentle rise for half the length of the field kept the exact point from our view. The declivity would be seen in a moment, and I called "Halt!" My misgivings, or I may say my fears, had increased. I calculated upon a catastrophe — an unpleasant one. I said, "We shall be overmatched and routed, or we shall be over taken, and I, being the most convenient size, may be gobbled up, and while I am going down into the creature's belly, my companion will escape." Of course I said all this mentally. I had, however, amid these thoughts, considered a few words of advice and caution, which, on halting, I imparted to my friend. In an undertone I said, "Don't be in a hurry; take good aim. You fire first; let me see the result, and I will be in reserve."

With this we topped the hill, and could see the brakes and briers, which were waving in a gentle wind, and reflecting the sun's rays, brightened up by a hoar frost that yet hung about the ground. I had no need to say, "Where is he?" for sure enough there he lay. I saw distinctly all my friend had described — the head, the eyes, the scales; but we had no time to reconnoitre, for in a moment off went his gun — Bang! bang! Doubtless many of my readers have heard of Crocodile Island — that desolate spot in mid-ocean given up by man to the amphibia. The verbal narration of an adventurer, who said he had been ship wrecked and cast alone on this island, so excited the sympathy of one who was listening to the marvellous tale of his friend that he suddenly exclaimed, "And how the deuce did you get off again?" "That," replied the professional writer — for he was a scribbler to the magazines and the monthlies — "is my dilemma. I have written my article up to that point, and how to get off again from that island I do not know. Here my pen refuses to go on; and cannot you help me?"

For my own part I am thankful to say I have no such difficulty. I have only to tell the reader — and I do so with a tinge of shame —that our crocodile was only an old straw hat. The aim had been so good, and the concussion so great, that the dingy old thing was lifted high over the hedge into the adjoining field. A few more words will explain how our mistake occurred. My friend held some meadow land and was taking a short cut to visit his pastures, when it occurred to him that a hare might be found in the brakes and briers already described; and casting a searching glance on the spot, two glaring eyes met his own — imaginary, nevertheless real to him. His blood chilled, his hair stiffened, his pace quickened, until he arrived at the bottom of the field, when he paused a moment, and, concluding that he had seen a crocodile, came straight away for me and his gun. The difference between an old straw hat and a crocodile is so great, that one can hardly believe two sane men, as we certainly considered ourselves to be on that special morning, could suffer such delusion. Nevertheless, all the leading points in the narrative are strictly true. The conclusion shall be a hint to all: Never allow yourself to be surprised. Look, think, reason, and then quietly decide.

## Out of My Orbit: Reminiscences of Alfriston

I wonder how many times in my boy-life visits to Alfriston the sound of the tanner's hammer has come out to meet me; when I had left home with bounding heart and light heel anticipating joys that in those early days were rarely denied me? The tanner and his hammer are silent enough now; both have many a year been laid low. The walk was a pleasant one, and for a mile or two quite arboreal, the solitude being woke up by a general chorus of all our well-known birds, both singing and chattering. The squirrel frisked and bounded from limb to limb in the oaks that nearly met overhead.

My favourite way lay through Robbing Post Lane, wrapped in by two very extensive woods, perhaps two miles in length, and as many in breadth, partly in our parish and partly in Wilmington; in winter miry and impassable, in summer shady and delightful. In a boy traveller's mind there might have been some misgivings as to safety, and in case of molestation crying for help would little avail; but though danger might sometimes be talked about, no mis-adventure was ever heard of in this old by-way. On a Sunday afternoon or evening it was the Cacklebury lovers' retreat, where vows were made and future appointments entered into, and no greater witchery than love engendered ever belonged to the place. No ghosts stood in the way to pall or to terrify the midnight traveller. Smugglers there might be, but, notwithstanding the ominous name (Robbing Post), highwaymen, never. The passage was at all times perfectly safe, and the chances were you never met a fellow creature. The trail of the adder, where he had wriggled across the road in the dust, might be seen, and also the green lizard lying motionless, basking in the sun. He is a fire-worshipper. Put yourself between him and his god — that is, put him in the shade — and like all other creatures of fixed principles, he will soon resent the affront, and deliberately wriggle off into his home in the old oak stump, whence he had with drawn to worship and to gratify his longings.

Passing on to New House, the home of the Gosdens, we soon arrive at the old crossways, where, on a triangular bank, stood the solitary oak, said to have grown from a stake driven through the body of a suicide — a soldier tired of life, and buried here ignominiously. This, of course, was a haunted place, and had its terrors. It was said that the drum and roll-call had at times been heard here, but the poor fellow never gave in his name. He had paid dearly for his follies; drink had been the enemy that had vanquished him, and perhaps his desire was to be forgotten. The spot is now occupied by a snug cottage; smiling, ruddy children play about the lintels of the door. The well to-do woodman has his cow, and the wife her hens and chickens, and all is peace and plenty — a good example of cottage life, of thrift and industry.

Mountain Pin Green is next seen, a small waste yet unenclosed; and through the fields on the right-hand we soon find ourselves in a genuine old lane, now severed by the railway, then crossing the "New Road" close by Wilmington Gate. In a few minutes we are in the Running Field, a large meadow of Milton Street Farm, and on the eastern border of which stands the farm house. Here, on the soft turf, as our grandmothers have told us, was the May-pole set up, and the farm lads ran and wrestled for the prizes, and the lasses, dressed as became the day and the occasion, together with the lads, danced on the first of May (old style), and the prettiest girl was crowned queen for the year. Cricket is now allowed, and the young men and the boys practise and play the annual match in the Running Field. It was here-abouts that the boom of the tanner's hammer, in its regular sequence, generally met my ear, and I was soon over Longbridge, and settled down among my Alfriston friends. Perhaps some will say, "Why all this prosiness?" One reason is, I love to look back and dwell in memory on these little reminiscences of youth. The journey, the visit, and the welcome were all real pleasures, and I love to remember so happy a time —

.... When meadow, grove, and stream,
The earth, and every common sight,
To me did seem
Apparelled in celestial light.

But there were other affinities that tied me to the place, and Alfriston had become a rival to my native home. It was here in the old town that my mother, the eldest daughter of a yeoman of Hellingly, being maid-of-all-work, from the lady and her toilet to the scullery, at £5 a year, became betrothed to the shoe maker. Here they married, the bride walking to church across the Tye in her best pattens, the tanner and his wife, with whom she lived, giving at their own house the wedding dinner; and here the couple began life on eighteen shillings a week, with flour at three-and sixpence a gallon, and bacon, butcher's meat, and candles at eighteen-pence a pound; and they, as I have heard them relate, being determined to live within their income, managed every week to lay a trifle by for coming extra expenses. It was in the following year, 1813 (myself in embryo), we migrated to the promised land and pleasant town of Hailsham, and finally, out of affection to the minister, the chapel, and the people, it was there that I was taken, baptized, registered, and qualified for Christian burial.

Up to this date Alfriston had flourished. There was a considerable brewery, with its vans and drags, sleek horses and burly-faced draymen. There were the tanners, the tawers, and tallow-melters, the candle makers and the soap-boilers, master builders too, doing a good trade; maltsters and the Excisemen, coopers and shoemakers by the dozen. The butcher did a large business, and made money. The two old inns were always full of company; volunteers and militiamen filled the place. Drinking, cursing and swearing (as now) went hand in hand. Barges floated down the Cuckmere and round to Newhaven, returning with merchandise of all sorts. The old town was at the height of its glory, but the hour of change and decay was at hand. The day of Waterloo sounded the knell to the prosperity of many a town on the Sussex coast besides Alfriston. The barracks round about were swept away, the canteens were gone, and the soldiers disbanded and sent to their homes, and their many wants went with them. A vast amount of the nation's money had been spent along the Sussex coast, but with Waterloo the end had come.

There was one man in the old town who had seen the hand-writing on the wall. He had discovered the anti climax, and to him it was a precipice. His dead body, in his riding-dress and top-boots, was found in the river at the back of his home. In all his opportunity he had secured no provision for his wife and family; so he made short work of his troubles: a midnight plunge and all was over.

After Waterloo a gradual change and decay set in. Ultimately the brewery rotted to the ground, and the vaults and cellars became a retreat for dogs and truant boys and girls to skulk in. There was no sale for such property. The brewer's occupation was gone, there being not enough mouths to drink nor money to pay for the beer, and so what befell the brewhouse followed and swept away all the other principal trade buildings. The fine tannery became a desolation, and the work men drifted away into other occupations and other homes; and so it has came about that the grocer, the shoemaker and another one or two minor callings are all that is left of the once flourishing trade of Alfriston. The half-dozen better-class houses on the old Berwick Road are all there is standing to mark the prosperous times.

And now what can be said of the people? Why, this first, that they were eminently religious, earnest, devout — the men as well as the women. The great majority were Dissenters, Lady Huntingdon's people, and not to be deterred by trifles. A new chapel was wanted; the congregation had outgrown the capacity of the old place of worship. A new one was soon built. As in Nehemiah's day, so now. Here the people laboured with their own hands. Some collected flints on the adjoining hills; some carted these to the place of building; others made up mortar and mounted the scaffold. The walls were soon up, the roof was soon on, and the place ready for religious service; and a commodious and substantial building it is. It was a time, and a fit time, among these earnest people for rejoicing, the opening of this new chapel. A thoroughly good and well-educated man was George Betts, the first minister I remember. How reverend his look as he entered the pulpit, robed in his black gown and white linen bands! He reminded me of an illustration I had somewhere seen of Paul preaching at Athens. So good a face, so free from all rant, and such presence had he that, to look upon him, *he could be believed upon trust*! The choir was a study with him. Occupying the gallery, facing the minister, they sang with precision, power, and judgment, and the whole congregation joined. It was well-known miles round that the singing was good, and this, it was calculated, drew many into the fold; and, doubtless, the calculation was a correct one. The bass was well done by four stalwart, deep-voiced men standing boldly up in the front seat — the miller, the builder, the farmer, and the shoemaker; the trebles and second trebles sang effectively; and with the tenors, all together made up a well-balanced harmony. This with the Alfristoners was a happy time. The place had become a religious centre; they had made themselves heard round about among the hills, and for a few years all went well. They had become a marked, a spiritual people.

But alas for human frailty and man and woman's fate and misfortunes! Under all this glare, this radiance, this halo of religious life, Satan was among them. Asmodeus, that limping devil on his two sticks, had penetrated to the inmost chamber of the heart and the home, and he had *blabbed*. The itching ear of Scandal had caught the whisper, and Rumour, with her double tongue, had given it life and spread abroad the poison, and the sinning brother was caught up and gibbeted. Naturally, at first he recoiled, and then turned and defied his accusers and pursuers. The case of necessity came before the "Church," that lurid, self-satisfied tribunal from which there is no appeal; but personal explanation cannot wipe out scandal. Sins are not, upon earth, so easily forgiven. The "Church" and the congregation upon this became divided, and a rent was made that has never been healed up, and the consequences that followed were sad in the extreme.

The question now presents itself to me, Why should the tale be told? "And why not?" echoes my neighbour, the Churchman. " 'Twas only a free fight, was it, on a Sunday morning in the Dissenters' chapel, for the pulpit?" And he added, "Did you ever know a Churchman spared for his slips and slides, aye?" Well, there were other things doing at that time in Alfriston besides free fights, and these were not a few. The devil appeared to have possession of the people, and the place by degrees had acquired an ill fame. One characteristic of the women was street-gossiping, hanging about the door-posts, conjecturing the future, and talking of the past. "I wonder what has been going on to-night?" said Mrs. Snarley to the pale faced baker-boy, as she took the hot roll from his basket. "I wonder what we shall hear of next? The carts have been running again like mad. Did you hear them?" "No," said the boy; "I slept through everything.

I don't know. Master said, though, as he was drawing the rolls, that the ghost was out again last night, and that it vanished at the old place on the side hill." "Ah," said Mrs. Snarley, "the White-way ghost you mean. We are sure to hear of something bad when that walks; we shall soon hear of murder again, I fear." "That we shall, sure," squeaked a wizen voice from the next door. Mrs. Dobbs had at that moment caught the fragrance of the rolls, and had stepped out to procure one for her breakfast. "That we shall," again said Mrs. Dobbs. "I heard the carts and the voices, and sure enough there has been evil afoot again to-night." " 'Twas the smugglers," said Mrs. Snarley. "Or something worse," said Mrs. Dobbs. "We shall hear of murder again, I fear, Mrs. Snarley," she added. Mrs. Dobbs, though she was fasting, was in her talking mood. "Mrs. Snarley," she said earnestly, "let me tell you what I have heard about the poor fellow's fingers being smashed. I had it from the mouth of one of the 'company.' The man said, 'We were all lying down in the furze expecting every moment to hear the call. The boat was nearing the shore, when the coastguardsman came along, walking his beat on the turf on the top of the cliff. There was no time for waiting; the tackle for lifting was all in its place. The men below were at the bows of the boat, and up the tubs must come. We could see the guards man just a moment; then there was a cry, and we were called forward. We saw no more of the guardsman that night; he, perhaps, was walking onward on his beat, marked out by a row of white chalk-stones. Perhaps the line had been broken, and the white marks taken on to the edge of the cliff, that the poor fellow might walk over, for, said the man, our masters did not stop at trifles them nights. However, we men soon shouldered the tubs, and was off.' " "Lord," groaned Mrs. Snarley, "what shall we hear next?" "Why," said Mrs. Dobbs, "next day the poor guardsman was found dead on the beach, just about the spot where the boat was worked. He might, you know, have walked over — a five-hundred feet drop — but some say he hung on and cried for mercy, and that his fingers were trod upon to make him let go his hold. Anyhow, next morning there he lay dead, and that is how they account for his fingers being smashed!" "Oh, Lord!" again ejaculated Mrs. Snarley, " 'tis always so when the ghost walks; 'tis

215

a wonderful thing, that ghost is." " 'Tis a wonderful thing," repeated Mrs. Dobbs; "and that it never comes townwards is more than I can under stand." "It always goes on towards Burnthouse, or is seen returning to that one spot in the hillside, where it vanishes," said Mrs. Snarley. "This is as great a mystery as the presence of the ghost *hisself*," said Mrs. Dobbs. " 'Tis a man ghost, then, is it?" said Mrs. Snarley. "So the walking-post always says," answered Mrs. Dobbs, "and he walks the road every night in the year, and has seen the young man, as he calls him, oftener than any other person about here. He is an oldish man now, is the postman, and he says it always goes into the hill just about one place." But the rolls were getting cold, and the crones separated to eat them.

It was no mere fancy, the foreboding of ill between these two old women. The place at that time was under a very dark cloud. There had settled down in the old town a young man, whose position and start in life promised success. The son of respectable parents, the husband of a young and good wife, himself of fine presence and robust health, with good business capacity and good capital, all things were a promise to him, and all might have been well, but he resisted not, and eagerly ran out to meet his fate. He became the leader of a party of smugglers who, for miles round, were known as the "Alfriston Gang" — a terror to the neighbourhood. The hills, the dales, and the cliffs of the downs were well known to them, and the old town by degrees became the centre of their meetings. Then it was that the disturbance among the chapel people had arrived at its height, and a row was looked for. Among these religionists the numerical strength of the rival parties was pretty equal. Moral right went with the minister and his adherents, popular feeling also; and though possession is said to be nine points of the law, their legal right was questionable. Money and property undoubtedly was on the side of the accused, the erring trustee and deacon, and he had determined, as persuasion and threats had failed, to fight to get rid of the old minister, Mr. Betts.

At that time there were among these good people a pair of blue eyes and a mellow voice that attracted me, and always welcomed my visits. These eyes acted as scout, and an intimation arrived, stating that next Sunday the trial of strength would be sure to come off. An early morning walk landed me in the street, and I soon saw preparations for the coming fray. The friends were gathering together in front of the minister's house. Their look was defiant. They were all ready to do their duty and stand by their old and reverend master. They wanted no change of minister; but sinners, they said, rich or poor, must be reproved. They had buckled on the armour and had come out to fight, to the help of the Lord against the mighty, and all, too, in their Sunday clothes.

We will now marshal out the opposing forces, or rather visit them in their citadel. They had stealthily entered the chapel and had been in possession the whole night. The Sabbath sun, as he rose from his slumbers, blushed upon them, if not for them, on their chosen battle-ground. They had improvised a parson and put him in the pulpit — alas! only to be shot at — poor, good honest man, who dared not refuse his employer. He had been for years an occasional preacher, a "supply" to various needs round about the country. With pale face, lank hair, in his amateur black, in the decline of life, he had been seen many a Sunday, miles away from home, to mount the pulpit steps, telling the good tidings. He was the least envied man that day as he stood a target for his enemies to shoot at, and at whom all the arrows flew. His was the centre of the position, and the cry was, "Out with him! Betts for ever!" Another force, not yet recognized, will by and by show itself. The back slums of the "George Inn" were within hailing distance from the chapel. The devil that day, if he would help, would be hailed by either party as a friend. A dozen frowzy, reeking men, some well-known, especially the leader — others were strangers — came at the captain's call. They were ready for any work — the rougher the better — they were wanted for. It might be some among them had seen the coastguardsman go headlong over the cliff, heeding not his cry, and they quailed not. An anticipated row, a fight in a place of worship, a place they looked down upon, with contempt — 'twas glorious! They lay like hell-hounds in the slips, too ready for the call, writhing and chanking at the restraint that held them, drinking success to the captain and the party the captain favoured. We shall see them make their dash before long.

The time for morning service is at hand. The side door of the humble dwelling near the market cross opens, and first out walks the constable of the Hundred, carrying his staff of office — that emblem of authority and order — erect. He looks grave; it may be he questions the propriety of his mixing up and siding with any faction even religious faction. Next the minister steps on to the neat gravel path that leads from his door to the street. He too is pale, and looks sad and serious. 'Tis a heavy hour with him, good man. He is robed in his gown; he limps in his gait as he follows his friend the constable, Mr. Jenner, farmer, of Winton House, and the two together head the company. The order is given, and they march. Chapel Lane is soon reached. There are many in the street looking on and conjectur ing which party will be the conqueror. "Providence favours the strongest battalions," said the greatest general in Europe. Well, the hour, the moment to settle that point — who shall win? — has arrived. The chapel door is challenged; there is no response. It is locked and barred. In a moment the bars and the bolts would have yielded to force. Luckily, or unluckily, at this moment an old lady stepped to the door seeking admission; she has given her name through the keyhole. She is a friend to the party within. The door moves cautiously on its hinges; a rush is made; in an instant the old lady is thrust aside, and the outworks are in the hands of the invaders, and they advance hastily to the grand attack. The bulk of the followers dash into the galleries, and the fray is at its height. Poor Master Sands! How much I pitied him. He has two *friends* with him in the pulpit — a body guard. The steps, too, are covered with determined looking men. A double row surrounds the sanctum, the Communion table and the desk. The defence is stubborn; but soon the double guard is broken, the stairs are stripped of the balustrades and the staves used as weapons. The men are seized by the heels and dashed on to the floor. Those in the pulpit throw back the assailants in front and side, and the stairs are again in possession of the first defenders. The final result is growing doubtful to those not in the secret. Blood begins to flow, coats are torn and rent up the back, dust rises in a cloud to the ceiling, women scream, daughters passionately entreat the father to retire from the disgusting strife. But at that moment there was to be no surrender on either side. The old minister stands aloof beneath the gallery, passive, motionless, helpless. A tear is stealing down his pallid cheek. Does he muse on the effect his preaching has had on these people? his ministry of so many years? Poor man! let us pity him, as he knew no way out of the dilemma, only that, as his friends had determined to fight, he must wait and abide the result. And they, too, must win. A drawn battle would make matters worse, and so at this juncture the ambush was signalled, and a dozen stout, swarthy roughs came bounding into the chapel; and they were not without their leader, a man in the prime of life, a resident, who had earned for himself a notoriety for miles round. He was known to be a smuggler, and suspected to be a thief. In a few moments Master Sands and his two friends were marched down defeated. The fight was over — discretion was deemed the better part of valour. The way cleared, the rival preacher mounted the steps, stripped of the protecting balustrades, and took his accustomed seat in the pulpit. Calm and serenity soon crept over his brow. He was reinstalled, and his party had triumphed. His grim opponent stood beneath him, unabashed, but, for the day, beaten. He was a man of matchless courage, or rather, stubbornness. He mounted a form, and would be heard. Railing shouts arose from the lookers-on; he was thrust down and defied. Blood was trickling down his pallid cheek; his dearest relations implored him to retire. At this juncture an old lady, standing  in front of the gallery and leaning forward, raised a cry that soon settled the wavering trustee and his party. "Betts for ev-er!" screeched the old woman. " Betts for ever!" resounded over the whole place; and for that day the question who should reign was decided. The vanquished then quietly retired; the people soon settled down into the seats. The service began by forthwith singing a hymn — it might be — but for this I will not vouch—

> God moves in a mysterious way
> His wonders to perform;
> He plants His footsteps in the sea,
> And rides upon the storm.

*Alfriston Church*

In the prayer and sermon that followed no reference was made to the fight that had preceded these devotions, thanksgivings, and praises. The text was "If God be for us, who can be against us?" The most notable thing was the presence of the ten or twelve swarthy men sitting in a line across the chapel to prevent a surprise and a recapture of the pulpit. The troubled waters and the billows that had heaved so high had subsided, but the calm was of short duration. There was to be no real rest for the conquerors. Their arrows had entered the soul of the vanquished, and left there a rankling that nothing short of submission (on the other side) would satisfy, and the case eventually went into the law courts, and there money and law won the day. The cry of "Betts for ever" proved to be a vain one. A stranger soon occupied the pulpit.

It will be but just to give some cause for all this hubbub. There is an old saying, that no misfortune befalls a man but a woman is at the bottom of it, and in this case, if the naked truth could be told, we should find the "deceased wife's sister" — that yet unlaid ghost, that "ecclesiastical cobweb" — to be the moving cause of all these troubles. The sin, if any, was venial, and might have been condoned. The case appears to read us this lesson — Christians, be not righteous over much!

Alfriston Parish Church at that time, to use a secular phrase, was at a great discount. Its influence for good was scarcely felt. The half timber-built vicarage house — a ruin — was occupied by the parish clerk and a labouring family. The churchyard was a scandal and a desolation. The inside of the church was a miserable hole; its walls damp and discoloured; green stains, narrowing as they descended, showed the leakage in the roof. Sparrows had taken possession through broken panes, and muted and besmeared the seats. Loose swinging ivy rustled and moaned on the outside of the windows. Truant pieces, finding their way through the loose flapping casement, hung sickly and pale, and the old high, dark-coloured pews formed a groundwork that gave a finishing touch to the sombre and melancholy interior. The Vicar was a pluralist and non-resident. The parish had the benefit of but "half a curate." Few indeed were the communicants, and the congregation was very small. Sloth had enervated and blighted the Church, and overheated zeal and strife had smitten and cursed dissent. Religion, and that which should be the fruit, industry and good morals, languished for many a year.

Alfriston, or King Alfred's town, as the antiquary would have it, is a quaint old place, having for its chief architectural curiosities the remarkable old inn, the "Star," and the market cross standing in the centre of the street. It is the antique town of the district, and carries our ideas back as far as — if not farther than — any inland town of East Sussex. Here it has lain nestling by the side of the Cuckmere, and lapped in by the hills for many a dark century. No history reaches its beginning, and the future promises but little change. Fifty years ago [1] a visit might have put a stranger under strange influences. Then it was enchanted ground, where stood the City of Somnambula, where the night queen reigned; when the houses were petrifactions, and whence the inmates looked out sleeping. Stranger!

[1] Circa 1830

221

*Star Inn, Alfriston*

now even if you need a change from every day life, visit the old town
and eat your mutton at the "Star Inn," kept by the widow Page. Fifty
years ago Mrs. Page was married at Hailsham (may the lady pardon
me). At that time she was the belle of our village — the pretty Ann
Wood. The two miles' walk from Berwick Station, or, better still,
over the Downs from Seaford, will give a sharp appetite, and if your
imagination be keen too, you may fancy you are in the same house
and under the same roof where good King Alfred ate his cake and his
Southdown mutton. Reader, despise not legend, for legend tells us
many a tale by which we have picked back through the dark, and
found, that "glittering gem," the truth. When "Dickey" Hutchings
kept the "Star," the management appeared to be in characteristic
hands. A little bit of antiquity was Richard Hutchings, dressed in
knee-breeches, grey stockings, and bright buckled high lows, as, on
a morning, he perambulated in front of the old house, shaking off the
fumes of the over-night tobacco, and setting his brain in order for the
day. He was a spare bit of humanity, no representative man, no

Boniface who had lived, eaten, drunk, and slept on his ale, who would say, "It's Burgundy, and worth ten shillings a quart." His face was innocent of blotches, and his thin nose told no tale of the brandy bottle. His hair hung lank on his temples and brow, and was of that unfortunate colour best represented by newly planed, unpolished mahogany. He was a quiet, unobtrusive man, never troubling his patrons with his talk, nor luring them on by any finesse to another quart. I cannot relate his exit nor his end, but I own to a glimmering recollection that his experience as "mine host" was not a success.

It was about the time that the house passed from his hands, and when the knowing ones were calling to drink the new landlord's or landlady's good health, and wish them success, that Mrs. Dobbs met Mrs. Snarley in front of the old inn. Mrs. Dobbs was coming out, and Mrs. Snarley going in, and Mrs. Dobbs waited her neighbour's return into the street. A drop of gin, at the new landlord's expense, had set them both up. They were at their best. They had both for that day done their duty towards life and health, and Mrs. Dobbs had her tale ready to tell; each had tossed down the twopenny worth, and both were ready for a gossip. In this respect, as a gossip, Mrs. Dobbs had a character to lose. She stood confessed the arch tell-tale of the place; she was looked to for the latest news, and she had the talent for collecting that village life-sustaining article. Be sides this, she was of importance with her charms — sure cures for ague, warts, cramps, and nightmare, though her remedy for the latter was a little uncertain in the action and result. If the Holy Bible, when placed under your pillow on going to bed, failed, Moore's Almanack, or Dibdin's songs stood next. In fact, she affirmed — and, as she worded it — "The songs carried the crack." She had been heard to say that, when she was young she had drunk tea and gin out of a silver cup with the gipsies at their camp beneath the shadow of Burlow Castle bank, and that she remembered the old man, William Hills, who had grubbed or unearthed for road-making the last stones of the foundations of that now forgotten ruin. She declared, too, that, by the light of the full moon, her mother had, on more than one occasion, seen the ghost of the black dog, with its glaring eyes and open, ferocious mouth, run down the "town field," take a look over

223

the flint wall into the road, and then, as it invariably did, run back again. She also held the monopoly of two important articles of home manufacture —penny pies and parched peas. The lingering fires of the last malt house of Alfriston gave her a costless cooking-place for these last-named popular delicacies, and with these two temptations she held the affections of all the boys and girls of the place. Ah, where is now the man who can, without a sigh, look back on those days of penny pies and parched peas? those luxuries of boyhood? My lips contract and pout as I write, thinking how the truant juices overflowed and tried to escape down the corners of my overcharged mouth. Then I indulged, and was not easy until I had spent my last penny. Altogether, Mrs. Dobbs found herself a person of importance; she was proud of her position and influence.

Mrs. Dobbs, when the two old ladies met that day, had something hanging heavily on her mind. Notwithstanding the gin, there was a tinge of sadness and melancholy hovering about her eye that told of anxiety. She had a great dislike to being forestalled. Had her neighbour heard the latest news? She was fearful and growing jealous. "Mrs. Snarley," she said, "have you heard about the White-way ghost again?" "No," said Mrs. Snarley: "what about that?" "Well then," said Mrs. Dobbs, greatly relieved, "I will tell you. I think 'tis likely we shall hear no more about the young man walking a-nights." "And a good job too," said Mrs. Snarley, a little snappishly. "I think when a body is decently buried it should lie still in the grave, and not go walking about a-nights, frightening us poor old mortals." "And so do I," said Mrs. Dobbs. "We quite agree about that." "I say," said Mrs. Snarley, suddenly, "did you ever hear the song of the White-way ghost? My father used to sing it when we were girls. I have never forgot one verse. Listen, and tell me what you think of it:—

> When evening closes in with shadows grey
> And ghostly vapours overhang White-way,
> And th' crescent moon hangs gloomy in the west,
> 'Tis then the spirit of young Chowne can't rest,
> But walks abroad, with melancholy stride,
> Adown the path that skirts the chalk hill-side."

But the listener did not tell what she thought of it. She had never so much as heard of the song, and that Mrs. Snarley should have this knowledge of a bit of the early history of the place was a vexation to Mrs. Dobbs' jealous mind. She cut the matter short by exclaiming, "Oh! I don't know. I will tell you what happened yesterday. Do you know, they found the skeleton of the young man, and have buried it — all the bones — in the churchyard?" "And where did you get that story?" said Mrs. Snarley. "Oh, 'tis settled now," said Mrs. Dobbs. "The doctor decided it was a man under twenty, and it has always been said the nephew was murdered! And they say now," she added, "the skull and the jaw were both broken." "Oh, 'tis dreadful!" said Mrs. Snarley. "There must have been rough work, then." "And the uncles lived on like gentlemen, and were buried in the church," said Mrs. Dobbs. "And 'tis my opinion, now that as the lad is buried in holy ground, his spirit will rest"; and upon this consolatory conclusion the two old women separated, and walked off to their homes.

It is somewhat remarkable in the history of the old town that Mrs. Dobbs' conjecture was a correct one. At that time the White-way Road needed widening. The side hill had by imperceptible degrees encroached on the highway. It had become too narrow for the traffic; two carts meeting could not pass, and in the night the passage was not safe. So the surveyors were driven to make the improvement, and men were employed to cut away the intruding side hill. In doing this they came upon a skeleton embedded in the chalk, and as it lay about the spot where the ghost was said to vanish, conjecture readily made out the case — that these were the bones of the lost heir of Burnthouse — and sadness ran through the old town. The bones were speedily buried, and from that day the White-way ghost has not been seen by mortal eye....

A few years later, and the captain of the Alfriston gang stood in the felon's dock at the County Hall, at Lewes. Smuggling had not flourished with him; profit had failed to meet the expenses and the waste of his dissipation; so he had gone from bad to worse, and stood charged with felony. He was facing Baron Alderson, and waiting the fiat of the twelve jurymen. His future liberty, if not life, depended

225

upon the words Guilty or Not Guilty. The case had been gone through, and the prisoner stood anxiously watching his judges. (I was standing in the body of the Court, almost close to him.) He was a tall, bulky man, with bushy, almost black hair, fiery grey eyes, high cheek-bones, defiant mien. He stood erect, both hands, with outstretched fingers, resting on the bar of the dock. Every nerve and muscle appeared to be rigid; the mental had over powered the physical. With strained eyes he watches the jury as the twelve men turn about and face the Clerk of Arraigns and the Judge. "What say you, gentlemen?" says the official; "is the prisoner at the bar guilty or not guilty?" "Guilty," answered the foreman. The prisoner was the first to hear the verdict. His overstrained nerves and muscles collapsed; his hands gave way and fell over the railing. For the moment he was unmanned. There was but one other agony left for him, and that was his ultimate fate. But in this there was no suspense. "The prisoner is transported beyond the seas for seven years," said the Judge, in solemn tones; and he, with the two gaolers, descends into that — to the public — unknown gulf beneath the floor of the Court, and is seen no more. An effort was made to speak as to character. A father and mother's love for the son had prevailed on a few old friends to give evidence; but the effort was as forlorn as thankless. James Kennett, butcher, of Hailsham, was the first to enter the box. The witness was an honest man, and dared not speak to the point, neither would he prevaricate. He "edged," and tried to avoid the questions as they became more and more direct. The Judge, seeing the dilemma, said, "You must speak to the prisoner's general character." "Then," said the witness, "*I'll tell you, my lord. If you want to beat a dog, you may generally find a stick to do it with!*" "Get down, sir!" said the Judge, indignantly; the evidence for character had collapsed.